WOMEN IN MEDIEVAL JAPAN

WOMEN IN MEDIEVAL JAPAN

MOTHERHOOD, HOUSEHOLD MANAGEMENT AND SEXUALITY

WAKITA HARUKO
TRANSLATED BY ALISON TOKITA

MONASH ASIA INSTITUTE
CLAYTON

UNIVERSITY OF TOKYO PRESS
TOKYO

English edition first published in Australia in 2006
for distribution in Oceania, North America, Europe and Southeast Asia
by Monash University Press
Monash University, Victoria 3800, Australia
www.monash.edu.au/mai

English edition first published in Japan in 2006
for distribution in East Asia
by University of Tokyo Press
www.utp.or.jp

Published on 26 February 2006

This book was originally published in Japanese by University of Tokyo Press, Tokyo, 1992,
as *Nihon Chūsei Joseishi no Kenkyū: Seibetsu Yakuwari Buntan to Bosei, Kasei, Seiai.*

This translation and its publication were made possible by a Grant-in-Aid
for Publication of Scientific Research Results from the Japan Society for
the Promotion of Science (JSPS), granted in 2004 and 2005.

Monash University Press ISBN 978 876924 45 4

University of Tokyo Press ISBN 4 13 027033 8

National Library of Australia cataloguing-in-publication data:

Wakita, Haruko.

Women in medieval Japan.

Bibliography.

Includes index.

ISBN 9 78876924 454.

1. Women - Japan - History. 2. Japan - History - 1185-1600. I. Tokita, Alison, 1947- . II.
Monash University. Monash Asia Institute. III. Title.

952.021

The cover illustration is the Kanpū-zu (maple-viewing) screen, a 16th century work by Kanō
Hideyori. The Kanpu-zu screen is a National Treasure held in the collection of the Tokyo National
Museum. Picture supplied by Image: TNM Image Archives Source.

Printed by BPA Print Group, Melbourne, Australia - www.bpabooks.com

Contents

Acknowledgments

The generous support of the Japanese Society for the Promotion of Science has made this translation and its publication possible. Professor Wakita's enthusiasm for having the book translated drove the project from its inception, and her continued support and availability for consultation have been invaluable. I thank her for her confidence in me for this task.

Mr Takagi Hiroshi of the University of Tokyo Press initiated and led the collaboration with Monash Asia Institute for a joint publication. I am most grateful to him and to Ms Emma Hegarty at Monash University for their work. All illustrations were kindly supplied by courtesy of University of Tokyo Press.

The translation has been assiduously checked at each stage by Mr Masahiro Tokita. The English manuscript has been exhaustively checked and improved by Ms Teresa Anile and Ms Cathy Edmonds. Two anonymous reviewers also made helpful suggestions. Any remaining infelicities and inadequacies are my responsibility.

All Japanese names are given surname first, except when referring to a person who publishes and works outside Japan.

Translator's introduction

Alison Tokita

The recent flurry of Western books on geisha testifies to the West's ongoing fascination with women in Japan, and their sexuality in particular. Even serious academic research on Japanese women often focuses on sexuality, exoticising gender (Katō 2004). It seems that Western attitudes have not changed very much since the days of *Madame Chrysantheme*, and her clone, *Madama Butterfly*. Such narratives can be situated in the Orientalist gaze, which sees the West as powerful and masculine, and the Orient as weak and feminine (Said 1978).

Japan is still the strongest economy and a political giant in Asia, and is the second largest economy in the world. Yet many aspects of Japanese society lagged behind industrial and economic development, with women not gaining the vote until the post-war constitution of 1947.

The first wave of Japanese feminism impacted only on the intellectuals in the Meiji period (1868–1911). During the militarist and colonialist period, women had to conform to the 'good wife and wise mother' (*ryōsai kenbo*) ideology in the service of the state, and support the men who fought for and otherwise created the Japanese Empire (Mackie 1997:37–41). Post-war Japan saw the rapid expansion of a consumer economy, which depended on the housewife as consumer of white goods such as refrigerators, vacuum cleaners and rice cookers. This newly-found leisure time gave mothers the capacity to focus on their children's education, creating the stereotype of the 'education mother' (*kyōiku mama*). Wakita discusses the academic debates surrounding the place of women in economic production, and the interpretation of women's history in the 20th century.

The impact of the second wave of feminism in the 1970s reached the popular level. It spearheaded counter-culture citizens' movements and consumer groups, campaigns for improved conditions and rewards for women in the workforce; and, after the International Year of Women in 1975, it led to a greater awareness of the international importance of gender equality as a mark of a developed nation. This period coincided with the time when consumer capability was highest and women had considerable disposable income, not only for household purposes, but also for self-development (adult education, artistic pursuits), personal consumption and leisure, including travel. This acquisition of consumer power and leisure time—which applied to housewives, but most significantly to unmarried women—was arguably more effective in achieving a new deal for Japanese women in a male-dominated society.

1

Wakita Haruko's experience as a working wife and mother in the academic sector reflects all of the above: the ideals of a woman being able to 'have it all' — marriage, motherhood, successful career, cultivated pursuits — without taking second place, without sacrificing ambition and ability to male interests. As an academic, she trained as a historian specialising in the commerce of medieval Japan. She was drawn into the second wave of feminism among academic women such as Ueno Chizuko, and threw herself into researching Japanese women's history, and into multi-disciplinary team research on women's studies. She was instrumental in obtaining grants for this work and, with colleagues, achieved major outcomes. The work from these research projects generated a lot of interest internationally, leading to team research in the United States, Europe and elsewhere. She tirelessly continues her work on medieval commerce, at present on a project about the Iwami silver mine and its role in East Asian trade in the late medieval period. At the same time, she is working on a project on discrimination on the grounds of impurity in a number of Asian countries, which encompasses women's issues.

Wakita's *Women in medieval Japan* was first published in 1992, and contains a large amount of her representative research. Naturally, it refers to secondary sources only up to that time, so research of the last 15 years is not here. However, it is clear that her work has had a great impact on the development of women's studies and women's history in particular — both in Japan and elsewhere — in the period since publication. The book is an indispensable source for understanding the dynamics of gender issues in medieval Japan, and it opens up myriad avenues for further research.

A key theme in the book is the critique of the simplistic view that in ancient times women 'were the sun' and enjoyed power, authority and privilege, which in subsequent centuries was eroded, specifically first by Chinese bureaucratic structures, and then by the culture of warrior (samurai) rule. This view was popularised by the first-wave Japanese feminists (such as Hiratsuka Raichō), and academically argued by Takamure Itsue, whose work Wakita uses as a point of reference. She acknowledges Takamure's importance as a pioneer in the historical research of marriage and family systems, but criticises her blind spots. She also critiques the Marxist historians who see the subjugation of women in purely economic terms. Wakita's thorough knowledge of commerce in the medieval era led her to view the situation in that period as much more complex: she refutes a single continuous downward trajectory of women's status, insisting that the process varied enormously depending on class, status, wealth, and social situation (household, monastery or itinerant).

Takamure's history of women focused on the change in marriage systems from uxorilocal (*tsumadoikon*, where the man visits the woman's dwelling; and *mukotorikon*, where the wife's family takes the man into the family name and business) to virilocal (*yometorikon*, where the woman goes to live with the man and joins his family) as the major factor in the decline of women's status. These marriage patterns co-existed in much of the pre-modern era, but the uxorilocal types were dominant up to the Heian period, and the virilocal, or *yometori*, type became dominant with the establishment of the *ie*-type family from the medieval period. Wakita, however, sees the key issue as being the establishment of the medieval 'corporate household' or *ie*, which she argues was the core social unit of all sectors of medieval society: domestic, government, production religious, performing arts and so on. Commercial development in that era was through the structure of the *za* (guild) which, she argues, was an amalgamation of groups of *ie*. The significant feature of the *ie* is that it was patriarchal, with a male head in nearly all cases. Even when a commercial or other social activity was actually performed by a woman, the business was registered, for tax and tribute purposes, in the name of the male household head—except in the case of widows or nuns (see Wakita 1984b).

Another key issue for Wakita is that within the large corporate households, which were the locus of both production and reproduction, the mistress of the house wielded great power; on the other hand, in a small or insignificant family, neither the male nor female had power.

Wakita strives to demonstrate that women in the medieval era were actively engaged in a variety of social and economic activities: from serving at court and in influential families, to being itinerant vendors, nuns and entertainers. She gives a persuasive analysis, supported by a wide range of documentary evidence, of the changes in attitudes towards women, women's work, motherhood and sexuality over the medieval period, arguing that women enjoyed much autonomy that was weakened in later centuries.

The high point of women's status in Japanese history could be said to have been in the Heian period (794–1185), when upper-class women created the great literary masterpieces of Japanese writing that formed the classical canon and the basis of later literature of both men and women. The great tradition of diary writing was an adjunct to this literary activity. At the same time, the content of this writing, both fictional and diaristic, so often expressed the pain and frustration of women who lived as one among many in a polygamous system; marriage in the Heian period allowed a man with earning capacity to have multiple wives and concubines, whereas women typically were confined to waiting for their husbands to visit them.

The greatest strength of the book is that it not only presents arguments and concepts, but its strong empirical methodology draws on a wide variety of texts to illustrate the lived experience of women in the period under question. Naturally, Wakita's methodology as a historian is based first and foremost on written documentary sources. In the best tradition of Japanese scholarship she quotes and summarises many conventional documentary sources (*komonjo*) from public and private archives and temples, to form the substance of her grounded narrative. Such documentary scholarship inevitably prioritises the history of the literate ruling classes.

Wakita's innovation as a historian is in her use of fictional narratives—such as the *Tale of Genji*, tales (*setsuwa*), and *nō* plays, as well as diaries—and in occasionally drawing on archeological evidence, such as pottery, housing and toilets.

Particularly noteworthy is the use made of nō and kyōgen plays as source materials. This derives not only from a deep knowledge of them as written texts, but also from her experience of performing *nō* throughout her life, through which she has imaginatively entered into the female characters that were created in the medieval period.

The book introduces important diaries such as those of Yamashina Tokitsugu (1507–79) (*Tokitsugu kyōki*, extant for 1544–45); Prince Sadafusa's *Kanmon nikki* (covering 1416–48); and the *Oyudono no ue no nikki* (more precisely, a daily log book, written by women serving at court, extant from 1477 to 1826). These diaries are frequently used by historians in a fragmentary way—for the information they yield about daily life and culture. However, Wakita's use of them to illustrate the culture and way of life of the women who are featured in them, or who wrote them, is something quite new. She enables the English reader to understand the rich nature of these documents as sources, as well as their limitations. These diaries produced by people in the imperial court naturally provide a rich insight into the lives of the women who served there. Wakita emphasises that this was the principal way in which aristocratic women could work, even though their work of managing royal households overlapped their concubine-like role and their function of producing heirs.

However, Wakita is ambitious enough to want to cover all types of women in her study.

Aspects of the social labour of all classes, except the aristocratic, are discussed using the pictorial evidence of the early 16th century *Shokunin utaawase* scrolls (see Chapter three) and the *Rakuchū rakugai* genre-themed folding screens depicting life in and around the capital of the late 16th century.

Here we learn about gender role division in a wide variety of occupations, and the life cycle patterns of many women.

Other literary sources she draws on include the *Nihon ryōiki, Konjaku monogatari, Kagerō nikki, Shin-sarugō-ki, Menoto no fumi, otogi zōshi* and *Shaseki-shū*. Fictional works enable us to enter imaginatively into the worlds of many different types of women, and to extrapolate the social context that gave rise to such writing. Wakita weaves from these a rich tapestry of women's experience covering all classes and all roles in the medieval period.

The first chapter lays out the key issues of the book to set the scene for more detailed analysis. The breakdown of the bureaucratic structures was paralleled by the rise of the *ie*, which became the key unit of society and was the site of production and reproduction based on the conjugal partnership of the household head and his wife. The relationship between this and changes in marriage customs is explored—from the looser parent–child focus to the more fixed husband–wife focus. The contribution of women to high culture is argued, as the women of the Heian period court created an indigenous literary tradition (whose pinnacle was Lady Murasaki's *Tale of Genji* [Tyler 2003], which was avidly taken up by men in the medieval era and became the foundation of the national literature. Finally, drawing on the 14th century collection of tales about the origins of shrines, the *Shintō-shū*, Wakita outlines some of the implications of gender status change for religious practices, as Buddhism took root alongside the indigenous *Shintō* cults, and expounds a view that male–female conjugal relations among the common people were characterised at that time by equality and devotion. This, she argues, was the positive aspect of the stabler marriage system in which the wife entered her husband's family fully for life. She further draws on *nō* plays and *sekkyō-bushi* narratives to support her argument that medieval culture was earthy, wholesome and not regulated by the ruling class's ideas about fidelity and chastity that devalued women.

Chapter two explores views of motherhood in the medieval period, and the ambivalence found in many texts about women's sexuality. In the early medieval period, there is strong evidence that motherhood was highly venerated not as a symbol of fertility in general, but because men who held absolute power relied on the official wife to produce a legal heir. The downside of this was the growing emphasis on chastity for wives, and the increasingly limited scope for women to participate in social labour. This meant that upper-class women's energy and ambitions came to be focused on bearing a child to the emperor or another noble, so that their child might become that person's heir. By examining several versions of the legend of the Buddhist saint

Mokuren, whose mother was condemned to hell, Wakita shows that the 'sin' she committed evolved from lack of faith, to a general karmic sin engendered by motherhood, to greed and ambition for her child, reflecting the changing conditions of women in medieval Japan. The pattern of women's ambition is further illustrated by an exploration of the medieval text *Menoto no fumi*, a primer written by the nun Abutsu-ni about strategies whereby a woman could succeed at court. The concept of identification of mother and child which emerges from this discussion is further illustrated by reference to reunion narratives between parent and child in *nō* drama and other performed genres. These narratives contrast with those produced in the court in that they do not impute guilt to mothers for ambition or attachment to their children.

Chapter three takes up the issue of women at work. Despite a growing disparagement of work for upper-class women, one group of women at court worked as administrators and scribes, conveying the wishes of the emperor to the court and beyond. Their work is extensively and amusingly discussed from analysis of the diary of courtier Yamashina Tokitsugu (*Tokitsugu kyōki*). The working lives of itinerant shamanesses (*miko*) and nuns, women in agriculture, performers, and the artisan and merchant classes are also studied in detail. A full analysis of one of the early 16th century scrolls depicting a poetry competition between pairs of artisans, the *Shichijū-ichiban utaawase* (*Poetry contest by 71 pairs of merchants and artisans*) provides a basis for understanding the gendered nature of work in the late 14th century.

Chapter four's central concern is an exploration of the life cycle of women, including working women. The experiences of women who formed part of the *ie*—whether wives, concubines or servants—and their daily work is complemented by the experiences of women who existed outside the *ie*—such as those who retired to nunneries, and itinerant vendors and entertainers. A central part of the discussion is of Prince Sadafusa's diary, the *Kanmon nikki* ('Record of things seen and heard', also known as *Kanmon gyoki*, covering the years 1416–48), and what it tells about the lives of the women in several generations of his family. Particularly noted is the importance of nunneries in looking after the frail and dying, taking on the function of hospice.

In Chapter five, Wakita takes as her central material the *Oyudono no ue no nikki* (a daily record, written by women serving at court, extant from 1477 to 1826) to examine the life and work of women in the Imperial Court in the late medieval period. The chapter points to the high levels of literacy of court women, and links up with the discussion of the creation of a national literature by women in Chapter one. This 'diary' is contextualised in the broader history of the diary in Japanese culture. The particular role of women's speech (*nyōbo kotoba*) is also discussed as it is the language in which the *Oyudono no ue no nikki* was recorded. Wakita argues that the culture and language of the court women and their self-effacing attitude of service had a palpable influence on female culture in Japan as a whole, one that continues to the present day.

This book will make available in English a body of work by one of the foremost scholars of women's history, dispelling some of the misconceptions that Japanese women have always been subservient to men and withdrawn into domesticity. It will hopefully change the way Japanese women are viewed from outside. Wakita's contribution to women's historical studies in Japan has been great and can now reach internationally, not only to Japanese studies scholars, but to medieval studies and women's studies in general. The arguments are made most powerfully, sometimes with previously little-used materials, often with new interpretations of readily available documents. Wakita recovers and rediscovers the important roles played by women in the medieval era.

Note on periodisation, calendar and dates

Much Japanese historiography is strongly influenced by Marxism and other Western thought systems. While Wakita does not use the word 'feudal', the key term for this book is *chūsei*, a Meiji-period neologism for medieval, or Middle Ages. For the purposes of this study, it loosely applies to the period 1100 to 1600 at its broadest perimeter.

Other broad eras named in the book are:

Genshi - primitive

Kodai - ancient   700–1100

Chūsei - medieval   1100–1600

Kinsei - early modern 1600–1868

Kindai - modern   1868–1945

Gendai - contemporary 1945–

Specifically named periods that most frequently occur in the text:

Nara   710–794

Heian   794–1185

Kamakura   1185–1333

Nanboku (Southern
and Northern Courts) 1333–1392

Muromachi	1392–1477
Sengoku (Warring States)	1477–1573
Azuchi–Momoyama	1573–1600
Edo or Tokugawa	1600–1868
Meiji	1868–1912
Taishō	1912–1925
Shōwa	1926–1988
Heisei	1989–

These period names are important in most discourse about pre-modern Japan, and are retained in this translation: Nara, Heian, Kamakura, Nanboku, Muromachi, Sengoku, Edo. The modern era coincides with emperors' reigns—Meiji, Taishō, Shōwa, Heisei—and are also important for modern Japanese cultural history.

The calendar of pre-modern Japan is the lunar calendar. In the translation, years have been converted to the Western common-era years, months are numbered, and no exceptions are made when the 12th month corresponds to the following Western year. For days, sometimes the old system based on the zodiac signs is used—that is, the day of the mouse instead of numbered days.

Names are given in Japanese order, surname first. Japanese terms are romanised according to the modified Hepburn system, which is standard in Japanese studies in the English language.

The text draws on the abundance of Japanese historical documents (*komonjo*) that customarily have been used in historiography as far back as the Heian or even Nara periods. Most often written in Chinese (at least in Japanese-style Chinese or *kanbun*), or in classical Japanese, these have been quoted and referred to liberally in the text. In most cases they have been translated into understandable modern English. Similarly, frequent reference is made by the author to literary texts that, while usually fictional, are useful in illustrating the place of women in society at the time. Where English translations already exist, these have in most cases been used, with due acknowledgement.

Specialised historical knowledge of social structures and of the functionings of court and military government are often taken for granted by Wakita—knowledge that is not even necessarily possessed by the average Japanese native reader, and certainly not by the foreign reader—such as the ranks of the women in the imperial court who looked after the emperor's every need, from bathing, eating and bedroom needs, to the issuing of important documents and the running of the imperial household. Some background can be found in Yoshikawa's chapter in Wakita, Bouchy & Ueno (1999); and for the wives of the military aristocracy, Tabata's chapter in the same volume. The Cambridge history of Japan (Heian and Medieval volumes) is also excellent. While every effort has been made to make the translation readable as well as comprehensive, the reader is advised to refer to the index, where Japanese terms are listed and glossed.

The formation of the *ie* and the position of women: motherhood, household management and sexuality

This picture shows the kitchen of a noble household: a young woman is fanning the large log fire while a middle-aged woman is stirring the cauldron; male servants are chopping ingredients and placing food on the serving table; the woman at the back is taking another cooking pot into the kitchen. (Tyler 1990).

Introduction

Pioneering research on Japanese women's history aimed to prove the existence of women's glorious past and, by demonstrating that women's abilities were no different from those of men, to overturn assumptions about the inferior capabilities of the female sex enshrined in the common phrase *danson johi* (respecting men, despising women).

The attempt to idealise a primitive period of gender equality, which was later debased, during which women enjoyed status and power, too easily slips into a schema in which women are equated with nature and men with culture. Women's history is then trapped in the bind of associating woman with nature, the primitive, childbirth and childrearing, and the effects of those functions. However, historical processes are not so simple that gender equality and mothers' rights steadily declined to *danson johi* equally across all sectors of society. It is important to tease out the complex interrelationship between class, or status differences, and gender and age differences from the point of view of the class society that formed in the medieval period. The all-important *ie* or corporate household has been treated solely from the perspective of the rise of patriarchy and the subservience of the wife. It is important to consider the interactions of both men and women with class and status differences, which women's history—with its strong tendency to talk only about gender differences—has excluded from view to date.

In medieval Japan, all social organisations—including politics, the military, commerce and the performing arts—were based on the *ie* in the various class and status strata. The husband was the household head and the wife was the domestic head of the *ie*; subservient to her husband, she was nevertheless totally responsible for what happened within the household. If we consider their combined male and female servants and subordinates, the position of the wife was high. In medieval society the household comprised a husband and wife and existed in a class society with many strata. If the *ie* is seen as a fixed entity, the power of the husband is in inverse proportion to that of the wife. If, on the other hand, the *ie* functions differently in different classes within stratified master–vassal relations, the household head and his wife are both very powerful in the *ie* of an overlord, whereas in the household of a vassal neither the household head nor his wife has much power. In the pre-modern period, the *ie* was the site of production, as well as of politics and performing arts, so the status of the wife was completely different from the modern housewife.

In this medieval social ranking, the *ie* was also the site of reproduction, which comprised the family nucleus: the couple and their children. It was a system of reproductive relations, through the sexual love of husband and wife, and childbirth and childrearing. Therefore, while the wife had overall responsibility for managing the household, her most fundamental duties were motherhood, ensuring the succession of the *ie* and sexual love, which is the source of motherhood and a symbol of prosperity.

Medieval Japan possessed a bureaucracy predicated on the *ritsuryō* statutory system of ancient Japan and on Buddhist thought, both imported from China.[1] These formal principles did, indeed, govern all of medieval society, but a whole world of actual behaviour modified them—the realm of the human experiences of love, suffering, ageing and death, which centred on the *ie* and the family. Medieval culture and religion were deeply shrouded in a very human vulgarity.

Although the medieval period tends to be interpreted as a remnant of the primitive period, or as the revival of indigenous conditions triggered by the atrophy of the *ritsuryō* system of centralised, bureaucratic rule, this chapter considers the status of women in relation to the *ie*, which was the backbone of medieval society. Of the many important institutions formed during this period, we look at the establishment of the *ie*, in which, due to changes in marriage practices, the couple was the core unit. We will discuss the wife's household management of the *ie*, the specific nature of women's culture (particularly the literature generated by court ladies), the religious role of female shamans (*miko*) and their religious tales, including 'gods who protect conjugal relations', and the growth in cults of female deities.

The pre-modern ie and changing marriage systems

Takamure Itsue (1894–1964) believed that women in the primitive period had power, which they increasingly lost over time. This way of thinking coincided with the schema popularly held in the West: nature = woman, civilisation = man.[2] However, Takamure was unique in labelling civilisation as evil and called for a return to the more natural state of the primitive period. She also considered *tsumadoi-kon* or 'wife-visiting marriage' to be a survival of the customs of the primitive age.[3] Yet, *tsumadoi* marriage surely had a different meaning in the earlier, classless society than in the period when patriarchy was firmly established.[4] Takamure (1963) somewhat simplistically ignored this difference, viewing both *tsumadoi* and *mukotori* or 'adoptive' marriages as uxorilocal and, hence, matriarchal rights as strong (Wakita 1983; 1978). Sekiguchi Hiroko, however, has pointed out that in *tsumadoi* marriage the patriarchal rights of the father can be discerned (Sekiguchi 1977).

The model proposed by Takamure of the transition from *tsumadoi/mukotori* to *yometori*-type marriage, where the wife is taken into the husband's home, and the concomitant fall in women's status, applied to women who had position and property. A woman such as the author of *Kagerō Nikki,* who was without position and property, expressed a strong desire to be taken into the residence of her husband Fujiwara Kaneie.[5] Takamure also points out that the author of *Sarashina Nikki* wanted to be 'placed' (*sue*) with a constant man; to be 'placed' is none other than the precursor of *yometori* marriage (Morris 1971).[6] Women who lost position and property as a result of the spread of patriarchy actually came to wish for *yometori* marriage, in which the wife's status was secure. The establishment of patriarchy and the subsequent decline of women's position resulted in changes in marriage practices.

Whereas Takamure only considered women of high social standing, Inoue Kiyoshi looked only at women of the lower classes who lacked status and property. His view was that with the rise of a class society, discrimination against women and the suppression of women suddenly became more severe and, with the gradual shift from slave to serf to labourer, the status of women rose. In my work, I have tried to integrate these two positions and have argued that it is necessary to look at each class separately (Joseishi 1982).

Modern patriarchy was brought to the common people in the Meiji period through the popularisation of a diminished version of the *ie*. The systems of production, administration and economics of the pre-modern *ie* lost their function and, as Ueno Chizuko points out, retained only the function of reproduction (Ueno 1990). In this kind of *ie*, the status of the household manager inevitably declined; however, with the later popularisation of the *ie*, the respected status of *okusama*, which previously had been possessed only by the wives in the *bushi* class, spread to the common people.

In contrast to the new form of *ie*, the pre-modern *ie* covered all social systems: political, economic, commercial, artisanal, agricultural (see Chapter four). As Ueno states, the pre-modern *ie* was an indivisible unit of productive and reproductive processes (Ueno 1990).

As Chapters three and four show, there are many differences between household labour in the pre-modern and the modern *ie*. In the pre-modern era, values were not measured only in terms of financial exchange. The *ie* was a social organism equivalent to a company today, and there was no split between consumption labour and productive labour. Domestic labour was performed as social labour by upper-class women serving at court or in other aristocratic houses, while, among the common people, socially productive work was performed by wives and children as domestic labour.

Chapter two builds on my earlier work on the historical development of the role of motherhood, changes in its status and the implications of these changes for women who were excluded from motherhood (Wakita 1986). Whereas Takamure idealised maternal rights, I explored concrete experiences of motherhood, including the relations between mother in law and daughter-in-law. The five-volume work *Nihon josei seikatsu-shi* (*A history of Japanese women's way of life*) (Joseishi 1990) examined changes in simple reproduction and changes in women's life cycle in the context of the *ie*. Commercial and economic progress and social change were linked with changes in productive relations and improvements in standards of living. This work argued the necessity to consider changes in the position of women in relation to these processes. However, there were limitations to this earlier research: the issues of production, reproduction and motherhood were presented in a disconnected way, without showing how they worked together in the pre-modern *ie*—it is therefore necessary to create a synthesised logic to organically link these.

Ueno sees the modern *ie* under the capitalist system as evincing the separation of reproduction and productive modes, and regards the productive mode as being subordinate to the reproductive mode in the pre-modern hereditary homestead-style *ie* (Ueno 1990). However, in the pre-modern case it is important to consider more closely particular periods and social groups. The centralised bureaucracy promoted the separation of productive and reproductive modes, as did the government offices and workshops of the earlier *ritsuryō* state bureaucracy. According to Ueno, there existed a household unit in which the productive mode was subordinate to the reproductive mode. At the time of the *ritsuryō* system (Nara to Heian periods), the *ie* had not generally matured, so this reproductive system could be called the 'household community'.[7]

As the *ritsuryō* system declined, the medieval *ie* emerged, and the means of production, which had been separate under the bureaucratic system, came under the control of the head of the *ie*.[8] In the early stages, the head of this *ie* was not necessarily male. Even in the later stages, phrases such as *nyōbō no sanmi ke no mandokoro* indicate that a court lady of the third rank or higher could set up a house administrative system (*mandokoro*)—if a person (man or woman) had the capacity to earn, they could establish an *ie*.[9] Having said that, the patriarchal *ritsuryō* state ensured that mostly men obtained status and power. Chapter four shows that *yometori* marriage was made possible by the male's ability to provide: the general appearance of this type of marriage in the medieval period shows that the patriarchal *ie* had been established.

The significance of the patriarchal *ie* for the position of women was that it required a *yometori* marriage, whereby the status of the official wife, who bore the heir to the *ie*, was firmly established. In the earlier *tsumadoi*-type marriage, parent–child relations were the basis of the family, and conjugal relations were unstable: this system allowed a husband multiple official wives through formal marriage ceremonies,[10] as well as multiple concubines. In *mukotori* marriage the husband lived with the family of the main wife, and the material position of the wife's father was at issue — the bridegroom did not need sufficient assets to set up a household. Therefore, as long as he had a household to accept him, he was free to engage in a *tsumadoi* marriage elsewhere. However, in the case of *yometori* marriage, the woman left her natal home and entered another household, in compensation for which she alone was the main wife. As long as she was not divorced and sent home, on the whole she enjoyed a stable status, the fixity of which naturally resulted in the lowering of the status of other wives and concubines, and was an eventual factor leading to discrimination against prostitutes. *Yometori* marriage led to a kind of monogamy (but included concubinage). In this way, the head of the household reintegrated the production and reproduction modes, and was able to control both.

If we believe that the general spread of *yometori* marriage was responsible for the establishment of the medieval patriarchal *ie*, then Takamure is right to say that in the primitive period women were equal to men, and that the position of women continued to decline over time, receiving a fatal blow through the establishment of *yometori* marriage.[11] Ueno, denying the anthropological bind that man is civilisation and woman is nature, focuses on the equation of reproductive function and maternal function, and seems to believe that the position of women has continued to decline from the primitive period onwards (Ueno 1990).

If we look only at the household head and his wife, and consider the difference in their absolute power, we must conclude that the establishment of patriarchy resulted in the subordination and the defeat of women everywhere.[12] This was not a problem for women alone, however, for under patriarchy only a few men became rulers: the majority of males were subjugated under their domination. Both ancient and medieval Japan were status societies — the early stage of a class society — so it is not very meaningful to highlight gender relations without considering lord–vassal relations, status relations and other hierarchical relations. If we deal with the organic connection between these two approaches, the historical process becomes more complex and richer.

The medieval *ie* was undeniably patriarchal, and was dependent on the father's status and power, and his resources of private property. However, the internal running of the household was controlled by the wife by virtue of her motherhood and her household management skill. The *ie* was ruled by the male head, to whom the wife was subordinate, and there is no doubt that the wife was a chattel of her husband.[13] However, rather than repeating the phrase 'establishment of patriarchy is the subordination of women', we will better ascertain the nature of medieval society, and the position of women in it, if we look at the complementary status of the household head and his wife, as shown by their roles within their joint jurisdiction of household management.

As the basic unit of medieval society, the *ie* was an organisation of people — some related by blood and others not — at whose apex was a husband and wife team. In her position as the official wife who bore the successor to the *ie*, and with her authority as supervisor of the household, a woman may in some ways have held greater power than in the primitive era. However, the male household head held final authority, even over the elder-like status of the steward of a Fujiwara Sekkanke household or the butler of a *daimyō* household.

The status of women deteriorated within the context of the decline of the structure of the family estate system, through the refinement of the bureaucracy that developed in the medieval and early modern periods, and with the corporate organisation of the modern period.

The medieval ie and the role of the wife — aristocratic families

The *ie* became the basic social unit in medieval society as a result of the withering of the *ritsuryō* bureaucracy. It is known that the political and economic affairs of the Fujiwara Sekkanke regent family were handled in the household government office (*mandokoro*). The bureaucratic structures remained only in a ceremonial way in the court, and the control of each domain was performed in a *mandokoro* office (Satō 1983),[14] to which officials such as the *keishi* and *shimokeishi* were appointed. In the *ie* the governing relationship was between the couple at the head of the household and the retainers, which was different from the *ritsuryō* bureaucratic structure in which women were excluded from the system (except for the women's quarters, as shown later).

In order to compete with the dominance of the Fujiwara family, the imperial household also formed a property-based *ie* household, which was different from when the emperor was head of the *ritsuryō* state. It is widely accepted that the rule of the retired emperors (11th–13th centuries) and the formation of domains for their retirement can be explained as property-based control structures to resist the Fujiwara family. The imperial family thus added to its ceremonial bureaucratic structures, and successfully created a parallel structure of control in the form of a medieval-type *ie*.

By the 14th century, the imperial family had long lost its actual power to rule, and the bureaucratic structures were the site of ceremonies only. While these ceremonies legitimised the nominal continuance of the imperial family as the highest authority, it was, in fact, just like any other *ie*—one of the powerful houses carrying out its domain management.

We know a lot about the ways of the imperial family from the communal diary *Oyudono no ue no nikki* (1469 to mid-19th century; see Chapter five) and about the Fushiminomiya family from Prince Sadafusa's diary *Kanmon Nikki* (1416–48) (see Chapter four), and what they tell us is essentially the same: in the 15th century, the emperor did not have a consort, and neither was there an official wife in the Fushiminomiya family. In the imperial family, the *suke* and *naishi* were in charge of running the household, and in the princely families the *shijo* ran the household. Among the latter, those with sexual experience were given names such as Hisashi no onkata and Higashi no onkata, based on the status ranking of the imperial household. The marriage custom of the imperial family and the princely families should be called one of one husband and multiple concubines.[15]

The case of the Sekkanke family was different, in that there was often an official wife (called *kita no kata* or *kita no mandokoro*). There was also an elder woman called *senji no tsubone*, a role corresponding to the *kōtō no naishi* (senior handmaid) in the imperial household, who was in charge of generating women's documents. Similarly in the Ashikaga *shōgun's* household, as Chapter five shows, the *shōgun's* wishes were conveyed in equivalent women's documents. Where there was an official wife, she had final responsibility for household affairs. We know how Hino no Tomiko, the wife of the eighth Ashikaga *shōgun*, Yoshimasa, actually grasped political power—not only by her outstanding talent, but because she was able to most effectively wield her status and responsibility as the wife of a noble (*midaidokoro*) (Wakita 1984a). Konoe, the wife of the 12th Ashikaga *shōgun*, Yoshiharu, performed a similar role: in negotiating with those under her she skilfully managed the Ashikaga *bakufu*.[16] This shows the kind of authority that came with the position of *midaidokoro*.

In the medieval *ie*, the power of the patriarchal head was supreme, but the wife, who understood her husband's intentions and acted on them, controlled household affairs and was the second most powerful. Whereas the husband was active outside, she occupied the most powerful position in domestic affairs.

Moreover, the wife bore the child who was heir to the *ie*, both to its property and to the authority that the *ie* symbolised. She had the capacity by which the *ie* could reproduce itself, as well as the function of production. In Japan, with the exception of the *ritsuryō* bureaucratic structures and the *bakuhan* system[17] of the Edo period, for the most part the productive modes combined with family management structures and were simply enlarged *ie*-like structures. The reproductive function and the productive function were inseparable, with the former taking precedence over the latter, and with the housewife able to integrate both functions.

Although this is a picture of the *ie* in the ruling classes, it operated essentially in the same way for the subordinate classes, but on a different scale.[18] This is what characterises medieval Japan: whether farming families, artisan families or performing artists, the basic unit of management was the *ie*. The occupational guilds (*za*), for example, functioned as a federation of patriarchal heads of the basic family unit, the *ie*.[19] Although it existed under the authority of the house head, the actual running of affairs was carried out through the co-operation of the couple. The management involved family labour and some vassal labour, so the wife had a broad sway of influence. This is similar to the family focus of management practices in small and medium enterprises today.

The 10th-century book *Shin Sarugō-ki* offers a portrait of a man (not a member of the subordinate classes, but a high-ranking samurai in charge of the court guards) called Uemon no jō, whose three wives have stereotypical roles of the time.[20] The first wife is positioned as the child-bearer, and the third wife as the playmate, while the second wife is set up as an outstanding household manager. This role included handling the basic areas of clothing, food and shelter, as well as buying and selling, the annual taxes, caring for the armour and military equipment, and looking after the servants and vassals. Even in an artisan's household, although the scale might have been different, the wife could be required to have the same ability as Uemon no jō's second wife. In this case, unlike the equation of female with nature, which is inherent in the child-bearing and the playmate roles, a wife was expected to have sufficient household management ability to control the *ie*.

In large-scale household management and in the nobility, the status of the main wife was very high. At that time, not having to work was seen as dignified, so work was delegated to the court women (*nyōbō*), especially the role of royal wet nurse (*menoto*), who looked after another woman's child and continued to exercise influence after that child grew up. However, there were some noblewomen, such as Hino no Tomiko and Konoe, who went as far as controlling the political sphere. The Portugese Jesuit Luis Frois (1532–97) noted that Japanese women were able to write documents and that this was not looked down upon.

The absence of empress in the imperial family and official wife in the Fushiminomiya family was in part due to a lack of resources to establish such positions, but it can also be attributed to the scale of such a status. For example, rather than just being the official wife of the emperor, the empress was the head of her own separate establishment or *ie*, with its own retinue and ranks (see Chapter five). Even the *nyōbō* above the *sanmi* (third) rank could have their own *mandokoro*, and could in turn set up their own *ie*. To have an empress on the throne meant the existence of a compound institution, consisting of an *ie* centring on the emperor and an *ie* centring on the empress. By the Warring States period (1460s to 1560s), it became impossible to afford the empress's establishment, which was rooted in the operating mode prior to the formation of the *ie* based on *yometori* marriage.

In the fictional depiction of aristocratic practices in the *Tale of Genji*, when Genji is exiled to Suma, his wife Murasaki takes full responsibility for his household, although it is the responsibility of her wet nurse, Shōnagon no Tsubone, to actually manage everything. However, Murasaki is not Genji's official wife, having only been 'placed' in an establishment,[21] but in the story she holds the highest status because of Genji's love for her. Genji eventually took as official wife the imperial Princess Onna Sannomiya. Murasaki constitutes an idealised portrait of a court woman who longs to be 'placed' (*sue* in Takamure Itsue's words), as the sign of a man's sincerity.[22] The logical extension of this was the position of the wife in the *yometori* marriage system.

By contrast, the empress was the head of her own household; she was not the housewife of an *ie*, which was based on the *yometori* marriage system. In the Warring States period there was no empress, and hence there was only one imperial household, not two. The court ladies were simply servants, some of whom were also concubines and bore children. There could hardly have been a more convenient arrangement from the emperor's point of view. The other princely families probably followed this lead. This system of several concubines for one husband, and no official wife, turned the husband–wife relationship into an unequal one of overlord and subordinate. The subordinate court ladies and female attendants faithfully served the emperor and princes who were their husbands and lords. There can be no doubt that the sexual mores of these princely families had a negative influence on other social groups.

Putting aside the imperial and princely families, the *yometori* marriage system created the medieval *ie*, whether of the ruling class or the ruled. This firmly consolidated the status of the official wife through her husband's earning power—she was no longer dependent on the earning power of her father, as in the earlier *tsumadoi* and *mukotori* marriage systems. Although patriarchal authority was strong, in the household the wife's authority as manager was secure. The debate up till now has considered the relative power of both husband and wife to have been in inverse proportion, and has viewed the couple as sharing the same things. However, not unlike the contemporary company, if the scale of the *ie* grew, the wife's management authority increased in proportion with the rise of patriarchal authority. Of course, a wife in a *tsumadoi* marriage who had no father could not be an independent self-sufficient manager. This can be compared to the way that the pre-modern self-managing small farmers and small enterprises were absorbed as labour into large enterprises in the emerging capitalist system, or to executives today in large corporations who have little jurisdiction because they are neither the president nor independent managers.

The medieval *ie* rested on the principle of monogamy. It was an organisation that integrated production and reproduction, and in which both men and women were subordinated. While the housewife had full command of the management of the *ie*, her power was in proportion to the patriarchal authority of the household head.

Chapters three and five look in detail at the imperial family in the Warring States period, and show that its household management was equivalent to that of the court. Suffice to say here that the court was fully controlled by the minor court ladies (*nyōkan*), most of whom were *kōtō no naishi*.[23]

In the imperial family of the period, there was neither empress nor *naishi no kami*. The *suke* and *naishi* were merely direct servants of the emperor. The highest class of *suke* was *dainagon suke no tsubone*, who administered internal matters, while the *kōtō no naishi* administered external matters. These two areas of responsibility were not clearly differentiated, as they would be in the modern court. Further, since it was a system centring on the emperor, it had the peculiar character of placing more weight on the minute personal needs of the emperor than on external matters.

The *kōtō no naishi* had full responsibility akin to a secretary-general: handling and writing documents that petitioned the emperor and decrees that made the emperor's will known to subjects, and handling general administrative work, accounting, personnel matters, annual court ceremonies, appointments of official rank, and lawsuits. The *nyōbō hōsho* documents issued by the *kōtō no naishi* carried weight equal to *rinji*, which shows the importance of her status.

Women's role in the establishment of national literature

Japan stands out in the world for the low status of its women. The educator Fukuzawa Yukichi declared in the 19th century, 'Japan is a hell for women'.[24] Yet it is no exaggeration to say that women's writing was the mainstream of Japanese classical literature and forms the core of the national literature. Another characteristic of Japanese culture to be discussed further in Chapter five is the highly developed female speech, which has its source in *nyōbō kotoba* of the medieval court.[25] It is vital to think carefully about the significance of these two phenomena.

I used to think that the existence of women's language and female speech in Japan was simply the result of the low esteem in which women were held (*danson johi*), but the situation is not so simple. There is also the view that an absence of female speech means that the expression of a specifically female experience must be swallowed up in male forms of expression,[26] and that if women are to be true to their own specific values, they need a language that can reflect that peculiarity. Japanese women's language serves as a means for their oppression, for it has elements that pander to those men who seek refinement in a woman. Yet, at the same time it is the expression of a culture created by women themselves in order to survive in certain adverse social conditions of the past. Could it be that this language contains a somewhat devious form of self-assertiveness by women?

In the Heian period, the language of prestige, of officialdom and of public documents was Chinese (*kanbun* and *kango*), which therefore became the norm for men's speech and writing. The spoken language of the day and the *kana* syllabary were used to express private matters and, as such, developed principally as a means for women's expression. This led to the schema of 'man = public, woman = private'. However, as in the *Tosa nikki* by Ki no Tsurayuki (about 870–945),[27] there were some attempts by men to use the *kana* syllabary to describe emotion and feelings. Tsurayuki, in his opening sentence, framed the literary fiction of a woman impersonating a man writing the diary: 'I intend to see whether a woman can produce one of those diaries men are said to write'(Miyake 1996:41)˙ We can surmise that Tsurayuki created such a complicated device because otherwise he could not have written in *kana* prose and expressed emotions naturally. Women were supposed to write only in *kana*, which gave them the literary advantage of providing a fertile soil in which

Heian-period women's literature became the kernel of the national literature. The *kana* preface to the *Kokinshū* (905),[28] written by Tsurayuki, argued that it was often impossible to express in literature matters of indigenous Japanese culture without relying on the native language and writing.

The culture of the ensuing medieval era was predicated on courtly aristocratic culture, with women's literature as the kernel. The *nō* drama, for example, which arguably is the heart of traditional performing arts, cannot be understood without reference to the popularisation of the *Tale of Genji* and the *Tales of Ise*. *Nō* drama rode the momentum of the rise of popular culture, and served to bridge all classes and people, regardless of age, sex and status. It brought local performing arts to the attention of the nobility and regional culture to the capital, as well as enabling the exportation of the culture of the capital to the provinces.

The classes that enjoyed *nō* drama extended from the upper echelons to the very bottom of society—from the shogunal government (*bakufu*) and the nobility at the top to the feudal stewards (*shugo*), the *daimyō* in the period of the Warring States, landowners and local gentry, and down to the communities that conducted festivals in local temples and shrines (Wakita 1990b). It is largely through the influence of *nō* that references to these classics appear even in the *senryū* comic poems of the Edo period.

The classical culture—including *nō* and the Heian classics of *Genji*, *Ise*, the *Kokinshū* and, of course, *renga* (linked verse)[29]—showed a remarkable degree of pervasiveness. The great scholar Sanjō Nishi Sanetaka (1455–1537) responded to requests from regional lords, from Mutsu in the east to Satsuma in the west, to correct and improve their *waka* and *renga* poems and their interpretations of the *Genji* and *Ise*, as well as their calligraphy. The breadth of this cultural layer is astounding (Wakita 1990–91).

Why was there such a widespread reception of the classics? The answer does not lie only in the desire of the *bushi* class to emulate aristocratic culture. If there had been no-one to satisfy the cultural craving of the *bushi* class, which was busy fighting continuously, surely they would have been bored with the study of the finer literary arts and would not have developed a passion for their acquisition. It is said that Asakura Takakage (1428–81), in the midst of unceasing warfare, spared a whole day to copy a sutra and to mourn at the burial ground of Minamoto Yoshitsune and Satō Tsugunobu.[30] Tales of battles and loyalty could be experienced in the *Gikeiki* (*Chronicle of Yoshitsune*) (McCullough 1966)[31] and in *nō* dramas. This anecdote shows Takakage's sincere personality—a warlord would not have valued the literary classics merely to win favour with his superiors.

Both *nō* drama and *renga* formed an indispensable part of the cultivation of the samurai, and *renga* in particular was understood to be the culture of the nobility[32] and could not be mastered without an education in classics such as *Genji* and *Ise*.

Nō drama and *renga* both originated as plebeian arts and were enjoyed by the *bushi* and common classes (by enjoying *nō* drama the *bushi* could become familiar with the *Genji* and *Ise* tales). The important question to ask is why *nō* and *renga* drew on the court literature and developed into great arts. To take this a step further, remember that not only the *bushi* class but also those who carried the court literary culture were male power holders: Nijō Yoshimoto, Ichijō Kanera and Sanjō Nishi Sanetaka were all powerful figures at court. Why did these men, as part of their life work, throw themselves so completely into the study of the *Tale of Genji*? Set in the era of the greatest flourishing of the imperial house and the Fujiwara family, the novel provided a model for court ceremony to those who wanted to learn about court ranks and stations. Further, there was a fascination with the world depicted in these literary classics. The great *renga* master Sōgi and the *nō* drama genius Zeami, by absorbing these classics, brought their work to completion. This was connected with the broader cultural reception of the classics. Consideration must be given to why these tales, with their themes of sexual love and adultery, which should have been trivial and personal matters, became writ large for medieval audiences, especially the *bushi*.

First, the Heian period was a transitional stage in the formation of the *ie*, and women's literature consisted of tales of its formation. In a society based on the *ie*, private family matters took on a certain universality. The medieval *ie* was formed by the man's ability to earn a living and take a wife (*yometori* marriage). The *Kagerō nikki* (*Kagerō diary*, 974, see Arntzen 1997) shows an early example of this: the husband, Fujiwara Kaneie, builds a new house and installs his wife Tokihime, who contributes to his wealth by bearing him several children. The author of the diary, known only as Michitsuna's mother, was one of his other wives, and she bore a grudge because she was not taken in by Kaneie. This confirms that a woman who experienced *tsumadoi* marriage desired to enter into the husband's establishment. Further, although fiction, in the *Tale of Genji* the eponymous prince builds the vast *Rokujō* mansion, where he gathers almost all his lovers—the ultimate expression of a man's ability to form an *ie* and support his wives. Genji is depicted as the hero, the ideal man of power, prefiguring the *ie* that was to follow in the medieval era.

In this tale, written by a woman, no lover is rejected and all are welcomed at the *Rokujō* mansion: wife, concubine or lover, they are all depicted in a highly idealised way as cohabiting without any quarrelling. This is consistent with the anxiety felt by women at that time about being cast aside and their longing to not be rejected. Murasaki had no relatives to rely on; Genji loves and looks after her, which beautifully illustrates the wishes of women at that time. Murasaki embodied the idealised image of the treatment of women by powerful males in the custom of polygamy.

This tale, which expresses most skilfully men's desire for both political power and sex, became male reading material, as well as the central object of research on the Japanese classics for literati such as Ichijō Kanera, Sōgi and Sanjō Nishi Sanetaka. Prince Genji is portrayed as an idealised patriarchal power figure in a medieval-style polygamous system, and the court ladies are happy when they can bask in his love. This is the most basic premise of the work. Whether or not Murasaki or the writer of the *Kagerō nikki* achieved self-realisation through their writing would have been of no interest to these men.

The major theme of Heian period literature was the new patriarchal type of *ie* — the ill-treatment of stepchildren in tales such as *Ochikubo monogatari* supports this theme. In *tsumadoi* and *mukotori* marriages, even if there was a stepfather, there could be no stepmother. So this problem did not occur until the formation of the *ie* based on *yometori* marriage (Gorai 1976). It could only have been a matter of concern in an era when the continuation of the *ie* was important. Regardless of this, it is hard to see tales about maltreatment of stepchildren, even if they were about the *ie*, as the reading matter of men. They were surely written for the enjoyment of women. In contrast, the central themes of both *Genji* and *Ise* contain a high degree of political and erotic interest for men.

The second reason for men's interest in these works was the issue of adultery and power. The *Tale of Genji* is basically about how a child born of an adulterous relationship becomes emperor, whereby his father, Genji, acquires political power. Although personal in nature, the secret family affairs of the imperial family take on a public aspect because of the family's position. This is a feature of a society in which power is hereditary and inseparable from reproduction. In a modern secular state, if the head of state causes a scandal, he or she becomes the target of moral criticism, which may lead to loss of power but cannot be the source of power. However, in medieval society, where landholders were also hereditary, the behaviour of the imperial family was not irrelevant — it was seen as having universal application. In order to command sexual love in a system of polygamy — or rather in a system of monogamy plus concubines — and to control motherhood, it was necessary to produce legitimate children. Seen from this point of view, there is nothing more interesting than adultery, which can be called property trespassing (Ueno 1990).[33] The *daimyō* and warlords of the 15th century who read the *Tale of Genji* saw Genji's erotic and political adventures as based on the *ie*, the basic social unit of their time. In the period of the Warring States, from their perspective and with their culture of seizing land, Genji was a peace-time hero.

The tale acquired universality because it dealt with the imperial family.[34] The *daimyō* who served in the shogunal court were familiar with the culture of central power, and they knew that Kiso Yoshinaka had fallen because he lacked knowledge of court diplomacy and finesse. Oda Nobunaga, on the other hand, dressed appropriately and made no breaches of etiquette. In Japan's centralised power structure, the high status of the culture of the capital, Kyoto, and the court culture which was at its heart, demanded imitation by small and middle-scale local rulers. Ashikaga Yoshimitsu, by introducing Chinese culture and fostering the *nō* drama, tried to protect his own culture in opposition to the court culture (Wakita 1989). Later, however, the shogunal court, especially under Ashikaga Yoshimasa, stopped having its own cultural agenda and was included and assimilated into the imperial court culture. The *nō* drama, in spite of its role in the education of the *bushi* class, turned towards the court and the central power symbolised by the emperor. The first category of plays (god *nō*) in particular are close to the imperial cult of *Ise Shintō* (Wakita 2002a); the third category of plays (women *nō*) attempted to re-enact the Heian period by bringing the characters from the *Genji* and *Ise* tales onto the stage.[35] Those who enjoyed *nō* thereby were able to deepen their knowledge of the classics and simultaneously acquire knowledge about court culture, which was the model for the shogunal court culture. The court and the emperor, by the power of that culture, could retain their status. As we have already seen, the *nō* drama popularised the classical world in the community festivals of towns and villages (Wakita 2002a). At the centre of that classical world of court culture was women's literature—its creators, the court ladies (*nyōbō*), can in no way be reduced to woman as nature, procreation and motherhood.

Gods in the medieval era: sexual love and motherhood

In the medieval era, Buddhism taught that because women possessed the five hindrances they could not attain Buddhahood; consequently, as polluted beings, women were forbidden to enter sacred precincts (Taira 1990). This section considers whether this was only an official attitude or whether, in practice, women really were excluded in this way.

The female shaman, or *miko*, was the bearer of magical powers in primitive religion: one who could hear the voices of the gods and transmit their oracles. It is generally accepted that in the process of the religious development that occurred through Buddhism, the activity of the *miko* was severely restricted. As its influence rose, Buddhism fused with the indigenous religion (*shinbutsu shūgō*) and incorporated the native gods, who had previously spoken through the *miko* but now became beings in need of salvation. These gods were interpreted as bearers of retributive karma and were expelled as heretical and harmful because living creatures had been killed and offered as sacrifices to them. Later, sacrifice was replaced by the practice of releasing fish, birds and other captive creatures (*hōjō-e*).

These changes had repercussions for the class of people who were discriminated against and whose vocations included the slaughter of animals (Wakita Haruko 1985; 2002b), but they were also of consequence for women's history, as *miko* were the carriers of these religious practices. Did the gods who demanded living sacrifices and were expelled as pernicious disappear with the flourishing of Buddhism or did they remain beneath the surface? Did this coincide with the relegation to a low social status of the people who were connected with these religious practices?

It is generally held that *miko* originated as the wandering women who attended at the imperial burials in the ancient period: they performed spirit placation and summoned the spirits of the dead (Gorai 1982). *Miko* existed in all places, not only around those in power. In the medieval era, *miko* always conducted séances (*kuchiyose*) to contact the spirits of both dead and living people, and they performed everyday divinations and fortune-telling, healing and interpretation of dreams. Even members of the intelligentsia, such as Prince Sadafusa, the writer of the *Kanmon nikki* (*Diary of things seen and heard*), constantly used their services, as Chapter four shows. Apart from *miko*, a large number of women, like the Kumano *bikuni*, who were *miko*-like nun figures, carried out medieval-style Buddhist proselytising and teaching from pictures (*etoki*) (Katō 1990).[36] They can be said to belong fully within the Buddhist framework, but were a typical phenomenon of the medieval era. There needs to be a reconsideration of what these women preached, and what they brought to the women who heard them speak about the realms of hell and heaven.

Should the religion disseminated by *miko* and *bikuni* be dismissed as vulgar superstition belonging purely to the world of folk religion? How should we distinguish between commonplace cults and 'respectable' religion? Perhaps the *miko* found today in major shrines are simply a relic of primitive beliefs, remaining as a formality and performing *kagura* dances. What kind of religious role did *miko* play in the middle ages? In the process of Buddhist–*Shintō* fusion (*shinbutsu shūgō*), what happened to the gods who had made their appearances through the oracular voice of the *miko*? I have wondered whether the gods existed only as shadows, the so-called temporary form of the Buddha, and have long doubted the nature of a religion that teaches that women are sinful creatures who cannot easily obtain salvation and should become nuns (Hosokawa 1989a; see also Chapter four).

Abe Yasurō has studied a significant group of stories (*setsuwa*) such as *Sotoba Komachi*, in which a woman argues with an eminently virtuous priest and makes her way into a forbidden precinct (Abe 1989). Even earlier, the mythical nun Tōro attracted scholarly attention, but there was a strong tendency to interpret her as the bearer of a primitive religion that had retreated in the face of Buddhism.[37] Female religious practitioners such as *miko* and *bikuni* have been understood as either being aware of their pollution and sin, to be reformed by a great priest, or as wielding a primitive magical power. Abe astutely points out that the supernatural power of the *miko* has a medieval character and functioned in the medieval world.

Abe also writes about the *miko* who served at the Wakamiya hall of the Kasuga Taisha, proving that *miko* and *shirabyōshi* (female entertainers) played an important religious role at large shrines, and that priests had extensive arguments about the appropriateness of this (Abe 1987). We can observe the oracle of Kitano Tenjin in the *Kitano Jinja Engi*, delivered through Ayako, the *miko* in the picture scroll of *Kasuga Gongen Reigen-ki* (Tyler 1990);[38] or, further, in the *Hōgen monogatari*,[39] when the *miko*, on the occasion of the retired Emperor Toba-in's pilgrimage to Kumano, foretold that his lifespan was up by repeatedly clapping her hands. Numerous examples show that even people in the ruling classes believed the oracles of *miko*—although these folk beliefs were excluded from official Buddhist dogma. If they were recognised at all, they were understood as a necessary means (*hōben*) to greater faith. However, if we look at Ippen's faith in the (*Shintō*) gods, such as those at the Kumano shrine, we see that Buddhism at the time was surprisingly close to the gods, despite Shinran forbidding their worship. In the Kamakura period, as the new Buddhist faith was promulgated to the common people, we can assume that a conscious decision was made about whether to tolerate the gods who formed the spiritual reality (the gods of the common people were local gods, not necessarily connected with the divine ancestor of the imperial house) or whether to confront them.

Local beliefs and cults involved gods of the mountains, the sea and the ancestors. From the late Kamakura to the Warring States periods (14th to

16th centuries) there were many attempts to raise the status of such gods by linking them with the ancestral gods of the imperial house (Wakita 1990–91; 2002a). However, in the early to mid-Kamakura period, there was no apparent connection with these centralised gods. There was a strong tendency for people simply to create origin myths (*engi setsuwa*) to raise the status of their gods (Sakurai 1976).[40] For example, in the *Shintō-shū*, a collection of *setsuwa* of the Agui sect of Buddhist preaching, many of the tales have their origin in eastern Japan (the Kantō region), not in the central area of strongest court influence. Many of these tales are about a malevolent spirit who suffers much hardship, journeys through hell (*jigoku meguri*) and finally becomes a god. Such stories are the essence of medieval myth.[41] Even the single deity devised by *Yoshida Shintō* was a deification of a dead spirit, as can be seen in the legend 'Fukushima bōrei shinkon'[42] found in the Miyazaki district, Hyūga Province. This is *not* a revival of primitive and ancient beliefs.

The appearance of such medieval gods—the beatification of ghosts—is often achieved via *miko*. Apparently, in an earlier version of the *nō* play *Tomoe*, the ghost of Tomoe possesses the *miko* of the shrine dedicated to Kiso Yoshinaka (Itō 1989); in the *Nenchū gyōji emaki* (annual events picture scroll), there is always a *miko* walking alongside the *mikoshi* carrying a deity.[43] In order to hear the words of the deity, it was always necessary to employ a shaman, who was often a *miko*.

It is essential to clarify the position of female religious practitioners, female deities and women in general in the syncretic medieval religion of *shinbutsu shūgō*. If we think of the nature of the gods, and not just the fact of possession, I believe that *miko* and the gods they served emerged as a medieval social phenomenon, not as some remnant of the primitive and ancient periods. Taking the example of the story of the wizard Kume no Sennin, Abe has concluded that 'the act of falling into, and being covered by, the common dust of woman, is a necessary turning point for the transformation of the mountain wizard (*sennin*) of the ancient period into the mountain ascetic (*hijiri*) of the medieval period'. He also points out that 'the (sexual) union of yin–female and yang–male (*in'yō wagō*)' is the central theme of medieval myth (Abe 1991). Very appropriately, Itō Masayoshi expresses this as 'vulgar and human medieval *Shintō*' (Itō 1989).

In the medieval period, gods familiar since the ancient period changed in character. In the north-eastern part of Kyoto the shrine called Kibune-sha enshrines the god Takaokami, originally invoked to bring or to stop rain. At that time, the court made offerings of sacred folded paper to pray for rain; however, among the common folk, this god was believed to protect conjugal love. In the *nō* play *Hanjo*, there is a passage in which the woman prays to the god of Kibune to discover the whereabouts of her departed lover; in the play *Kanawa*, a woman comes to worship at this shrine at the hour of the ox (two to four o'clock in the morning) in order to curse and kill the man who rejected her. The Kibune-sha had become a shrine for the protection of male–female love by the mid-Heian period, and Izumi Shikibu composed a *waka* there. An amusing version of this legend is included in the *Shaseki-shū* collection of tales from the mid-Kamakura period, where a *miko* celebrates the 'Festival of Love' (*Kyōai no matsuri*) (Nishioka 1956; Izumiya 1984). We cannot know the truth of Izumi Shikibu's involvement, but we can be confident that *miko* probably conducted 'festivals of love'. This is persuasive because of the anecdote in *Shin Sarugō-ki* about Uemon no jō's first wife going to pray at many shrines to reclaim her husband's love.

The Kibune-sha was not connected with sexual love in the ancient period, but as the *miko* came to conduct 'festivals of love' the nature of the god changed to one that protected male–female relations. In this medieval situation, it was more effective to teach about gods who had shared the same experiences as humans, for such gods would have greater impact on the lives of the people who believed this. The medieval gods were therefore explained as being no different from humans: experiencing sexual love and maternal affection, having families and suffering both love and hate. This is why they can be called both vulgar and human.

Although in the medieval period the official attitude was that sexual love was sinful, there was no other era in which sexual love was propounded so much and occupied such a basic position in people's lives. The *nō* play *Ominaeshi* depicts a woman who kills herself out of resentment at the unfaithfulness of her husband. The man then follows her in death. The play intones, 'the demon of lust tortures the body', but it is also a song of praise for mutual love and respect. Research is needed on issues such as why sexual love formed the basis of literature and drama in this way, whether this sexual love was based on the male prerogative of possessing polygamous sexual love, and whether women had any agency in sexual relationships.

One story in the *Shintō-shū* expounds the provisional form of the Kumano deity, the Kumano *Gongen* (or avatar). The lady of the Gosuiden hall obtains the love of the king and incurs the jealousy of the other ladies when she becomes pregnant. It is decided to kill her and her baby who was born at five months. In death, she gives milk to her child and so is deified as the mother god with her child. Similarly, in the *Uji shūi monogatari* collection of legends,[44] a mother who dies in childbirth falls into hell; and in a legend introduced from China a woman turns into a bird and kills other people's children (she is called *ubume-dori*) (Yamada 1990).

The Kumano legend has the woman give birth before being killed, so she is not cast as *ubume-dori*, although she calls herself the *ubume-dori* in the tale *Kumano Gongen no koto*, thus gaining narrative consistency. However, instead of becoming a malevolent ghost, the spirit of the murdered woman is deified. This story is related to the oral tradition of hunters, who came to the assistance of a woman who spilled blood while giving birth in the mountain; in return the mountain god gave them the right to hunt in the area (Kishi 1967). This oral tradition and the Kumano story of the Gosuiden lady are both characterised by a portrayal of the deification of motherhood, in the form of a woman who loses blood while giving birth.

In the medieval era the female sex as mother was imbued with the pollution of blood, which hindered its salvation; women were considered creatures of deep sin, destined in death to be thrown into the pond of blood in hell.[45] The *Kumano no honji* (*Origin of the Kumano Temple*) narrative, which the Kumano *bikuni* are said to have preached, is no exception: it, too, teaches this hindrance of women. Notwithstanding, the woman who is soaked in her own blood while giving birth becomes a god. This is the same narrative device as the Kōga Saburō story in *Suwa engi no koto*, where a malevolent spirit goes through great torment and suffering on a journey through hell before finally being saved and made a god: deification is the result of descending into hell due to (female) blood pollution. As Gorai Shigeru writes, in Japanese folk belief hell exists side by side with heaven, with an ordeal in hell holding the promise of a pathway to heaven (Gorai 1990). Gods in medieval Japan—who, when living in this temporal world, accumulated more than the normal suffering—had to be worshipped or else they would bring curses as malevolent spirits. For women, the torment of a mother who shed blood while giving birth, then died leaving the child alone, was surely the greatest unresolved grudge that could be borne.

From a male perspective, sexual love with women brought trouble. As pointed out by Sakurai Yoshirō, Kōga Saburō's sexual feeling for the woman he loves is the reason for his sojourn in hell in the tale *Suwa engi no koto* (Sakurai 1976).[46] His beloved Kasuga-hime is abducted by a *tengu* (long-nosed goblin) and when Saburō finally rescues her she has to return to retrieve the precious mirror she left behind. Kasuga-hime commits nothing but blunders, thus causing Saburō (who has been killed and thrown to the underworld by his elder brother) to wander in the nether world and tread a path of suffering until he is rescued by another woman and is able to return to this world as a god. In this way, both the processes of suffering hardship and of being raised to the status of a god are connected with a woman. The theme of the story, then, is that through sexual love a woman leads a man to hell. According to Sakurai, the concept of the *miko* as 'bride of the god' is behind this narrative, and Saburō's journeys and his adventures as the god (Saburō) were narrated by wandering *miko*. Itinerant *miko* and Kumano *bikuni* proselytised the *Shintō-shū* and, one can imagine, elaborated and expanded the *setsuwa* as they recited them over and over. The audience for whom a story was narrated should also be considered as a part of the formation of the *setsuwa*, for the listeners were men and women who managed an *ie*, the site of daily life, based on monogamous sexual love. Belief in a god who had also lived in this world as a human being—a god who had suffered far more than most people in order to become a god—would have made it easy for people to accept as normal the schema of a husband's sexual love and the pure love of the wife responding to it. If the *miko* and Kumano *bikuni* embellished as they recited these *setsuwa*, it was surely in response to the listeners' demands.

However, man as agent, saved by a wife's pure love, is not the only formula in the *Shintō-shū*. The *setsuwa Nisho Gongen no koto* tells of the origin of two avatars (objects of strong faith for the Kamakura *shōgun* family): the *Izu-san Gongen* and the *Hakone Gongen*. The latter is also sung about in the *nō* play *Hanjo*, as one of the list of gods (Ashigara, Hakone Tamatsushima, Kibune-ya Miwa no Myōjin) who protected conjugal love. This is a typical tale about the maltreatment of a stepchild. Set in India, it concerns a stepdaughter and a younger sister who takes pity on her. The two young girls, who have been chased away by the stepmother's servant, fall into an abyss in the mountains and are near death when they are rescued by two princes who are hunting. The princes marry the girls, much in the pattern of European folk tales (Chūsei Eikoku Romansu Kenkyūkai 1986). Moreover, when the young wives say they are returning home to Japan with their father, the husbands accompany them. The story states that it is the natural way of the world for husbands to follow their wives, and admonishes couples to behave this way.[47]

This is the gist of the *Shintō-shū*, which is substantially different from both Buddhism and establishment *Shintō* sects such as *Yoshida Shintō* and *Ise Shintō*. It is said that the *Shintō-shū* is underpinned by, and shows a strong influence of, the Lotus Sutra (Fukuda 1984). Certainly, its virtues are expounded on every page; furthermore, the concept of blood pollution can be seen. Apart from that, the stories manifest a religious world completely different from Buddhism, which creates a barrier that women are forbidden to cross.

The main themes of these medieval myths are the mother who loses blood when giving birth and the sexual love that forms the relationship between a man and a woman. Human pain is woven around this axis, leading to tragic deaths and restless ghosts who are forced to journey through hell before eventual sublimation: this is the path to becoming a god. A passage in one *Shintō-shū* tale, *Komochiyama engi no koto* (*Concerning the origins of the great deity of Komochiyama*), describes this:

> *Shintō*, which reveals the traces of Buddhas and Bodhisattvas, is necessarily dependent on causes; when Buddhas and Bodhisattvas enter our country, they always borrow human wombs and are born as human beings; they suffer physically, and after enduring many trials, are tried and, after all these, become gods and save living beings in bad times (Kishi 1967).

Sexual love and childbirth were central to life in a medieval society in which the *ie* was pivotal and where even the gods took on the appearance of family members when revealing themselves. Even though the active agent of this society was always the male family head, at times, in a polygamous situation, the image of woman differed: in later times, she became a passive creature, always the object of love,[48] but in the early medieval period woman possessed a positive and active will. She responded to love, and was chaste and faithful to her husband, but she was not the 'ideal woman' of men's imagination. On the other hand, men were willing to wander and carry out sacrificial acts for the sake of the women they loved. Here is a love that is close to being equal. The image of a marriage relationship in which the woman was absolutely subordinate to her husband did not exist among the common people in medieval Japan.

Such an image can be seen not only in the *Shintō-shū*, but also in *nō* plays such as *Ataka*. Itō wrote an essay about the passage that attributes the motive for Emperor Shōmu building the Great Buddha (*Daibutsu*) in Tōdaiji temple to his desire to memorialise his beloved wife, the Empress Kōmyō, who, according to legend, came back to life after her death. He writes that this legend was widely believed in the middle ages. There are numerous examples of stories in the middle ages in which sexual love becomes the impetus for desiring to practise Buddhism. The construction of the Great Buddha of Tōdaiji temple in the 8th century is known historically to have been a highly political strategy; it is interesting that in the medieval period the motivation for its construction changed and was attributed to a personal matter of sexual love, characteristic of the medieval world.

The *nō* play *Utaura* has a section called the *jigoku no kusemai* or hell dance: it speaks of the inevitable trajectory from this world, in which the heart suffers because of love, to the next (hell); that is, the love and affection of this world are contrasted with hell. This is not the official world of politics, but a very human and real world with a simple view of the gods.

A similar structure can be found in *sekkyō-bushi*, a late medieval form of musical story-telling that developed from the arts of the outcast groups of *shōmoji*, as did the *nō* drama. Oguri Hangan is killed because of transgressive sexual love. He is returned to life through both the pure love of Lady Terute, and through the miraculous hot water of Kumano (that is, by the agency of the gods). Indeed, both Oguri and Terute become gods. In another *sekkyō-bushi* narrative, Shuntokumaru, because of the calumny of his stepmother, was banished, but the karmic illness he was afflicted with was cured through the love and sacrificial spirit of a princess, resulting in a happy end to the story. The women in these stories constantly offer their devoted love to the male characters, and it is this selfless love that breaks the spell binding those characters. However, the structure of the earlier *Shintōshū* tales (14th century), in which men proffer love towards women who are active and outgoing, disappears by the time of *sekkyō-bushi*. The extant texts of the *Shintōshū* and of *sekkyō-bushi* date only from the early Edo period, so they may have been modified substantially over time.

The *nō* play *Yorobōshi*, a masterpiece written by Zeami's son, Motomasa, uses the same subject matter as the *sekkyō-bushi* narrative *Shuntokumaru*. In early versions, it appears that Yorobōshi (Shuntokumaru) was accompanied by a young woman, but in the version performed today he is a solitary blind beggar who loves elegance. The scene of his daily meditation, facing the direction of the setting sun, has strong philosophical and religious overtones. The romantic connection with the woman has been completely cut, reflecting the influence of aristocratic tastes in the changing reception of *nō*.

Thus there was another world separate from the official philosophy of Buddhism, which stopped women from entering its inner precincts and regarded women as contaminated by blood. In the world inhabited by the common people, distinct also from the political sects of *Shintō*, there existed a body of tales and performing arts, which treated seriously the relations between men and women, and motherhood and childbirth. These were in no way in conflict with the official religions of Buddhism and formal *Shintō*. Rather, these stories stripped away the outer layer of the official religions, embellished them and formed a compromise with them. The many and complex ways in which this occurred is still not completely clear and needs further research.

In the medieval age there were many instances where the nature of deities changed, as in the case of the Kibune-sha shrine, whose deity became the god who protected relations between men and women. As with the gods in the *Shintō-shū*, many took the form of couples and parent–child pairs. One example, which stands out as distinctive, is the gender transformation of male gods into female gods. Since the pantheon of gods was constructed to reflect the world of humans, it is not surprising that both male and female gods should exist. However, female gods dominated: not only those surviving from the primitive and ancient periods, but many that were created in the medieval period. This can be thought of as reflecting a peculiar quality of the medieval period. In ethnology, the theory of a *miko* as the bride of a god implies that the god whose oracle the *miko* conveys is a male god; but this is not necessarily so, given that there were more female than male deities in the medieval period, as the following few examples show.

The deity Yamato no Katsuragi, called Hitokotonushi-no-kami, appears in the Yūryaku-ki passages in the chronicles *Kojiki* and *Nihon shoki* in the male form of the Emperor Yūryaku.[49] Perhaps the gods of the ancient world could take on any form at will when appearing to a living human being. The next time this god appears is in the record of En no gyōja, the story in the Monmu chapter of *Zoku Nihon shoki*, in which the help of the gods was called on to construct a rock bridge between two cliffs.[50] This story was expanded into a *setsuwa* tale in which the god, ashamed of his ugly appearance, built the bridge at night and disappeared in the morning. As a result, the name Katsuragi became a synonym for ugly looks: by the time of *Kagerō nikki* we can already see in a poem, which Fujiwara no Michitsuna sent to a woman, that this deity was understood to be female.[51]

In the *nō* play *Katsuragi*, the female deity dances a *Yamato* dance on the snowy Mount Katsuragi—a most suitable setting for a god play (*kami nō*, or first category plays). In the medieval period it was thought that the High Plain of Heaven and the Heavenly Rock Cave were situated on Mount Katsuragi, according to Itō Masayoshi.[52] Furthermore, this mountain was also the centre of *Shugendō* religion, which took as its theoretical core the document *Yamato Kazuragi Hōzan-ki* (Ōsumi 1977). The founder of *Shugendō* was En no gyōja, who was called on to build the bridge. The image of the female deity who bears the 'suffering of the three heats' is directly reflected in the sun goddess, Amaterasu Ōmikami.

It is from Kannami's time that *nō* (*sarugaku*) became steeped in *Shintō* thought (Wakita 2002a). Zeami, who wrote many god plays, wrote 'Sarugaku is *kagura*'. The fact that he made the Katsuragi deity female was the result of medieval *Shintō* theories, not a revival of primitivism; neither was it trailing after the folk residues of such things. Of course, there is the possibility that

Shugendō ascetics shared the mountain with hunters, who believed the mountain god to be female, and were possibly influenced by them in making Katsuragi a female deity. Just the same, it is very interesting that this myth was universally accepted in this medieval world—a religious world dominated by Buddhism, which promulgated prohibitions against women (*nyoninkinsei*) .

While in the ancient chronicles the sex of the Katsuragi deity is indistinct, that of the Miwa deity is much clearer. In the *Kojiki*, the Miwa deity was a man who regularly visited the lady Ikutama Yoribime; in the *Nihon shoki* the deity was the *Ōmononushi no kami* who regularly visited the goddess. As the main character of a divine marriage myth, it is obviously a male deity[53] and the external form of the god was a snake. However, in the medieval *nō* play of this name, a female deity appears, dances *kagura*, and re-enacts the ancient marriage tale. The *kyōgen* interlude states that 'this god is known as both female and male', which suggests that the *nō* actors felt uncertain about the gender.

Itō has argued that the text shows that the *honji* Dainichi Nyorai was the manifestation (*suijaku*) of both the Miwa deity and the *Ise* deity, who both narrate the story of the Heavenly Rock Cave and appear as female deities (Itō 1989). In that case, why is it that the Miwa deity seeks the Dainichi Nyorai as its *honji*? The *Ise* deity is the sun goddess, so this is logical, but it is difficult to see the same necessity for the Miwa deity. There was an oral tradition that, before Dainichi Nyorai became its *honji*, the Miwa deity was a female form: that is why Dainichi was the *honji* and became associated with the *Ise* deity.[54]

In the *nō* play *Tatsuta*, the eponymous deity is a female wind god (*fūjin*) of the Tatsuta shrine, which the story claims stands in the path of the wind. According to the *Konjaku Monogatari* (*Tales of times now past*), during the wind festival (*kaze matsuri*) a wild boar was sacrificed and ceremonially eaten.[55]

Why are there so many instances of gods—even those who had clearly been depicted in male form in the ancient period—who subsequently became female? The most common explanation is that the god borrows the human form of the *miko*, who receives and communicates its messages. I agree with Itō that this interpretation derives from the perspective and logic of contemporary scholarship (Itō 1989:'Miwa'; Wakita 2005). In *nō* plays there is a clear distinction between dances in which gods such as Miwa and Katsuragi appear on stage, and dances in which a *miko* is possessed and delivers an oracle. When the *shite* actor plays a god and dances *kagura*, he performs a stomping action called *jo* (called *henbai* in *onmyōdō* practice), which is not performed when the *shite* plays a *miko*. Thus, in the god plays *Miwa* and *Tatsuta*,[56] this movement is performed: in *Miwa* the deity appears as female because it was thought that the god was female.

In the *nō* play *Makiginu*, the Kumano deity enters a *miko* and delivers an oracle in order to rescue a man who is about to be punished for a crime. The man, a vassal, had composed a poem dedicated to the deity. However, this case is clearly no more than a *miko* possessed by a god, not the god himself. The aim of this play is the possession of the *miko* and not the appearance of the god, whose sex is not discernible. Therefore, the *shite* actor plays the *miko*, not a god, and when *kagura* is danced the stomping movement *jo* is not performed.

This shows that the *miko* is treated separately from the god who possesses the *miko*, and so we cannot accept the argument that the female deity is reflected in the sex of the *miko*.

A second interpretation, which should be considered, is that these gods own the suffering of the three heats and are seeking salvation and pardon from this guilt. They are gods who remain in this unhappy world and take upon themselves the suffering of ordinary mortals. According to Itō, the way for humans to achieve release from guilt is by narrating the karmic events of their former lives. Gods who vicariously bear the suffering of living creatures are most suitably female forms. The simplest way of understanding *shinbutsu shūgō* is as Buddhism overwhelming the native belief, making inroads into the world of the common people and fusing with the indigenous gods. *Honji suijaku* theories are a kind of conditional surrender, and a salvation of the gods by Buddhism. It is fair to say that the native gods were relegated to a lower position. According to this view, it is for this reason that they took on the female form: for defeated and rescued gods, a female form was the most suitable. While this interpretation is not unreasonable, I think it came about after male-centric thought strengthened. Are female deities always begging for salvation and alleviating guilt?

In Zeami's play *Furu*, the deity has a female form, and as a god of war she appears carrying a sword; she is not necessarily a god praying for salvation and forgiveness. The existence of this play is an exception to the interpretation that a female form is assumed in order to achieve forgiveness and salvation.[57] Perhaps this is the reason that the play dropped out of the performance repertoire from the late Muromachi period: it no longer suited the growing patriarchal system to have a female god of war or gods who did not plead for forgiveness and salvation. *Shintō*, including the academic theories of the *Ise* and *Yoshida* branches, which were both patriarchal and political, donned a new garment—the local beliefs of the people fused with the ancestral deities of the imperial family and gradually became woven into *Yoshida Shintō.*

Just as humans form families, in this era, in which the housewife (the official wife) held a very important role in the *ie*, the gods also formed families, appearing as husband and wife with children and as gods who protected conjugal relations.

Conclusion

In order to escape the bind of 'woman–nature–primitive' and 'man–civilisation', this chapter has put forward an alternative narrative to investigate the establishment of the medieval *ie* from the viewpoint of women's history. The *ie* and the family operated in society as an organisation encompassing politics, economics, industry and culture. We have considered the inner workings of the *ie*; the status of the woman, who occupied a central role in household management; the mother who bore the heir who ensured the continuation of the *ie* and the sexual love that was the basic task in this; and the religion and culture surrounding all these. The position of the mother was high, but her value did not exist solely in childbirth. As the chief manager of house matters, she was expected to have high-level abilities in household management.

I have argued that within the *ie*, women were not restricted to being wives. In the pre-modern era a large number of women were not included in the *ie* system. However, I have chosen in this chapter to focus on the *ie* because medieval society was formed with the *ie* as its basic social unit. Irrespective of whether dominant or dominated class, those who formed *ie* were on the whole involved in the basic relations of production, from which some people were excluded from these relations. Scrutinising both the inside and outside of the *ie*, we can see the aspects which are prescribed by the *ie* as the basic social unit, extending to religion and culture. In this way, we have a methodology to surmise the status of women, even though we cannot see into the innermost workings of the *ie*.

Because medieval society had the *ie* as its axis, it had to place importance on male–female conjugal relations. Of course, it cannot be said that sexual love was an equal relationship, for, although monogamous, the system allowed multiple concubines. However, in this system the status of the official wife was secure, unlike the *tsumadoi* or *mukotori* marriages of the Heian period, where the wife's status was precarious. Accordingly, it is one-sided to paint the medieval *ie* uniformly as a patriarchal authority. Whether considering the primitive classless society or patriarchy, equality or subjugation, it is simplistic to think in terms of only two dichotomies. There is not necessarily a contradiction in the coexistence of patriarchy and the authority of the housewife. It is essential to include both class differences and gender differences in one's view of a status and class society. It is inappropriate to theorise gender differences in isolation from class differences, and to see class status as a homogeneous abstraction.

Notes

1   The Chinese-inspired *ritsuryō* system was a national administration formalised by the Taihō reforms of 702 AD. It comprised both a penal and administrative law, established as the country's fundamental legal code. The general populace, which had lived under the domination of near-autonomous wealthy families, became subject to the control of a centralised administration, through intermediary offices in the capital region and in the outlying provinces [trans].

2   Takie (1979) applies Lévi-Strauss's theory of a nature versus culture schema to women and men, and criticises Sherry Ortner's (1987) schema of woman = nature, man = culture ('Are women and men the same relation as nature to culture?'), as she believes that the role of women is a combination of culture and nature. Further, the way of realising equality between the sexes must be found in working out how to engage with both genders: on the one hand, pinning down cultural and artificial causes and liberating the natural fact of sex and, on the other hand, supplementing and remaking cultural equality out of the natural inequality that exists in sex.

3   *Tsumadoi-kon*: 'wife-visiting marriage', where husband and wife lived separately in a duo-local arrangement and the husband visited the wife, who resided with her family, was one of two (with uxorilocal) predominant systems of marriage in the 10th and 11th centuries. The wife depended on the husband's visits, and divorce was a simple matter of suspending either the visits or correspondence. This was the most unstable form of marriage, with a high incidence of divorce. In the case of secondary wives, duo-local was the rule. Neo-local marriage, in which principal and secondary wives lived together (as in the *Tale of Genji*), was rare (see Wakita 1984b). *Mukotori-kon* is the adoption of a husband into the family. In *Yometori-kon*, a woman marries into a man's family [trans].

4   Takamure Itsue (1963) views the *tsumadoi* marriage depicted in ancient poems (*Azuma-uta*) and the *tsumadoi* marriage of the Heian period nobility as the same. Despite their similarity, we must also consider the differences that evolved between these two chronologically separate marriage practices.

5   *Kagerō nikki* 974 (see Seidensticker 1994). The author, known only as Michitsuna no haha (Michitsuna's mother) was a member of the middle-ranking aristocracy of the Heian period (794–1185), and wrote an account of 20 years of her life (954–74) centring on her relationship with her husband, Fujiwara no Kaneie (Arntzen 1997; McCullough 1990:102–99) [trans].

6   Retiring and shy, the author was known as the daughter of Sugawara no Takasue—a Heian middle-class woman (born 1008). She preferred to dwell in the fantasy world of fiction, which she read with religious zeal, and thus was never a success

in polite society or at Court, where she served intermittently as a lady-in-waiting [trans].

7   We should not imagine that the household community (*setai kyōdōtai*) and the systems of production were completely separate in the ancient period. Rather, the bureaucratic organisations and the official workshops probably existed on top of the foundation of the widespread existence of an inseparable household community—even in the nobility. There was a sutra-copying office, for example, in the residence of Fujiwara no Kuzumaro, son of Fujiwara Nakamaro (see Sonoda 1966).

8   With the dissolution of the government workshops (*kanga kōbō*) in the mid-Heian period, some craftsmen entered workshops in the establishments of the nobles (such as *mikuramachi* and *tsukumo dokoro*); others set up workshops in their own *ie* as independent managers (see Wakita 1969b). Even though many commodity-producing industries, such as ceramics production and brewing, relied on the active involvement of women's labour, the goods were often contracted out in the name of the male head of the business—except in the case of a widow, where the woman's name was often used (see Wakita 1988a).

9   Among *nyōkan* (*nyōbō*), the high ranking ones formed their own *ie*, and those above the fourth rank, like their male counterparts, had *mandokoro* administrative offices. For example, the document 'Nyōbō no sanmi ke no mandokoro no kudashibumi' (holograph, 'Hōshakuji monjo', in *Ōyamazakimachi-shi: shiryō-hen*) was issued by the daughter of Ichijō Sanetsune (1223–84), Banshūmon-in Hanshi, the court lady Shōshi of Go-Nijō-in, who held the sub-third rank.

10   In the Heian period, if a man visited a woman for three nights in a row, the relationship was acknowledged and celebrated by the woman's family by the eating of ceremonial rice cakes, called *mikago no mochi* [trans].

11   Not everyone has argued that the position of women was highest in the primitive era. For example, Hora (1956), applying the theory of Couneau, argues that the rights of the mother came into being because of the invention of agriculture by women.

12   It is common to position the establishment of patriarchy as coinciding with the development of a dominant class from a classless society. It even seems that the rise of patriarchy is seen as synonymous with the creation of a civilised state, without any clear definition of what this might mean. Furthermore, female emperors in the primitive era, such as Himiko, are simply explained away as shaman queens: female emperors under the *ritsuryō* system are explained as filling a gap before a child emperor is able to rule, or as puppet-like rulers. The nature of power in these situations has not been properly addressed.

13   The crime of adultery came to be regarded more seriously from the early medieval period to the later medieval period (Katsumata 1979; Tabata 1982). The fact that it applied only to wives, not to husbands, signifies that the wife was the possession of the husband. Gomi Fumihiko demonstrates conclusively that a wife who was supported was in effect enslaved to her husband, whereas a wife who possessed property in her own right was treated quite differently (see Gomi 1982). If so, she may also have been treated differently in relation to the crime of adultery.

14   On the transitional *ie* of the Heian period, when living in the wife's house and production were separate, see Fukutō (1991).

15   See Wakita (1990c), and Chapter four. The unusual situation at this time, with no empress in the imperial family and no official wife in the princely families, relates to the gap between the medieval *ie*, which is predicated on the union of a married couple, and the legal *ie* in the form of the marriage system of the imperial era (Nara–Heian). In the *ie* based on imperial legal status, as can be seen in documents such as *Nyōbō sanmi kasei-dokoro shimofumi*, anyone above the third rank, whether male or female, could establish their own *mandokoro*. This was based on the nature of court rank. Therefore, the empress set up an *ie* separate from that of the emperor. It is probable that an official wife in the princely families was chosen according to rank. This means that the *ie* of the imperial and princely families are not an integrated group with the emperor and empress at the summit. Rather, both emperor and empress had their own establishments, served by different *nyokan*, but were married to each other. Therefore, in the 14th and 15th centuries, the marriage practice of the emperor consisted only of the emperor's household. Since the emperor from time to time formed liaisons with the *nyokan*, this system should be called one man and multiple concubines. The households of the imperial family and the princely families found it difficult to form the medieval style of *ie*, with the couple as its nucleus.

16   *Tokitsugu kyōki*, entries of the 13th year of Tenmon, fourth day of the fifth month; 29th day of the ninth month; and 20th day of the 12th month tell of a lawsuit by Yamashina Nishi no shō: he made a request to the *Buke* Midai (Konoe) through her servant Matsui Magosaburō, and received her support. The entry for the eighth day of the 11th month in the same year tells of Yamashina Karei being chastised, but Midai apologised on his behalf; for this he was pardoned by the *Buke* and also received an imperial pardon. This indicates that Konoe was no less powerful than Hino no Tomiko.

17   *Bakuhan* system: the government system of the Tokugawa shogunate (also known as the Edo *bakufu*,1603–1867)– a mixture of central authority and local autonomy, which characterised the Tokugawa polity. Literally a combination of *bakufu* and *han* (the domain of a *daimyō*) [trans].

18   Kawane (1971) posits that in the 9th and 10th centuries the *ie* consisted of the couple: house head and mistress. However, this would only have been possible in a *mukotori* marriage, not in a *tsumadoi* marriage. If there had been a master and a mistress, it would not have been a couple but siblings. The change in the nature of the *ie* must be thought of in terms of changes in the nature of marriage practices.

19   *Za* carries many meanings: seat, position, status, guild, community, theatre. The commercial *za* of medieval Japan was much the same as the Western guild: a confederation of bosses. Each boss was head of a house, which was the basic unit of the guild. On the Japanese medieval *za*, see Wakita (1969b;1988a).

20   The *Shin Sarugō-ki* was written in the mid-Heian period, a transitional period for marriage practices. The first wife seems to be in a *tsumadoi* marriage; Uemon no jō has set up a house which is managed by the second wife, who is like the

42 WOMEN IN MEDIEVAL JAPAN

ie nyōbō of the later period. The third wife is depicted as either in a *tsumadoi* marriage, or just set up in a separate establishment.

21 Shimizu Yoshiko pointed this out to me. Murasaki no Ue is the daughter of a prince, but her father does not treat Genji as a formal son-in-law, for Genji brought Murasaki to his residence and lived with her informally.

22 Takamure Itsue (1963) uses the word *sue* to express the situation of a woman with no means of support who enjoys the love of a man either at her own home or at another place.

23 This position was the head of all the *naishi no jō* (see Wada 1983:228) [trans].

24 See Kiyooka (1988) [trans].

25 This specialised secret jargon of court ladies dates back to the early Muromachi period and gradually spread to the ladies of the *shōgun's* court and then to the townspeople classes. It involved, among other things, a duplicate vocabulary, so that, for example, *yukata* (summer kimono) was called *yumoji* (Takeuchi & Takayanagi 1974).

26 Nishikawa Yūko has pointed out that in France there are people who argue that, because the culture itself expresses the oppression of women by men, not possessing female language leads to the inability to express specifically female experiences (see Tanasawa 1981).

27 See *Tosa nikki* (1990), an anthology of *waka* poems connected by prose, in which the first person narrator is a female writing in the Japanese syllabary (or *kana*) [trans].

28 *Kokin wakashū* is an anthology of 1111 Japanese poems compiled and edited early in the 10th century. Conventionally abridged in Japanese to *Kokinshū* and translated as 'Collection of old and new Japanese poems', the poems are divided into 20 scrolls or books (*maki*), each of which bears a title referring to conventional poetic topics (the seasons, love, parting, mourning, miscellaneous topics) or to genres. The great majority of poems in the collection are in the form today usually called *tanka* (short poem or song) but traditionally referred to as *waka* (Japanese song/poem) or simply as *uta* (song, poem) because this was the predominant canonical form of Japanese poetry from perhaps the 8th century until the late 19th century (Rodd 1984; McCullough 1984) [trans].

29 *Renga* is a traditional linked poetry of 5–7–5 or 7–7 syllables. In *renga* meetings, people would produce continuous stanzas called *haikai no renga* or *renga* in the medieval period (12th to 16th century). *Haikai* means comical; *renga* means linked poetry. The opening stanza of the *renga* chain (the *hokku*) later became the basis for the modern *haiku* poem. For further reading, see Miner (1979) [trans].

30 'Eulogy on the occasion of the 33rd memorial service for Asakura Takakage (1428–81)' (*Dai Nihon shiryō* 1968:8-13; Wakita 1988b).

31 In this companion piece to the famous *Heike monogatari*, the unknown 15th century author traces the story of Yoshitsune, the dashing young Genji general and half-brother of the founder of the Kamakura *bakufu*, whose meteoric rise to fame during the Genpei War (1180–85) came to a poignant halt when the slanders of rivals caused Yoritomo to turn against him [trans].

32   Nijō Yoshimoto laid down the prescribed form for *renga*, which later became a favourite pastime of the nobility.

33   In the early medieval period there was a system of equally divided inheritance (*bunkatsu sōzoku*), so a wife who brought property to a marriage had a different treatment and position in the household from a woman who was completely supported by her husband (Gomi 1982). By the late Middle Ages, the practice had changed to individual inheritance (*tandoku sōzoku*), in which a woman's right to own property disappeared, so the sense of woman as possession (chattel) became stronger, and the status of women plummeted (see Wakita 1984b).

34   In the medieval period, when individual spheres of influence and decentralised rights jostled against each other, the emperor was a symbol of centralised power, so by bringing the emperor into the story, universality was acquired. For example, in Zeami's *nō* play *Yōrō*, this universality is achieved when the local mountain god is encountered by an imperial messenger (see Wakita 1990b).

35   Among plays that take their subject matter from the *Tales of Ise* are *Izutsu*, *Kakitsubata*, *Unrin'in*, and *Oshio*. Plays based on the *Tale of Genji* include *Yūgao*, *Hajitomi*, *Aoi no ue*, *Nonomiya*, *Ukifune*, *Tamakazura* and *Genji kuyō*.

36   This article differentiates the *miko* as dealing with things in the present life, and *bikuni* as dealing with matters of the next life.

37   Yanagita Kunio pointed this out a long time ago (see Gorai 1982).

38   This is a book of 21 picture scrolls (*hon e-maki mono*) depicting various aspects of the supernatural associated with the Kasuga shrine and its deity, the tutelary deity of the Fujiwara. Paintings by Takashina Takakane (flourished 1309–30), head of the imperial office of painting (*edokoro*); stories compiled by the Kofukuji monk Kakuen (1277–1340) in consultation with two senior monks of the same temple; text written by the former Regent Mototada and his three sons. The Tokyo National Museum copy (Tokyo Kokuritsu Hakubutsukan-bon) number 1 was copied from the original in 1845 [trans].

39   This chronicles the Hōgen incident of 1156, an abortive coup d'etat, which marked the emergence of the military class as a political power in Japan (Wilson 1971) [trans].

40   The *kusemai* narrative section in Kannami's *nō* play, *Shirahige*, is also relevant.

41   At the Katsuō-ji temple in Minō, in 1243, the Yakushi and the Kannon statues in the Main Hall were opened for public showing in order to raise money to restore the temple. On that occasion, the temple requested the Agui sect to create a picture scroll on the temple's origin (Minō-shi-shi [History of Minō City]). In particular, the Sengoku period saw a boom in the upgrading of temples through the creation of picture scrolls of origins. Many stories in the Agui sect's *Shintō-shū* are said to have originated from eastern Japan, which suggests that the addition of the name Agui had a close connection with the raising of the status of gods by creating origin tales (see Fukuda 1984). The *Shintō-shū* referred to are Kondō (1959) and Kondō & Kishi (1968).

42　Tadatomi Ōki, entry for the 23rd day of the 9th month, 1498. See also Wakita (1990–91).

43　See 'Gion goryō-e (The Gion festival for spirits)', a scroll published in Komatsu (1987). Gomi Fumihiko (1984) mistakenly takes this picture as depicting the Imamiya goryō-e. *Nenchū gyōji emaki*, the subject of Komatsu (1987), is an illuminated picture scroll of annual court ceremonies. It is attributed to Tokiwa Mitsunaga, an important member of the Painting Office (*E-dokoro*) attached to the imperial court, and was produced between 1158 and 1179. Although the original scrolls of this series were destroyed in the great fire at the imperial palace in 1661, copies of seventeen of them are still extant in the Tanaka Collection in Tokyo.

44　See *Nihon ryōiki* II-9 (Nakamura 1997). This book contains early 9th century tales (*setsuwa*) on the karmic retribution of good and evil from the oldest collection of Buddhist legends in Japan. Kyōkai was a contemporary of Saichō and Kūkai, founders of Japanese Tendai and Shingon sects, respectively. See also *Uji shūi monogatari, Konjaku monogatari-shū* 27-43 (Mills 1970) and Katō (1985).

45　In the *Jigoku-zōshi* (hell-tale scrolls), it seems that those struggling in the 'Pool of Thick Blood' are not necessarily only women (Komatsu 1987). However, in the Tateyama mandala illustrations of the 'Pool of Blood', all are women. There is one clear instance of this belief to be seen in writing in the famous *Kabuki* play *Kenuki* in the lines, 'it is pre-ordained that women who die in the blood of childbirth will be plunged in the Pool of Blood'. The hell-tale scrolls are 12th century Heian period scrolls depicting the tortures of hell in the collection of Nara National Museum. In Japan, this vision of hell was popularised by the Tendai monk Genshin (942–1017) in his work *Ōjōyōshū* or 'The essentials of salvation', according to which the key to avoiding the torments of hell lay in chanting the *nenbutsu*, an appeal to the saving power of Amida Buddha. This scroll was painted at the behest of emperor Go-shirakawa (1127–1192), but the artist and calligrapher are unknown.

46　Kondō Yoshihiro (1959) also points out that there were places where only women could recite, arguing that women were also teachers of Buddhism (that these were *shōdō* texts recited by women).

47　'A husband ought to obey his wife' (Wakita, Bouchy & Ueno 1999:57).

48　In *sekkyō-bushi*, as we will see later, male agency and female passivity are the norm.

49　See *Kojiki*, 'Yūryaku-ki', and the *Nihonshoki*, 'Yūryaku-ki', item for 4th year, 2nd month (Aston 1956; Inoue 2001:32).

50　*Zoku Nihonshoki*, Monmu third year, fifth month, 24th day. Also in Nakamure (1997:1(28)).

51　See *Kagerō nikki* (Seidensticker 1994).

52　'Katsuragi: Kōten no hara no Iwato no mai' (Itō 1989).

53　*Kojiki*, 'Sujin-ki', *Nihon shoki*, 'Sujin-ki', entry for the tenth year, ninth month.

54　Syncretistic tendencies were formalised in the theory of *honji suijaku*. This theory regarded indigenous Shintō deities (*kami*) as trace manifestations (*suijaku*) of buddhas and *bodhisattvas*, who were their original ground or true nature (*honji*). The theory appears to establish a hierarchical relationship, with the *bodhisattvas* as more basic and important than the *kami*, and thus Buddhism as more fundamental than Shintō (Maraldo 1998), www.rep.routledge.com/article/G101SECT5, viewed 16.10.2005 [trans].

55   'Mikawa no kami Ōe Sadamoto shukke no katari' (Konno 1993–99). *Konjaku monogatari* is a collection of short stories compiled by Minamoto no Takakuni at the end of the Heian period (c1120) from the popular oral tales of that epoch. It contains more than 1000 tales divided onto 31 volumes and covers the histories of Japan, China and India (mostly Buddhist sources).

56   In the play *Katsuragi* the female deity performs the *jo* movement in the *Jo no mai*, even if there is a note to perform *kagura* in the *Yamato mai* (personal communication from Urata Yasunori, a professional performer in the Kanze School).

57   According to personal communication from Urata Yasunori, there are differences among female deities dancing the same *kagura*. Miwa does not perform the *tatsuhai* movement, whereas Tatsuta does. This can be read as performing the difference in status between the two gods. This difference may also be due to the sources on which *Tatsuta* was based—the *Jinnō shōtōki* volume 1 and the *Tatsuta Daimyōjin no koto* (in *Zoku gunsho ruijū*, volume 48) dated 1396.

Changing views of women in medieval Japan: veneration of motherhood and women's bad karma as seen in medieval texts

2

These town dwellers are laughing at the awkward spectacle of Fukutomi. The father of the family is leaning out of the open window, while the mother nurses her baby, with a little girl by her side. This street scene could have been found anywhere.

From an anonymous e-maki mono from the Muromachi period, The tale of Fukutomi (roll 2), about an old man called Hidetaka who becomes rich from his amazing art of farting. He lives next door to another poor man, Fukutomi, who wants to learn this art but fails in front of a rich patron and is ridiculed. The story is also found in *otogi-zōshi* collections.

The scroll is held by the Shunpoin (Myōshinji) in Kyoto (Takeuchi & Takayanagi Mitsutoshi 1974:817; Pigeot & Kosugi 2001)

Introduction

All women are true mothers of all Buddhas of the past, present and future, whereas all men are not true fathers of all Buddhas. Why? Before a Buddha was born, he had been in a woman's womb. Needless to say, when a Buddha is born from a woman's womb, a father does not have this union of yin and yang. A human is given a body, hair and skin by a mother, not by a father. There is no reason or truth that a 'father bears a child', therefore a woman is superior to a man...' (*Gyokuyō*, 28th day, 11th month, 1182)

Kujō Kanezane (1149–1207) recorded this sermon by the priest Chōken, who was renowned as the greatest preacher of his day, in his *Gyokuyō* diary at the time of the Genpei conflict (1180–85). He writes that the elegance and power of the message — that, because women were mothers they were the mothers of all Buddhas, and were therefore superior to men — had the congregation weeping and wiping away their tears. It is clear that this idea was different from the accepted views of the day, because Kanezane added the comment, 'unusual but interesting'.

However, this is not simply an interesting piece of rhetoric in the sermon. Rather, in this chapter I argue that it formed one strand of the thought of the following centuries: that is, veneration for motherhood and its corollary, the strengthening of the stress on chastity for women. Furthermore, as seen already, in inverse proportion to the respect for motherhood, the role for women became quite restricted in various spheres (the court, local rituals and festivals, and work in the society as a whole). The value of women was relegated to motherhood, and women's labour and other activities were gradually gathered under the control of the *ie* as a help-mate for men. Women who had no choice but to exercise their abilities outside the home, like *shirabyōshi* and *yūjo* (entertainers and prostitutes), often lived and worked on the outer margins of respectable society.

This chapter looks in detail at the changes that occurred in the medieval period to ideas about the respect for motherhood, especially as reflected in literary texts.

It is questionable whether medieval women had to live solely within a framework of identity as mothers, living only to serve their children, who were an extension of themselves and their status. In the 16th century, Portugese missionary Luis Frois wrote that in Japanese towns there was a lot of abortion, infanticide and abandonment of children (Frois 1977–78): there were also cases where children were sold to slave traders.[1] While one cannot say all these were the responsibility of the mother, there were many cases where the mother was forced to do this, or at least permitted these acts to occur. How can we know what women felt in this situation?

The function of bearing a child in the medieval period was at times highly respected and at other times regarded as a nuisance. This chapter plots the oscillation between these two poles in the view of motherhood in medieval Japan.

Strengthening of the veneration of motherhood

The spreading trends among the nobility of despising work, of excluding women from social activity and of upper class women not showing their faces were accompanied by a growing respect for motherhood.

The veneration of motherhood expounded by Chōken (as noted by Kanezane in his diary) was not just paradoxical rhetoric by a talented preacher. This philosophy became even more pronounced in the *Gukanshō*, written soon after in 1220 by prominent Tendai high-priest Jien (Kanezane's famous younger brother, 1155–1225). From the perspective of Buddhist teaching, the author explored the significance of the existence of women emperors in Japan in ancient times when the country was developed by women.

Jien writes:

> It was during these 36 reigns that reigning empresses appeared. Two occupied the throne twice: Kōgyoku, who was Saimei in her second reign, and Kōken, who was Shōtoku in her second reign. The truth of the old saying that in this country women provide 'the life-giving touch' (a metaphorical use of *jugan* [inserting the eye], the final touch when completing a statue or painting of a Buddhist figure) was revealed by the appearance of these reigning empresses. In trying to understand the basis for this in Buddhist teachings, I conclude that the phrase 'birth of the human world' clearly points to the fact that people are all born from the wombs of women. Since causal effects (*inga*) are both good and bad, those born of women include the good as well as the bad—holy men (*hijiri*) of the two vehicles and Bodhisattvas, as well as non-Buddhists like Devadatta and Kokāka. All have received the female–mother blessing. Therefore, the principle of taking care of and revering one's mother was followed. Reigning Empresses Jingū and Kōgyoku were placed on the throne because each was the wife of the previous emperor and also the mother of the crown prince (Brown & Ichiro 1979:37).

Women emperors were not necessarily mothers, as in the 8th century example of the woman who ruled twice, first as Kōken (749–758) and again as Shōtoku (764–770).[2] This shows that Jien's view was based on a misapprehension of fact. However, it could be said that, in contrast to earlier periods, the early

Kamakura period when Jien wrote was characterised by a strengthening of the veneration accorded to motherhood, and so it was inevitable for a woman emperor to be justified through her function of motherhood. Jien's philosophy of the veneration of motherhood was a kind of 'mother origin' theory, predicated on women giving birth to both bad and good people.

Jien writes that 'women have begun bad things too', referring to an abortive disturbance called *Kusuko no ran* in 809 when Kusuko (?–810), the lady in waiting to Emperor Heijō (774–824; reigned 806–809), plotted against him.

At the time of the *Gukanshō*, the Kamakura *bakufu* was controlled by Hōjō Masako (1157–1225) and her brother Hōjō Yoshitoki (1163–1224). In the court a woman known as Kyō no Nii (1155–1229), Fujiwara Kaneko, the nurse of retired Emperor Gotoba-in, held the de facto reins of power. Jien wrote: 'The Kantō region is controlled by a sister and brother, and the capital is controlled by Lady Kaneko. Verily, Japan is a country where women give life to all' (Brown & Ichiro 1979:Juntoku).

The *Gukanshō* also vividly describes the activities of mainly noble women in the context of the shifting contemporary political situation. This was not because Jien had a high opinion of women's abilities but because he saw women's function of giving birth as the source of all things—the purpose of existence for women emperors was their ability to bear children, not their ability to rule. He wrote that it was necessary for an empress to have a good aide, and that when there were good subjects it was better to have a woman emperor (Brown & Ichiro 1979:149). Therefore, in the time of Fujiwara no Kamatari (614–669), it had been appropriate to have a woman emperor, Kōgyoku (594–661; reigned 642–645), for since that time the Fujiwara family had monopolised the positions of chancellor and regent and hence had dominated politics. Later, even if blessed with a good aide, the realm had become difficult for a woman emperor to control; consequently the position of *Dairan*, or person in charge of state affairs, was created for the father of the imperial consort. According to Jien, this suited Japan—a country where women were the life givers and which fulfilled the obligations of filial piety by showing gratitude to mothers. He argued for the necessity of the Fujiwara family, of which he was a member, which for centuries had helped its daughters to become empresses through marriage, thus acquiring the positions of chancellor and regent for the Fujiwara family. The logic totally suited his own purposes: in Japan women gave life as a tradition, which was interpreted as veneration of motherhood, and he further linked this to the contemporary political situation, beautifully demonstrating a feature of the culture of the early Kamakura period.

Historical fact does not always accord with Jien's statements about female emperors. Suiko (554–628; reigned 592–628) was not made emperor because she was a mother; furthermore, there were also unmarried women emperors such as Kōken-Shōtoku. Neither can it be said that all women emperors were blessed with good and loyal subjects. Kōgyoku-Saimei, mentioned by Jien, did not always use a Fujiwara as her aide. However, as is well known, the chancellor–regency politics of the Fujiwara clan depended for its authority on the womb of its daughters to put the resulting boy child on the throne, with the maternal grandfather becoming the prime political mover. Jien turned back to ancient times in order to advance his theory of the veneration of motherhood, which suited his need to maintain the status quo of the politics of his time.

However, it is simplistic to think that the concept of veneration of motherhood emerged simply in the particular context of the Fujiwara Sekkanke family; it is more logical to assume that it had a broader base in society.

In the politics of the Fujiwara family, the maternal grandfather of the young emperor was first a guardian in imperial politics, later taking control of broader politics. It is hardly necessary to state that this practice was established against the background of *tsumadoi* and *mukotori* marriage, in which a strong father acted as a support for his son-in-law and, by extension, as a mentor for his grandchild. Veneration of motherhood emerged within this framework of the relatively strong status of the mother–wife. However, accordant with Jien's view, the strength of a woman's status did not depend on her individual talent, for even in *tsumadoi* and *mukotori* marriage her position existed in the shadow of the patriarchal authority of the father or the husband.

This can be confirmed by revisiting the *Shin sarugō-ki*, written by Fujiwara no Akihira (?–1066) in the mid-Heian period (Yamagishi 1979; see also Chapter one), which describes the family of Uemon no jō, a man from Nishikyō (West Kyoto), as the family watches a *sarugaku* performance. His first and principal wife is 60 years of age, 20 years older than her husband, and unashamedly exposes her aged ugly appearance; the second wife is not particularly beautiful, but has talent as a household manager and is the same age as her husband; the third wife is only 18 years old and is very attractive—this is a stereotypical family arrangement.

He married his first wife when he was a young man apprenticed to a bureaucrat because he wanted the influence of his future parents-in-law. Even though she is now full of faults, the account says that he cannot get rid of her because she has borne him several children. This means that the position of the principal wife is assured not so much due to her household management, but owing to her father's status and position, and her maternal function of

bearing children. Here is a unique type of patriarchal system: with the backing
of the wife's natal family, the man was able to have a successful career in the
bureaucracy and support his wives and children. We can conclude that in this
system the mother that could produce children for the patriarch was more
highly valued than household management or good looks.

Therefore, in the veneration of motherhood preached by Chōken and Jien,
and in the marriage system (*tsumadoi/mukotori*) of the nobility of the Heian
period, as well as in the bureaucracy, the positive evaluation of motherhood was
due to the function of childbirth, not to an appreciation of women's individual
aptitudes. In this world, and in the Buddhist world, male power was firmly
entrenched—women were respected as mothers for bearing the successors
to this authority. However it may have been in reality, the consciousness of
respect for motherhood can be interpreted as a male consciousness located
in noble society. This was somewhat different from the motherhood that was
respected in primitive society as the bearer of the next generation of the whole
community.

The mother who descended into hell

In the Heian period, a Buddhist belief, which was different from Chōken
and Jien's theory relating to motherhood, entered Japan. It was the teaching
of filial piety and prayers for one's mother. Mokuren (Mahāmaudgalyāna)
belonged to the inner circle of the Buddha's disciples and was esteemed for
his psychic powers. When his mother went to hell and became a hungry ghost,
he offered services for her and saved her.

This legend was the origin of Japan's *urabon* services (Iwamoto 1968).
The *urabon* was practised as early as 606, and after 733 it became a regular
celebration at court. From the 'Suzumushi' chapter in the *Tale of Genji*, we
know that the legend of Mokuren was current in Heian society.[3] It also appears
in the *Hōbutsu-shū* by Taira no Yasuyori.[4] In the *Konjaku Monogatari* there
are many tales involving Mokuren, but none about his saving his mother. In
the *Gaki zōshi*, which was created shortly after in the late 12th century, the
legend is pictorialised, and the accompanying text tells the story this way:
Mokuren meets his mother who has fallen in the *gaki-dō* hell, and offers her
some food; however, the food immediately catches fire and she cannot eat it.
Mokuren asks the Buddha how he can overcome this problem and save her.
The Buddha answers that if he offers food and drink to a priest and gives his
mother the leftovers, she will be able to eat without it burning her.

It is important to consider the reason that Mokuren's mother is condemned
to hell. In Gukan Jūshin's *Shishū hyaku innen-shū* (*Private collection of 100*

karma tales) (1257, volume 3), in the first tale 'About the wizard Mokuren', Mokuren's mother, Seidaijo, went to hell and suffered unbearably because she was mean and greedy. According to Iwamoto, this shows the influence of popular Chinese literature, for in Chinese versions of the legend the main cause for going to hell is the bad deeds of the mother; whereas in Indian versions of the tale it is because Mokuren's mother does not believe in Buddhism. This is characterised by a spiritual salvation for a problem of faith, not a release from physical suffering.

Urabon services were carried out for the salvation of all people, male or female, who had done bad deeds or whose faith was deficient and caused them to suffer in hell. The practice appropriated the legend of Mokuren saving his mother, showing that mother–child relations were very important.

However, some later *setsuwa* state that the sin that sent the mother to hell was not a specific deed, but the condition of motherhood itself. Whereas earlier motherhood had been venerated, in these later tales it is perceived as a sinful state. In the mid-Kamakura period, Mujū Ichien wrote a collection of *setsuwa* called *Shaseki-shū* (1283), in which the tales about mothers are quite shocking.

A priest called Sanuki-bō dies and is resurrected. When he goes to hell he sees many hungry ghosts (*gaki*) in a field, just as in the scroll pictures. One of them chases after him saying, 'There! That's Sanuki-bō, my child, over there. I raised him and thus accumulated lots of sin and karma and now I suffer hunger and thirst, I am helpless. I am going to eat him'. A Jizō[5] helps him escape and explains:

> Yes, that really is your mother. By raising you, she acquired karma. Yet, even if she eats you, her hunger will only be satiated for a moment. It would have been a pity to have lost your life without a supremely happy memory, so I deceived your mother in order to rescue you. Alas! You should conscientiously offer services for your mother to relieve her suffering, and to make your own next life better (Morell 1985:115).

It is by no means clear just what sin this mother committed in raising her child. Is it the sin of killing living things, such as fish, in order to feed her child? For a human being to be born, raised and to live, many living things must be sacrificed and killed, and that sin seems to have been laid at the door of the mother.

Another possible interpretation is that in order to raise and feed her child, the mother goes hungry and, as a result of her craving for food, after she dies and goes to the hell of hungry ghosts she wants to eat her child. This interpretation, however, does not amplify the phrase 'acquire many sins' and seems a bit too abstract. In the same collection are tales of a priest who does not preach and does not cultivate fields, but lives off other people; and of farmers who incur sins by killing insects and other small creatures in their cultivation. This supports the interpretation that a mother cannot avoid incurring karmic sin in the process of bearing and raising a child. All the sacrifices that accompany the birth and raising of a child are characterised clearly as the sin of the mother, not as the original sin of humans as a whole.

This effectively argues that the whole process of bearing and raising children is achieved at the cost of the mother's guilt, and shows the extent of a mother's role. If there were no women prepared to make such a sacrifice, the human race would not exist. Therefore, it is necessary to hold services for one's mother, a duty bound with the strong ties and inseparability of mother and child (*boshi ittai-kan*). This is the other side of the coin of the veneration of motherhood expounded by Chōken and Jien, where the close identification of mother and child paradoxically becomes a negative for women.

Therefore, the view of the identity of mother and child rests on both the veneration for motherhood and on women's guilt. The child is what the mother has created, whether respected or condemned as sinful, and cannot become totally separated from her because birth and upbringing are possible only through the sacrifice of the mother.

From this identity of mother and child, two trajectories of mother–child relations can be seen. One is the sight of Sanuki-bō's mother in hell, trying to escape from the suffering of hunger by chasing after her child, a part of herself, in order to eat him. The grotesque idea of eating the child belongs to the world of fiction, but the implication is that, having undergone great sacrifice and privation to raise the child, it is only natural that the child, in return, should make sacrifices for his mother after he has grown up. As a kind of hell in this life, the practice of infanticide or 'thinning out' as a means of population control was not unusual in medieval Japan (as in medieval Europe).

In the 16th century, Luis Frois wrote in his *History of Japan*:

> It is very common for women to carry out abortions in Japan. Some do it because of poverty, others because they have too many daughters, and yet others because they are in service and otherwise cannot continue to work properly, and many other reasons. Moreover, normally no person feels angry or upset about this. Some people kill the child soon after birth by treading on the child's neck and strangling it. Others take herbs to induce an abortion. The town of Sakai is big and has a large population, and in the mornings if one walks on the riverbanks or along the edge of moats, one often sees children who have been thrown away here. If the mother feels some emotion towards the newborn who is to be abandoned, the child is placed at the seaside, so that it can live

until the tide comes in and drowns it, or the child is thrown into the moat. It is
then usually eaten by dogs.

This passage, written by a foreign missionary, does not make it clear
whether the mothers killed of their own accord, or because of pressure, or
whether fathers did the deed. However, it is probably true that mothers did not
really feel so sad about it. The identity and unity of mother and child meant that
the child was considered a part of the mother's body and a personal possession.
Infanticide might have been as painful as cutting a part of one's body, but it
may also have been carried out as a necessity for one's own good.

Another trajectory of maternal love is blind or deluded love. From the Heian
period, a parent's love for one's child was commonly called 'the darkness of
the heart' (*kokoro no yami*). A poem in the *Gosenshū* by Fujiwara Kanesuke
reads:

> Although a parent's heart is not in darkness, he might lose the way because
> of wishing the best for his child.

Kanesuke wrote this poem when his daughter became one of the emperor's
wives. In the poem he openly conveyed to the emperor his deep feelings for
his child. And yet, as time went on, the phrase 'darkness of the heart' gradually
came to be applied only to a mother's feelings, with the negative connotation of
blind love. Kanesuke's poem is quoted in the *nō* play *Sumidagawa* to express
the mother's feeling of longing for her lost child.

In the Chinese and Indian versions, and early Japanese versions, of the
legend of Mokuren's mother, the reason given for the mother being in hell
is either her own wrongdoing or the sin of killing living things. However, in
Mokuren no sōshi, the *otogi zōshi* version which appeared in the late medieval
period, it is the result of blind love: the heart of a mother who pushes others
aside for the sake of her child constitutes a sin which warrants going to hell.

In *Mokuren no sōshi*, a mother who is mean and greedy goes to hell and
becomes a hungry ghost. She is 'as black as charcoal' and shameful in her
desires. She is speared through with a pike and whines like a mosquito when
relating why she is in hell. The mother is the wife of the king and her wish is
for her only child, the prince Mokuren, to become king and acquire riches.
After Mokuren becomes a priest, she says how happy she would be if her
son was the most superior of all scholars; she prays that even if 500 or 1000
enlightened beings have to die, her own child should be respected by all kings
and people. Because of this sin of arrogance she is sent to hell.

The inscription at the back of the only extant copy of *Mokuren no sōshi*
(in the Tenri University Library) is dated the second day of the fifth month,

1531. This could be when the tale was written, or when it was copied. On the back of the cover are the words, 'in the brush of Kunisuke', suggesting that the copyist was Prince Fushiminomiya Kunisuke. As the prince died in 1563, the book was possibly written in 1531. It appears likely that the book was read among the upper classes.

Unlike the *Shaseki-shū* version, the sin of Mokuren's mother derives from her arrogance and greed for her beloved child, a more refined and spiritual reason. It depicts exactly the psychological structure of noblewomen (such as consorts of emperors or *shōguns*) in the 16th century. We can speculate that it served as a primer for such ladies and for those who aspired to their positions because, in the system of one husband and multiple wives (concubines), a woman's greatest wish was that the child she bore should become the successor to the ruler or, at least, become a priest and rise to the highest rank of holy orders and control the spiritual life of the ruler. While the scale of this wish varied depending on the position of the mother, the wish was common to all women who wanted successful careers for their children. There is no doubt that excessive love for one's child and the ambition for the child to occupy a high position can be seen as a condition of 'darkness of the heart', not unlike the 'education mothers' (*kyōiku mama*) of our time.

Fathers were also ambitious for their children to succeed in life and inherit position and power. Yet we do not find stories about fathers going to hell for this sin, or stories in which emperors are sent to hell for engaging in political struggles to ensure that their children will succeed them. An exception is the story of the Hōgen rebellion (1156), which arose because the dream of the Emperor Sutoku (1119–64; reigned 1123–41) to have his child enthroned was shattered. He raised a rebellion and was exiled to Sanuki Province in Shikoku, where he became a vengeful spirit because of his desire to maintain control of power as a retired emperor, not necessarily for the sake of his son. This tale lays more weight on the emperor's own dreadful attachment, than on his paternal love.

Why is it that only maternal love condemned one to hell? The story in the *Shaseki-shū* teaches that in order to bear and raise a child, inevitably living things must be killed, and that this 'original sin' is laid at the feet of motherhood. This is similar to the way in which riverbed people and outcasts, who had no choice but to engage in slaughtering and handling dead bodies, and who were considered the lowest of professions including slaughterers and spirit merchants, were condemned to hell in early Japanese Buddhism. When the *Shaseki-shū* was compiled, the cause of the mother's condemnation to hell was consistent with the view that killing living creatures deserved hell. However, by the time of the *otogi zōshi* version of *Mokuren no sōshi*, it was assumed that women normally go to hell, and that the cause was exclusive blind love. This is a psychological cause, and is thus a cautionary tale against such blind love. This change occurred because women (and men) of the nobility had no reason to incur the sin of killing living creatures in bringing up their children and such a cause would not have been convincing.

Paternal love was probably just as exclusive as maternal love, but only maternal love was charged as sinful. A second possible reason for this is that the scope for women to engage in active work had narrowed, and they were locked into maternal love and the function of motherhood. The reward for women's hard work in this situation can only be located in the careers of their children, for women were evaluated only as the mother of someone. This is no doubt why they focused exclusively on their children. The next section further discusses the background to this.

The identification of mother and child

Fortunately, there are several extant writings from the medieval period that were produced as guides to female behaviour and encapsulate the wisdom of women in the noble class of the time. These include *Menoto no fumi* (*Letter from a wet nurse*), *Menoto no sōshi* (*Tale of a wet nurse*) and *Mi no katami* (*The keepsake*), all printed in the collection *Gunsho ruijū* (Hanawa 1928–34). *Menoto no sōshi* and *Mi no katami* seem to have been written in the Muromachi period (1336–1573) and were directed at women in the aristocratic classes who might become members of the *shōgun's* retinue or women serving at the imperial court. *Menoto no fumi* (also called *Niwa no oshie—Homely Teachings*, a reference to the Analects of Confucius) originated at the end of the Kamakura period (1185–1333). The author was a woman with a high degree of accomplishment and refinement acquired as a result of her experience as a court lady. Written as advice for her daughter, named Ki no Naishi, it contains her own accumulated wisdom and experience on how to succeed at court. It is possible that this is a fictional device created as a vehicle for the rules of feminine behaviour—which range from realistic and practical cautions to cultivation of skills in singing and playing musical instruments, to detail how to handle servants.

This *Menoto no fumi* differs from other primers for women in that the writer, herself a *nyōbō*, writes out of ambition for her own daughter:

> That you (my daughter) bear a prince who eventually will be enthroned, and you are respected by everyone as the mother of the country, is my consolation in this hard world. Without that happy memory, in the next world I would sadly be lost in the darkness.

The writer tells that before her child was born, she had a mysterious but auspicious and trustworthy dream in which there was an oracle from the Kasuga deity foretelling that the daughter to be born would attain a very important position. She instructs her daughter:

> If your wish is not realised, this life is not worth living. If you finally feel you can leave this life, and take the path to enlightenment, and if you feel safe and calm, then be ordained and homeless and enter the path of the truth.

This advice (unimaginable today when women have so much choice) advocates setting a positive goal to install one's son on the throne, which *Mokuren no sōshi* later preached to be a sin worthy of hell. It is not something longed for after one's child is born; it is a wish to bear and bring up such a daughter who will obtain the emperor's favour and bear him a son.

Menoto no fumi is believed to have been written by the nun Abutsu-ni (?–1283?), who wrote *Izayoi nikki*, the record of her journey from Kyoto to Kamakura in 1279. Some think this is doubtful (Fukuda 1972),[6] but the contents make it a reasonable attribution. Shimizu Yoshiko states that Abutsu-ni's authorship is supported by the high value placed on the 'way' of poetry (Shimizu 1980). The book has a short dedication, 'To Lady Ki no naishi, from a person far removed from the court', which also indicates that this is a manual written by a cultivated mother (with a long experience of court service herself) for a daughter in court service. Furthermore, the desire to obtain the favour of the emperor, bear an imperial prince, put the child on the throne and become revered as the imperial mother shows accurately both the culture of the late Kamakura era and the personal wish of Abutsu-ni.

In the Heian court, if a court lady of low status and without substance or support received the emperor's favour and bore a child, normally that child was given the status of an ordinary citizen (in the emperor's service, but not as a member of the imperial family), as in the case of Hikaru Genji. A father powerful enough to have his daughter become the mother of an emperor could grasp political power, but a father with no political power to begin with could not hope to do this. Political power relations were closely connected with marriage relations. By the late Kamakura period, partly due to the dominance of the Kamakura *bakufu*, the power of the imperial family and of the Fujiwara family had weakened. Emperor Gosaga took as his empress the daughter of Saionji Saneuji (1225–92), called Ōmiya-in, after which it became common for an imperial consort to come from the Saionji family. The history *Masukagami* (*Jinnō shōtō-ki, Masukagami* 1965; see also Perkins 1998)[7] states that it was rare for a consort, a dowager empress or the wife of a retired emperor to come consistently from a family other than the Fujiwara.

Members of the Saionji family were often appointed as chief ministers, and many daughters of that lower rank family married into the imperial family and became mothers of princes and princesses. However, this was also often achieved by female entertainers such as *shirabyōshi* and *kusemai*. Retired Emperor Kameyama-in (1249–1305; reigned 1259–74; retired emperor 1274–87) was known for his amorous penchant, and among his wives was the daughter of a *dengaku hōshi* performer, who served the retired empress Ankamon-in. Kameyama-in fell in love with her, made her the adopted daughter of the minister Takatsukasa Kanehira (1228–1294) and gave her the title Hisashi no onkata (the lady of the corridor) (*Jinnō shōtō-ki, Masukagami* 1965). Then Prince Kaneyoshi was born. Abutsu-ni was also a lady-in-waiting to Ankamon-in, serving at first under the name Echizen, and later as Uemon no suke, and later again as Shijō. She undoubtedly had every opportunity to observe at close quarters Hisashi no onkata's path to success.

There were many other cases where a prince not born of a high-ranking mother became emperor. For example, the mother of Emperor Gonijō-in (1285–1308; reigned 1301–08) was the daughter of Minamoto Tomomori, who was appointed as minister of the first rank on the occasion of his grandson's enthronement. It was unusual for the child of a Minamoto mother to be chosen as emperor, and the *Masukagami* says that people felt uneasy that the boy's mother lacked political influence and authority. Even so, he could aspire to the rank of emperor, and his mother was granted the title Seikamon-in (1269–1355) as a special honour given by the court to the emperor's mother. Another example is Emperor Godaigo (1288–1339; reigned 1318–39), whose birth mother, Dantenmon-in (Fujiwara Chūshi), was the adopted daughter of the Interior Minister Morotsugu, and whose real father was Councillor Tadatsugu. Many birth mothers came from this councillor (*sangi*) class.

Thus, as *Menoto no fumi* expounds, there was always an opportunity for court ladies in the late Kamakura period to obtain the love of the emperor and bear an imperial prince, and for that child to be enthroned. It is of course possible that Abutsu-ni's daughter was also blessed with this chance, but it is not known what sort of life her daughter led. Abutsu-ni's granddaughter, however, became a consort of the Kamakura *shōgun* and the mother of a prince, actualising the lesson of *Menoto no fumi*.

Abutsu-ni, herself, as the adopted daughter of Taira no Norishige, was a *nyōbō* serving the empress Ankamon-in. She bore a daughter through a love affair with a noble, and in her thirties became a wife of Fujiwara Tameie (1198–1275), bearing him two sons, Tamesuke (1260–1328) and Tamemori, and a daughter. The incident in which she travelled to Kamakura for a lawsuit to protect Tamesuke's domain is well documented. As a consequence of this journey, she wrote *Izayoi nikki*. The blind love she had for her child was intense, and her ability to take action can only be called exceptional. Moreover, through her talent for poetry and her general refinement, she obtained the love of an influential man (if not the emperor himself), bore his children and thereby ensured her own position. She lived the lesson advocated in *Menoto no fumi*.

Within the marriage system of both the court and the Kamakura *bakufu* (one man having several wives), the court ladies were adept at grasping the opportunities available to them for advancement through becoming the mother of a prince. It is more correct to say that was the only chance for them to exercise their own ability. *Menoto no fumi* advocates that if a woman is not blessed with the good fortune of bearing an imperial prince, she should become a nun and pray for happiness in the next life. This state of mind of the author is heart-rending.

The political situation in the late 13th century was characterised by disputed imperial succession, with the court divided into two competing branches. The *bakufu* decreed the alternative succession of the two lines of opposing claimants, and kept imperial reigns short (see Yamamura 1990:164–68). Subsequently, there were many retired emperors and nobles who had a lot of spare time on their hands. This created a situation of total disarray for the sexual mores in the ladies' quarters. The memoir *Towazugatari* (1306?), written by Lady Nijō (Gofukakusa-in Nijō) (see Brazell 1976), relates the situation during that time. The book was Nijō's self-reflection on her numerous love affairs, and most of the women mentioned in it are seen as scandalous and are advised to become nuns. This is probably a warning against the moral climate that prevailed.

The later primer *Menoto no sōshi* was not written for a specific person, but for readers from the broader noble class. After writing about rules for women who aspired to the rank of imperial court ladies and imperial consorts, or wives of nobility, it goes on to advise:

> If your wish for getting on in the world is not realised and you go into service at court, you must be very careful about paying respect to your superiors.

By this time, if a woman's ambition to become the concubine of an illustrious person had been frustrated, she had to serve at court. Seen from this vantage point, *Menoto no fumi* was written for lower-station women whose only option was service at court, and who dreamed of making a fortune at one stroke and rising in the world.

Menoto no fumi advocates becoming a nun—the end of the road for a
court lady who did not become a mother was a lonely one. This is sung about
in the *Ryōjin hishō*:

Sights that cool the heart:
a broken shrine, no priests, no acolytes,
the palace fallen in the middle of the field,
the last years of a lady of the court
her children never born.
(Kim 1994:135–36)

Just like a shrine or a temple where no-one worships any longer, a court lady
without any children in her old age makes the heart silent and pained. Sung by
kugutsume entertainers, this song shows that court service, the only possibility
of work available to noblewomen, was not superior to having a baby, and that
a woman who did not have a child was to be greatly pitied.

Obtaining the love of a person of high status, bearing his child and
desiring the worldly success of that child was a kind of 'success hell' and in
the context of a marriage system of one husband and many wives there must
have arisen many disagreeable situations. The husband was not a disinterested
bystander. Although responsible for placing women into this competitive hell
of concubinage, he would have viewed their rivalries with distaste. This was
surely the background of *Mokuren no sōshi*, which implies a man's perspective.
Menoto no fumi taught, with absolutely no sense of blame, practical ways in
which a worldly, realistic court lady could advance and be educated; *Mokuren
no sōshi* preached guilt for the same thing: both were firmly rooted in the
identification of mother and child, and this identification could be seen as
resistance to the husband, who was the family head.

This identification applied mainly to the court world of imperial consorts
and ladies-in-waiting, not to society as a whole. And yet, the court at the time
was the centre of culture, refinement and learning, a model that the Kamakura
bakufu tried hard to imitate; in particular the ladies of the shogunal palace took
the court ladies as their model. When Abutsu-ni went to Kamakura, she wrote a
theoretical treatise on poetry called 'The evening crane' at the request of a noble
lady, probably the consort of the seventh Kamakura *shōgun*, Prince Koreyasu
(1264–1326; reigned 1266–1289) (Hosoya 1976). A woman poet from the
capital was highly valued in Kamakura, suggesting that the women's culture
of the time was sustained by the court ladies-in-waiting. Because court culture
held such sway, writings such as guides to female behaviour and *otogi zōshi*,
which emanated from the court, gradually infiltrated the whole of society.

In samurai society, also, the identification of mother and child formed a basic theme. A couple of cases of land inheritance, for example, illustrate this point. Nitta Yoshishige, who acquired extensive landholdings as the developer of Kōzuke Province Nitta Estate, handed over the ownership to his fourth son Yoshisue (called Raiō Gozen as a child), giving the rights to the child and his mother together. His will and testament dated 1168 reads:

> I have many children, but I love Raiō Gozen's mother especially, so I want her to have the lands of Nitta Estate and I leave her all undeveloped land in Kokan. So Raiō Gozen should not neglect his mother (*Gunma ken-shi, shiryō-hen* 1977–92).

These halting words express Nitta Yoshishige's love for his wife. The fact that we cannot tell whether the land was to be given to the mother or to Raiō Gozen shows that the mother and child were seen as one in this transaction. According to Minegishi, the rights of management were transferred to the mother and 13 units of land[8] went to her and six to Raiō Gozen, with the mother's holdings to be gradually transferred to her son (Minegishi 1989). Even in the multiple wives system of marriage, the status of the wife who brought up a child was higher than in later centuries, in that the whole domain passed from the husband to the wife, and then to the child.

However, over a century later, the 1311 will and testament of Sagara Rendō in Kyushu shows that women were no longer given landholdings; only male children received portions of land:

> The widows (wives) are the natural mothers of their respective children, and so it is not necessary to grant them land separately from their children. But the children must look after their mothers for the rest of their lives.

This is the same as the Nitta case, with mother and child considered as one unit. However, whereas Nitta placed more weight on the mother when assigning his land, Sagara granted no land at all to the mothers, but transferred all to the children, and stopped at obliging them to care for their mothers in a filial way. Sons were instructed to give to their mothers only ten *koku* of rice and 20 *ryō* worth of *ramie* cloth: this is a startling difference from the earlier instance of the mother who inherited the extensive Nitta domain.

The philosophy of mother–child identity in *nō* plays

This section considers how the concept of mother–child identity appeared in the sphere of literature and performance by focusing on the texts of *nō*, the most significant performing art of the medieval period.

Because of the influence of Buddhist thought, sexual love between man and woman was on the whole negated in *nō* drama. Yet at the same time the aesthetic of romantic love was lauded. In *Ominaeshi*, for example, the words of the character suffering in hell, 'Devils of lust are tormenting the body', realise exquisitely the pleasure and torture of love. Because of this attitude, a mutually loving couple does not appear on stage together. In the rare cases where this does happen, one is portrayed by a child actor (as in *Funa Benkei*), a script convention which avoids direct depictions of physical love.

By contrast, the attitude towards the love shared by mother and child is totally affirming. There is no sense of guilt. A story about a mother who descends into hell can be found in the play *Matsuyama kagami*, where the dramatic emphasis is on the way the daughter's services for her mother lead to the mother entering nirvana. Unlike the story in the *Shaseki-shū* and the *otogi zōshi* version of *Mokuren no sōshi*, in *nō* plays there is no exposition of guilt incurred by the mother because of original sin or blind love.

Other plays in the contemporary repertoire treat the theme of going to hell as a punishment for killing living creatures, including *Utō*, whose main character is a hunter, and *Ukai* and *Akogi*, about cormorant fishermen. Another play dealing with mutual love between a man and a woman, and the resulting obsession, is *Motomezuka*. In none of these does a mother go to hell simply because she is a mother; rather the theme is of women attaining salvation as a result of their child's prayers of filial piety.

A similar example is found in *Ama* (*Diving woman*), a strange play which has the atmosphere of medieval legend. Fujiwara Fuhito has lost a precious jewel obtained from China, called 'the jewel with a face and no back': whichever angle the jewel is viewed from, the face of the Buddha is seen. It is seized by the Dragon King at Shidonoura in Sanuki Province. In order to reclaim it, Fuhito disguises himself, travels there, marries a humble diving girl, and they have a child. He then demands that the diving girl descend to the Dragon King's palace in order to get the jewel. She extracts from him a promise that if she succeeds, he will acknowledge their child as his heir. She enters the sea, fights a fierce dragon guarding the palace and finally obtains the jewel, but in the process she dies. Their child becomes the state minister Fusasaki. When he turns 13, he hears the story of his past, and goes to Shidonoura, where the ghost of his mother appears to him in the form of a diving woman and narrates the story to him. After recounting the moment of taking the jewel, she disappears into the waves. Fusasaki performs Buddhist services of filial piety for his mother and chants the Lotus Sutra, through the merit of which his mother achieves Buddhahood. This story is the legend of the origin of Shido-ji temple at Shidonoura Bay.

In this play, the mother who asks that her child be made heir is praised for her sacrifice and devotion, and is not seen as sinful—exactly the opposite of the judgment made in *Mokuren no sōshi*. Even though the nobility loved *nō* drama, this play contains no sense of guilt because of the wholesome nature of its source, the performing arts of the common people.

This play is a *mugen* (dream) *nō*, in which a ghost appears and re-enacts past events. In contrast, in *genzai* (present-time) *nō*, one group of plays is about mad women. In these plays, a mother is separated from her child, goes mad and wanders around searching before eventually finding the child again. These are plays such as *Hyakuman*, *Miidera* and *Sakuragawa*. A major plot variant is the tragic *Sumidagawa*, in which the mother wanders around searching for her child unaware that it has already died. In another variant, in plays such as *Utaura* and *Tsuchiguruma*, the father is reunited with a lost child.

The mad-woman plays are very like the so-called mother plays (*haha-mono*), a genre in 20th century drama and cinema. In the medieval period, it was common for parents to be separated from their children, who were either sold because of famine or abducted while travelling. There were also times when, in response to severe hardship, children sold themselves into slavery or service, and gave the (ransom) money to their mothers or used it to hold Buddhist services for their dead parents. In other cases, fathers left their children and entered the religious life. However, these *nō* plays tell us that when mothers experienced separation, they lost their minds and roamed around searching for their children. The most typical play of this kind is *Hyakuman*.

Hyakuman was one of Kannami's best, and was originally called *Saga monogurui no nō*. It was revised by his son Zeami. The highlight of the play is the dance of the famous *kusemai* performer, Hyakuman. Like other mad-woman plays, the reunion of mother and child is a device to display the *kusemai* dance of Hyakuman. However, the *kuse* section of Zeami's version encourages maternal love and the filial piety of the child:

> 'The Dhamma of Ango was originally for Shaka's mother Maya; the Buddha also mourned his mother. One who was born into the human world, why not mourn one's mother. Accusing the child and complaining of the current situation in which I am in, I pray with heart and mind that mother and child would be re-united as my sleeves are embroidered in parrot design.' See how Hyakuman dances.

'Ango' refers to the wet season (16 April to 15 July) in India during which priests remain in one place to practise austerities instead of moving from place to place. The Dhamma of Ango refers to the sermon that the Buddha delivered when he ascended into the Trāyastriṃśa realm to comfort his mother Maya.

This story can be found in the Agon Sutra, which dates back to the very early centuries of Buddhism. In *Mokuren no sōshi*, the mother becomes a hungry ghost and requests the reciting of the Lotus Sutra and the Agon Sutra in a service, which is consistent with this story. The Lotus Sutra, which teaches the enlightenment of women, enabled the Dragon Lady to achieve enlightenment, and the Agon Sutra serves as a liturgy of mourning for Buddha's mother. Such references to these sutras in the play *Hyakuman* were possible because of their popularisation in *setsuwa*.

However, as a present-time *nō* play, *Hyakuman* is not about mourning for a dead mother but for a lost child. Hyakuman asks bitterly why her child does not miss the mother from whom he has been separated, just as the Buddha grieved for his dead mother. There is no trace of a mother's guilt or sin. The key concept is an obligation for the child to offer services and feel filial devotion towards his mother, even though she is still alive; there is a strong emphasis on the identification of the mother with the child she has borne and raised. The play also demonstrates, via the happy reunion of mother and child, the virtues of piety, which brings practical benefits in this life.

Hyakuman is set in the Seiryōji Temple in Saga, during the spring-time of the Dainenbutsu service. This rite was established by the head priest Enkaku Shōnin, himself an abandoned child who had prayed to the Jizō Bodhisattva to be reunited with his mother. Later, this prayer was realised and in gratitude he established the Jizō-in (Jōhoshin-in) temple at Seiryōji (Hosokawa 1987; 1989c). In later commentaries on the play, such as in *Yōkyoku shūyōshō* (Inui 1979) (1772), the child of Hyakuman is said to be modelled on the story of this priest. The choice of Seiryōji as the setting where mother and child reunite may retain traces of the priest's own story. There is no connection between the *kusemai* dancer Hyakuman and the priest's mother.

Historically there was an excellent *kusemai* dancer called Hyakuman in the old capital of Nara, according to Zeami's treatise *Go-on* (Zeami, Zenchiku 1974). He also writes that his father Kannami learned *kusemai* from a dancer called Ototsuru, who was in the performance lineage of Hyakuman. Kannami's play, *Saga monogurui*, and Zeami's reworking of it, *Hyakuman*, presumably sought to evoke this great dancer as the main character in order to create an eminently suitable context for this play. However, there are no legends of mother–child reunion associated with *kusemai* dancers such as Hyakuman's, so why was she chosen as the main character for a play of this theme?

Ethnologist Yanagita Kunio wrote extensively about the theme of mother–child reunions in mad woman *nō* plays (Yanagita 1989a). Yanagita pointed to the link between the miraculous parent–child reunions and the dance of the crazed person, suggesting that the female character donning the male court hat (*eboshi*) recalled the costume of both *miko* and *shirabyōshi*, and indicating that it was therefore the dance of a medium entered by a god. The mad scenes in *nō* represent a state of trance where a god or a spirit comes to dwell. Yanagita speculates that the combination of a crazed character and a mother–child reunion presupposes the ancient custom of itinerant religious women such as *miko*, who performed rituals for the safe delivery and growth of small children. He believed that the Kawanozomi festival of the yin–yang practitioners (*onmyōdō*)—consisting of prayer at the river's edge for the safety of a newborn and its mother—was a transformation of the *miko* profession, which had existed from ancient times.

Yanagita further claimed that the name of Hyakuman in *kusemai* dancing originates from the popular Buddhist practice of chanting the Amidha Buddha's name one million times (*hyakumanben no uta nenbutsu*), in particular by the lead singer of this ritual. Until the late Edo period, in Echigo Province there were *miko* called *Mannichi* (ten thousand days), who Yanagita believed to be the descendents of the *nenbutsu* ritual singers. On festival days these *Mannichi* performed a dance (*mai*), and carried out séance rituals in individual homes; *Mannichi* near Morioka were engaged at the beginning of spring to carry out rituals to bring good fortune. There was also the practice called *Mannichi no toriko* (adopting a child), where *miko* were asked to become nominal parents for children to make children grow up strong. Yanagita argued that this was the final relic of the Hyakuman legend.

In the background of the *nō* mad-woman plays, the fusion of the Buddhist practice of *nenbutsu* (invoking the name of the Buddha) and the *Shintō* practices of *miko*, as well as rituals of offering prayers for the safety of mother and child, can be seen. It is significant that in *Hyakuman*, the prototype of mad-woman plays, the main character is a *kusemai* dancer, and that *kusemai* dancers (together with their predecessors, the *shirabyōshi*) possessed religious powers to bring good fortune. Certainly, in the play, Hyakuman does lead the *nenbutsu* ritual and performs an offertory dance intended to draw a favourable response from the gods. This drama of the reunion of mother and child has an implied subplot. Hyakuman has the power to achieve a divine response in the form of a reunion with her child. Someone watching this play and praying for a reunion with a lost child might well have believed that such miracles could happen if they requested a *miko* such as Hyakuman to perform a dance-ritual prayer for them. Even in our day, the *miko* dance in *kagura* performance has the same meaning and function.

This play narrates the efficacy of the gods who respond to the masterful dancer Hyakuman. The dancer in the play 'goes mad' because the gods respond to her dance and possess her. This led to the convention that the mother must be mad before being reunited with her child.

However, even in *Hyakuman*, the main focus is on displaying the *kusemai* performance art rather than on the drama of the mother–child reunion. In later mad-woman plays, the wearing of the man's *eboshi* hat, the symbol that enables possession by the gods, is less common. In *Kashiwazaki*, the mad woman wears the *eboshi* as a keepsake of her dead husband; in *Sakuragawa* and *Miidera*, it is not worn even in the mad scene—longing for the child has become only an auxilliary of the scenes of great poetic beauty. *Sakuragawa* pursues exclusively the beauty of the falling blossoms and the melancholy mood of madness, while *Miidera* portrays the theme of the bright autumn moon reflected on the lake and the sound of the temple bell.

In *Sumidagawa*, the drama of reunion has disappeared because the lost child has already died, unknown to the mother. The present-time mad-woman play has changed into the dream play mode, seemingly without any of the religious power of the *miko*. This invites two possible interpretations: either the *nō* drama as a genre has left behind its connections with *shirabyōshi* and *kusemai* religious origins so as to develop as a drama rather than as a ritual; alternatively, in the voice of the dead child from the funeral mound, the power of the *miko* to make contact with the dead can be seen, like those *miko* who still practise divination and séances on Mount Osorezan today and derive from the medieval *miko*.

In its formative stages, *nō* drama—a highly developed art, which still moves us today— grew out of the fertile soil of the multifarious arts of the *shirabyōshi, kusemai* and *miko*, and was closely connected with the popular folk beliefs that sustained those arts. From that base, principally through Zeami's efforts in the early Muromachi period, *nō* rose to a high artistic level. It then entered a period of development as commercial theatre, with an emphasis on entertainment. Both *Hyakuman,* a mad-woman play, and *Sumidagawa*, a tragedy in which there is communication with the dead, can arguably be seen as products of those folk religion origins.

In *nō* plays about the reunion of father and child, such as *Tsuchiguruma* and *Utaura*, the plots concern an abandoned child looking for its father; there is not one story about a father searching for his child and thereby becoming mad. In *Tsuchiguruma*, the male guardian is the principal actor (*shite*), who takes the child around in a barrow seeking the father who has become a priest. The guardian feigns madness as a way of earning money, and the plot develops around status differences. In *Utaura*, the father is the one who goes mad, but this is because he is a shaman fortune-teller, not because he is looking for his child. The child draws a fortune-telling stick (*omikuji*) from the unknown fortune-teller; the poem he draws tells that he will meet his father immediately, whereby they realise that he is the lost child of the fortune-teller. After this revelation, to express the joy of reunion, the father dances the 'hell narrative dance' (*jigoku no kusemai*), during which he becomes possessed and becomes mad for the first time. These plots are devices whereby the male mad person and the male shaman can appear on stage; they do not have the same inevitability as the crazed woman seeking her child. This reinforces the view that the core of mad-category plays is the separation and reunion of mother and child.

Unlike the guilt and bad karma of motherhood expounded in the world of the nobility, in the common people's performing arts a wholesome identification between mother and child is affirmed. The *miko*, *shirabyōshi* and *kusemai* performers existed not only to entertain but to contribute ritually to the raising of healthy children and to effect the reunion of mothers and children who had been separated. *Nō* drama was located precisely at the boundary of the world of local folk beliefs and performing arts and of the world of elite culture. For that very reason, it was able to convey the atmosphere of the soil from which it emerged and was trying to rise above.

Conclusion

Literature on the theme of motherhood reached a peak in the *nō* mad-woman plays. By way of conclusion, I would like to touch on the trajectory of this theme as it developed in one subsequent literary example. The *otogi zōshi* story 'Izumi Shikibu' (Ichiko 1958) tells how Izumi Shikibu had a baby at the age of 14 and abandoned it at the Gojō bridge in Kyoto. The child grew up to become a priest called Dōmyō Ajari. He happened to go to the palace and, catching a glimpse of Izumi Shikibu behind a screen, fell in love with her. This led to incest between mother and child. When Izumi Shikibu realised this was the child she had abandoned, she took vows and became a nun.

This odd story has no basis in historical fact. It represents a degraded and sad end to the medieval sense of mother–child identification and the dramas of mother–child reunion examined in this chapter. One theory is that the taboo theme of incest reveals an unconscious desire (Ishikawa 1983). *Otogi zōshi* were read widely among the court and military aristocracy, and no doubt their principal readers were aristocratic wives, consorts and concubines, and the women who served them. In the Muromachi and Sengoku periods, both the imperial and the military courts were worlds of one man and multiple wives and concubines, all living together. A court lady who bore a child to a nobleman naturally wished to promote her child, as already seen. It is not beyond the bounds of reason that a woman's excessive and blind love for the child who is part of her, and is her one hope in life, might contain latent incestuous desires.

It is often said that when a culture becomes decadent, incest increases, and whether the incest is mother–son or father–daughter depends on the type of culture. In a strongly patriarchal society, women were excluded and developed very strong links with their children, leading to very close mother–child relations. Since the head of the family was raised under his mother's wing, his affection towards her was naturally very deep.

The clinging nature of the mother–child relationship is replicated in the next generation of mother–child relations. It is not surprising, therefore, that there have been many occasions when a mother took over the reins of politics if the head of the family was underage or sickly. Clear examples of this can be seen, especially in an extended period of unrest like in the Sengoku period, in Kitagawa-dono, the mother of Imagawa Ujichika (1473–1526), and in the nun Jukei-ni, who ruled for Ujichika's son, Ujiteru (?–1536) (Adachi 1931; Nagakura 1978).

This chapter has looked at different medieval views of motherhood: veneration, causes of sinful karma and mother–child identification. These views indicate that the role of motherhood became stronger in the medieval period when, with the rise of patriarchy, the base from which women could be socially active diminished and they could find their value and purpose only in the function of motherhood. In that sense, the veneration of motherhood did not match the strength of patriarchal authority, but rather was premised on it, and respect for motherhood did not necessarily emphasise the human value of women. In the world of folk religion, which was communicated in the mad-woman plays of the *nō* theatre, there was a wholesomeness which invoked smooth and positive mother–child relationships; but medieval motherhood was not venerated as a wish for fertility in itself, as in the primitive period, but was respected for its ability to produce heirs for the due continuation of patriarchal authority. Furthermore, in the Fujiwara Sekkanke family, motherhood was valued as a means of achieving political power. Therefore, women who did not exercise the function of motherhood were treated as worthless, and in some cases motherhood itself was viewed as sinful.

For the women's part, if their own sense of meaning in life was to be derived from motherhood alone, they had no choice but to exploit and enrich that avenue: mothers proceeded to extend to the utmost that part of themselves which was called 'the darkness of the heart'. By the Edo period, the term 'the womb is for rent' or 'borrowed womb' (*hara wa karimono*) shows that motherhood was no longer respected. Moreover, the saying 'a woman without a child must leave the marriage' (*ko naki wa saru*) shows that women were required solely for their ability to produce children. In the medieval period, women were fortunate that motherhood was respected at all, but the conditions that led to its devaluation in the Edo period were already present in embryonic form.

Notes

1   'Kamakura bakufu tsuika hō' (Satō et al 1978). This says that trading in children was frequently banned. *Nō* plays and *sekkyō-bushi* often tell about this practice, although there are no stories in which a child is sold directly by a parent. Rather, the child spontaneously sells him/herself in order to help the parent, or is kidnapped and then sold. However, in actuality, there is no doubt that parents did sell their children, as attested by documents from the Edo period.

2   She lived 718–770 [trans].

3   'The holy man Mokuren was close to the Buddha, and they say that he saved his mother immediately' (Tyler 2003:715) [trans].

4   Dates unknown; exiled to Kikaigashima in 1177 with Shunkan because of his involvement in the Shishigatani conspiracy; pardoned and returned to Kyoto in 1178 [trans].

5   Jizō (kṣitgarbha in Sanskrit)—one of the most popular Buddhist deities in Japan, regarded as a protector of children and of those beings suffering in hell.

6   On the other hand, Matsumoto Neiji (1983), supports her authorship.

7   *Masukagami* is a historical epic about the Kamakura period (1192–1333) and one of the four best-known *kagami* (records) of Japanese history. The document, which is attributed to Nijo Yoshimoto, was written sometime between 1333 and 1376 and narrates the historical events occurring from the birth of the emperor Go-Toba (1180) to the return of the emperor Go-Daigo from exile on the Oki Islands (1334).

8   The unit is *gō*, originally consisting of 50 households [trans].

3

Changing gender roles for medieval Japanese women: court attendant, vendor and nun

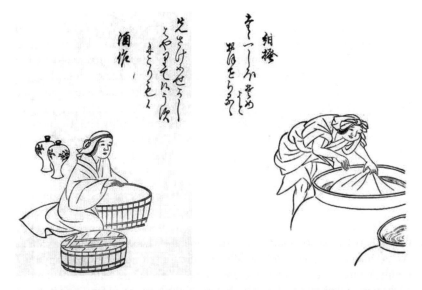

The gendered division of labour in the medieval period was very different from that in the early modern and modern periods. In later periods, it was said that sake would spoil if a woman entered the brewery, whereas in the ancient and medieval periods brewing used to be women's work. Indigo dyeing, fish-vending and pot-throwing, which later became men's occupations, were also women's work.
Shichijū-ichiban shokunin utaawase (Poetry contest by seventy-one pairs of merchants and artisans), volume 1, 'Brewing sake' (left) and 'Indigo dyeing' (right), from Gunsho Ruijū (Hanawa 1933).

7

71

Introduction

Why women, by virtue of their sex, were subjugated under patriarchal authority has been debated as a central issue of women's history. Engels suggested that the rise of patriarchy was the cause of women's subservience, not their devotion exclusively to childbirth, childrearing and domestic labour (Wakita 1983). He also believed, however, that the fixity of male–female gender roles, in which women engaged in domestic labour and did not participate in social labour, exacerbated the lowering of women's status, and he argued for the necessity of women's participation in social labour as a condition of women's liberation.

A historical understanding founded only on a division of social labour lacks a perspective of those fundamental parts of human life—childrearing and domestic labour. The change from a natural division of labour, based on sex and age, to a socially based division of labour raised productivity and created superstructures (such as society and the state); however, the *ie* sustained basic human life, so it is essential to consider the labour within the *ie* as a structural unit, which participated in the social division of labour. Marx distinguished between exchange value and utility value, and pointed out the contradiction of a modern capitalist society, which recognises only exchange value. Despite this, the modern social sciences adopted a perspective that took exchange value as the sole criterion for the concept of social labour. Domestic labour oversees the most basic part of human life, and thus has both utility and importance, but it has no exchange worth, and is not social labour, so it is not valued by society—this view has led to the abasement of the status of women occupied in domestic labour.

When applied to pre-modern society, two problems emerge from this attitude. First, at a time when society was not dominated by an exchange economy, the criterion of value was not placed solely on exchange values. Yet, that society has been explained according to our own modern exchange values. An exchange economy society falls into the trap of not evaluating anything highly, no matter how important, unless it is of exchange value. With the rise of the patriarchal system, the state embraced the patriarchal family as its basic unit of society. However, the full accomplishment of this system within the *ie* took a long time to complete. The establishment of the authority of the family head required several factors (such as private ownership of property, power and ownership of the means of production[1]), not the least of which was surely this lowering of the value given to domestic labour.

The second problem is that the *ie*[2] has had different social roles in different eras: in the pre-modern period, the *ie*, and before it the clan (*uji*), was the organisational unit both of social production and consumption. This is very different from the present day, when the *ie* is the unit of consumer life (however important that is for human life).

The existence of women's right to inheritance in the Heian and Kamakura periods undoubtedly served to strengthen women's status, and indeed women's high status may have brought about the right of inheritance. Both factors are in a causal relationship with each other. As a factor in the estimation of women, undoubtedly motherhood loomed large, but women's importance should not be sought in motherhood alone. Within the *ie* as an economic unit, the position occupied by the wife and the extent of her household management capacity was of great importance in the society as a whole; it was also linked to her economic value because politics and economics, production and distribution—all the functions of social reproduction—were carried out with the *ie* as the basic unit. In that process, the important role of women in the reproduction of the *ie* was not totally ignored. Even in the modern period, the standing of women in the *ie* and the family (*katei*) did not change, but the social role of the *ie* itself, as a political and economic structuring unit, became less significant. In the pre-modern period, the role of modern-day corporations was borne by the *ie* and the position of the mistress, who integrated all its domestic affairs, was much higher than in the modern period.

When dealing with the issue of gender role division in relation to women, there is a strong tendency for researchers to look only at women's social labour, leading to a perception gap about domestic labour. However, the impossibility of separating clearly the domestic and the social is a feature of pre-modern labour. The example of the work of the ladies-in-waiting who served in powerful noble families focuses this contradiction well. Serving at court was the most widespread social occupation for noblewomen, whose work entailed political and economic aspects of the organisations of the great families. In this context they undertook social labour, but their duties also extended to being glorified maids, a magnified type of domestic labour.

The high status of women serving in the imperial household is amazing when considered by modern standards. The importance of the *kōtō no naishi* is demonstrated in the 'women's documents', the *nyōbō hōsho*, which were created by ladies in service at court to convey the will of the emperor. The shogunal households in both the Kamakura and Muromachi *bakufu* were modelled, in many respects, on the imperial household and other influential families. This suggests that the duties of the *kōtō no naishi* show the status of women in the aristocratic institutions of all medieval households, whether court-centred or military.

Inheritance documents of the medieval period point to the achievements of women as wives and mothers, and suggest that they were valued for their practical ability, not purely as the bearers of children to perpetuate the blood line. This is shown also by the fact that wet nurses (*menoto*), who looked after children whom they had not borne, wielded considerable power (Wada 1912; Nishioka 1977). The situation was the same for common people. In medieval society, whether in farming or fishing villages or for merchants or artisans, work was carried out through the unit of the family, and the *ie* functioned as both workshop and shop. Artisans' guilds were collectives of the heads of individual *ie*, each of whom looked after skilled workers and apprentices in the *ie* unit. The role of the mistress in overseeing the basic aspects of daily life in the *ie*, as a unit of management, was therefore extensive.

In medieval society the *ie* was the unit of production and the economy, and the meaning of domestic labour differed from today, so we cannot distinguish between domestic and social labour as we do in contemporary society. In order to understand the social conditions of a given period, it is important to carefully consider the contrasting roles of the court ladies who served in aristocratic households and of the women at the heart of household management as wives and mothers. The social roles of the many women who did not create families, and who did not become housewives, must also be taken into account.

The ruling class introduced a patriarchal system of ethics, together with the *ritsuryō* system, and imposed it on the lower classes in a systematic way that included ideological coercion. Women's social roles were a large part of their lives, and this chapter looks at how their roles and the division of labour according to sex changed during this process. This chapter discusses the changing roles and status of women from the ancient to the medieval periods, especially the changes in women's religious roles. It then looks at the imperial household, the most representative of the household management structures of the dominant classes, and examines the status of the *kōtō no naishi*, the women who had total control of the imperial *ie*, and the documents that they issued. Finally, it looks at the social status of women's labour by focusing on the pictures in the *Shokunin utaawase-e* scrolls.

The decline in women's ritual role

In primitive and undeveloped societies, religion and politics were generally integrated. Ritual aspects tended to be carried out by women, and political or governmental aspects were the responsibility of men, which lead to a natural division of male and female roles (Ishikawa 1979). In Japan, the mythical Queen Himiko and her younger brother ruled together in the Yamatai kingdom and, according to Takamure Itsue, there was a system of shared power between a male and female leader (the *hime-hiko* system) (see Takamure 1966). Several 9th-century sacred songs (*Kagura-uta*) indicate that women were involved in sake brewing in connection with religious ritual practices; for example, 'Today the serving girl sweeps the holy Wine Hall, trousers and skirt trailing behind her' (Okada 1982).

Under the *ritsuryō* system both men and women participated in village rituals (Sekiguchi 1977), and these had an intimate connection with the system of official rice grain loans to farmers (Yoshie 1972). The *Nihon ryōiki* (*Miraculous stories of Japan*) has a concrete example of a woman called Tanaka No Mahito Hiromushi-me, the wife of a high-ranking official (Nakamura 1977: part 2(26)). She has a rice-seeding loan (*suiko*), which she repays in rice and money; but she tries to cheat in the measurement of the sake that she sells. According to the story, she commits an offence against the Buddhist law and meets an unnatural death. We can guess that her business practice possessed a religious element and that the ritual and the commercial were inextricably linked.

These kinds of local village rituals and festivals underwent reorganisation by the centralised state, and gradually focused on men. In 868, a document issued from the Daijōkan Council of State, dated the 28th day of the sixth month, lists all the small shrines in the provinces as having either celebrants only, both celebrants (*hafuri*) and priests (*negi*), or female celebrants only. It decrees that shrines that have both celebrants and priests should get rid of the latter. This is a counter-measure against serfs who would try to evade forced labour by becoming priests or celebrants: 'Most shrines should have celebrants, to perform the ceremonies, while priests have positions but no duties; therefore do not have *negi* but employ women to support the *hafuri*.'

This is an early sign of the trend for males to be central in religious ritual and females to be subsidiary; this was complete by the medieval period, when village festivals and rituals were officiated by men (Kawane 1982), with *miko* in supplementary roles.

Village rituals in the medieval period can be divided into two types: one took place under the control of local resident landowners who inherited the posts of village head (*chōja*) and of shrine head (*kannushi*) (Kawane 1977); the other type took the form of rotating *kannushi*, under the auspices of *miya-za* associations, whose members were influential but egalitarian villagers. Many were held in urban locations such as Rikyū Hachimangū in the port town of Ō-Yamazaki and Kamo-sha in Kyoto (Wakita 1981b), but there is also evidence of this phenomenon in the central region villages—in places such as the *mura-*

za of Zenjōji temple in Uji-Tawara (Kuroda 1974). Both types of rituals were already appropriated by men. In those rituals performed by rotating *kannushi*, as seen in Ō-yamazaki, all the males of *miya-za* families received the right to be members of the *miya-za* when they came of age (whether these men should be called patriarchs is an issue), while the women of these families seem to have formed a *miko-za* association (Shimamoto-chō-shi Hensan iinkai 1975–76). Yanagita Kunio has pointed out that in the Edo period, also, examples clearly show that some festivals—such as the *o-monoimi* of the Kashima shrine in Hitachi Province and the *tete* in Echizen Province—were conducted by hereditary female *Shintō* functionaries. He quotes another example from volume 12 of *Hitachi kokushi*: 'Occasionally, a woman called Miya-ichiko plays the role of *kannushi*. She has a husband who is, however, like a slave' (Yanagita 1989b). However, in most village shrine festivals the prerogative had shifted to men, under whose leadership female *miko* probably offered *kagura* performances and carried out the ritual of 'hot water' (*yutate*). But there were certain ceremonies and rites led by women which continued throughout the medieval period. Some of these were conducted by itinerant female religious specialists, such as *aruki miko* and *agata-miko*.[3]

In a *Ryōjin hishō* song, a ten-year-old child has left her parents' side to become an itinerant *miko*.

> *Almost a woman, my daughter, now*
> *I hear she is a wandering shrine-maiden*
> *When she walks the salty shore at Tago Bay*
> *The fishermen must pester her*
> *Squabbling about her prophecies, finding fault with whatever she says.*
> *Her life, how painful!*
> (Kim 1994:8)

The *Shaseki-shū* contains a story about a priest who prayed at the mausoleum of Shōtoku Taishi in Kōchi. The deity who appeared before him took the form of an *aruki miko* and granted his petition to obtain a relic of the Buddha (Morell 1985:book 2(1)).

These kinds of *miko* had their own particular gods, as seen in another song from the *Ryōjin hishō*, which teases them. Kim picks up the pun of *Kami*, meaning both god and hair in her translation:

> *The gods the girl next door serves are*
> *Hair gods: with curly hair, with frowzy hair,*
> *With hair rolling to her shoulders:*
> *A bungling, messy god at her fingertips,*

The god who walks in her soles
(Kim 1994:121).

Further, the *uchifushi no miko*, in whom Fujiwara Kaneie (929–990) fervently believed, was possessed by the Kamo Wakamiya deity and proclaimed its oracles (Konno 1993–99). The same connection can also be surmised from the shamanistic folk beliefs and practices in north-eastern Japan where puppets are used in rituals (*oshirasama, okonaisama* and *oshinmeisama*) which have been transmitted to the present day.

These itinerant *miko* had close connections with female puppeteers (*kugutsu*) and prostitutes, and may even have formed communities together. This is suggested by the fact that the *Ryōjin hishō* has many songs about *miko*, such as the *imayō* songs of *kugutsu* women in Aobaka in Mino Province.

In the medieval period, when the gods were reorganised at the centralised national level of *shikinai* (major) shrines, in the villages the *miya-za* were formed, focusing on local gods. It is tempting to see that the *miko*, who were the celebrants of *hyakujin* (100 gods), left the villages to become itinerant as part of this process, but this is not necessarily so. The *aruki miko* had the same lifestyle as the *kugutsu* groups, who were included among those occupations of a non-agricultural nature. As the saying went, they:

> do not cultivate any land, do not make silk thread, therefore they do not belong to official registers, and are not regular residents; they simply wander, not knowing the authority of emperor and official, and not fearing governor or steward; they are not required to perform labour and provide taxes, but live a life of pleasure (*Kairaishi-ki* 1979).

However, these groups most likely included refugees from villages, as is clear from documents from the Kamakura period relating to trading in people.

In all probability, primitive beliefs in nature gods existed among both itinerant people and settled villagers, but in the midst of the national, centralised formation of village rituals, and the male leadership in *miya-za*, the earlier beliefs only persisted strongly among itinerant people. Consequently, it is impossible to agree with the view that *kugutsu*, prostitutes and *miko* were of a different ethnicity. It can be seen that people who were originally of the same roots, took separate paths over time through changes in occupation and way of life. These religious rituals, which were the domain of *miko*, were not included in the general religious revolution of the time, but continued as they were, and dropped in status—their practitioners even became outcasts. This is a major factor of women's history of the period, and is discussed further in the section on performers below.

The shrinking role for women of the nobility and the disparaging of women's work

Recent research has confirmed women's rights to property and succession in the Heian and Kamakura periods, although not exactly as discussed by Takamure Itsue in terms of matriliny and matriarchy. The Hachijō-in Princess Shōshi (1135–1211) possessed large domains, making her possibly the largest landholder in Japan at the time. Such cases were rarer in the Muromachi and Sengoku periods, although women's rights to property and succession did still exist. Research is now questioning the nature of the society that allowed such rights for women, even while reducing opportunities for women to exercise their capabilities.

In the Nara period (710–784), noblewomen carried out estate management and harvesting. A poem in the 8th century *Man'yōshū* anthology shows a glimpse of a woman managing the autumn harvest: the poem was composed by Ōtomo no Sakanoue no Iratsume when she went to the family domains of Atomi and Takeda (Ishimoda 1973). The previously mentioned story in the *Nihon ryōiki* about Tanaka No Mahito Hiromushi-me portrays the great wealth gained from rice loans and sake brewing, and was a cautionary tale against greed. This shows that a negative attitude towards women doing socially active work was starting to appear in the 8th century, but it also indicates that it was not in any way unusual for women to engage in rice loans and brewing. Religious rituals and rice loans were conducted by village leaders who, in fact, attained their positions of authority as a consequence of performing these tasks. This indicates that originally these tasks were the privilege of both men and women and that, in the process of reorganising society on the basis of the *ritsuryō* system, the ruling (male) class appropriated these rights from women (Yoshie 1972).

The formation of private domains came about as a way to oppose ownership by the *ritsuryō* state, but was still based on *ritsuryō* bureaucratic appointments and court ranks. Possession of a rank was important in the ability to form an independent domain, whether of the land reclamation type or the land grant type. In order to acquire land, the central nobility wielded influence based on court ranks, and local gentry also used their positions as regional officials (*gunji*) and increased their power by military force. In contrast, those exceptional women who formed private domains—none more than women in the palace quarters—were able to do so because of their connections with powerful men: as mothers, wet nurses or wives. For example, a document shows that two individuals (Tamate Norimitsu and Tamate Noriyasu), who wished to win favour with the influential Higashi-sanjō-in (961–1001), presented land to one of his court ladies, Dainagon no tsubone, by virtue of her power as the mother of Emperor Ichijō and as the woman behind Michinaga (she was his elder sister) (Takeuchi 1974–80:Tōji hyakugō monjo – yo).

Such women were also given court rank. The basis of their rank and their ability to acquire private domains lay in their motherhood, that is, as mothers and wet nurses to powerful men. Women of lesser rank (*nyōbō*), however, had to depend on any influence they could gain in the palace structure.

Therefore, the majority of the landholdings of other women were the result of inheritance. Of course, wives also had inheritance rights—there were cases where they inherited property from their husbands—but the majority came from parental legacies. The Hachijō-in Princess Shōshi inherited 21 domains from her father, the retired Emperor Toba, and her mother Mifukumon-in, in addition to which she was presented with estates in 220 locations (Ishii 1988). A large number of these were managed by Buddhist temples or by the various middle or lower-ranking vassals and servants of the bureaucracy of the retired empresses, except the Yoshitomi domain of Ōmi Province, which Fujiwara Sadaie was commissioned to manage. Even so, we need to bear in mind that the staff surrounding the empress's household management consisted largely of female court women.

It is interesting to note from the fictional world of the *Tale of Genji* that when Genji is exiled to Suma, Lady Murasaki and her wet nurse Shōnagon are left in charge of managing Genji's property.[4] For court ladies and nurses to become responsible for household management was the same as the wife in an ordinary household having responsibility for managing the house but on a grander scale. In the *Kagerō nikki*, Kaneie goes to the writer (one of his formal wives) and asks her to look after his clothing. He is rebuffed and laughed at because his new wife and her servants do not have the knowledge to look after him (Seidensticker 1994). Again, the *Konjaku Monogatari* shows that, regardless of whether a man and woman live together or separately, it was considered a woman's work to administer household affairs (Konno 1993–99:26-5). In the Nara period, even the work of managing the harvest of the estate was part of women's household management; however, in the Heian period, household management structures of the great families, such as the *mandokoro* office, burgeoned and acquired a separate existence. This specialisation circumscribed the work of court ladies and wives, although there were differences between classes in this matter.

Therefore, court ladies were probably the only women in the Heian period who worked as domain managers and wielded considerable power. Through their hard work they were often awarded more estates. However, while these court women were proud of their place in the world of the court nobility, they also felt some shame at working (Shimizu 1979). Sei Shōnagon criticised as hateful those men who disparaged women for showing their faces even to humble people (Morris 1967).[5] Writing about the positive side of palace service, she boldly protested against the general court culture of despising ladies who uncovered their faces and worked. The passage reveals the prevailing court attitude in which women were looked down upon for being socially active. After the establishment of the *ritsuryō* system, women were shut out of the bureaucratic structures, and in both central and regional administration the important jobs were monopolised by men. Women's work was restricted to lowly and menial jobs, and noblewomen were supposed to remain concealed behind blinds, not showing their faces, and to be waited on by other people. With the emergence of a class society, among women of the dominant classes, a culture emerged which despised any engagement in social activity. Being a court lady was the only work that remained for women of the noble classes, and Sei Shōnagon states that even for the wife of a regional aristocratic landholder it is an advantage to have served in the palace. The culture of despising labour spread from high to low, from capital to countryside, not only among the local aristocrats but also in regional wealthy families. However, the custom of women concealing their faces did not extend to the lower classes, as in Islamic societies, and neither did Japan import the Chinese custom of foot-binding. We should be thankful for small mercies.

The role of women in agriculture, commerce and artisanry

A tale in the *Konjaku Monogatari*, called 'Mikawa no kuni: inugashira no ito no hajime no katari', relates the origins of *inugashira* thread, a famous product of Mikawa Province, but it also tells how the quality of silk thread improved through women's management (Konno 1993–99:26-11). A certain county governor had two wives. Because the silkworms of the first wife died, she became poor. The man stopped visiting her and took a new wife. Then, by a miracle, the silk thread business of the first wife flourished, making her rich again, so he went back to her. Like the story of Hiromushi-me in the *Nihon ryōiki*, this is a vivid depiction of a woman who has a leading hand in management. In contrast, the husband is depicted as actively engaging in an administrative position in local government and regional administration. This would seem to reflect the condition of the landholding class in the late Nara to the mid-Heian period, but what about agricultural workers, particularly upper class farmers from the late Heian period?

The members of a *miya-za*—the village community bound together by means of festivals and rituals—were the men of that community, while the women were only seen in the ancillary groups of *miko-za* and *nyōbō-za*. It

Table 1: Allocation of land belonging to Tōdaiji Daibutsu

Children's names	seal	Land area	Tax payable
Eldest son Norifusa	+	Myōden: 1 chō, 2 tan	2 to of polished rice, 5 hiki of silk
Second son Gyōgen (monk)	I	Myōden: 1 chō, 2 tan	5 to of polished rice, 4 hiki of silk
Yoshifusa	+	Myōden: 7 tan	3 to of polished rice, 2.5 hiki of silk
Suefusa	+	Myōden: 7 tan	2 to of polished rice, 2 hiki of silk
Kōhan (monk)	+	Myōden: 1 chō, 3 tan,	6 to of polished rice, 4 hiki of silk
Chinkei (monk)	+	Myōden: 1 chō, 2 tan	3 to of polished rice, 4 hiki of silk
Hando*	+	Myōden: 1 chō, 1 tan	5 to of polished rice, 4 hiki of silk
Kubota**	+	Myōden: 1 chō, 1 tan,	4 to of polished rice, 4 hiki of silk
Suenori	+	Myōden: 240 ho,	5 shō of polished rice, 0.5 hiki of silk

Father, Yoshinori (lay priest): signature and seal, 1104, second month.
+ Signatures (*ka-ō*) of all beneficiaries
*Yamamura elder daughter (Anenoko): seal Hando
**Yamamura middle daughter (Nakanoko): seal Kubota
Note: 1 *chō* = 10 *tan* = 3,600 *ho* = 119.34 *arl*
1 *to*–10 *shō* = 100 *gō* = 18.039 litres
1 *hiki* = 2 *tan* = 2.6 square metres (1 *tan* was enough material for an adult garment)

appears that by the late Heian period, men controlled village governance. Kawane has noted that women's names do not appear in documents such as land registers (Kawane 1982), and yet women's right to own property was still an indisputable reality. Fukutō takes the view that the custom of equal distribution of property was stronger among private owners than among the class of resident landowners (Fukutō 1990). These facts need to be drawn together to see what can be inferred about women's mode of existence and roles.

In Yamato Province Kohigashi no shō estate, a small property (of eight *chō* and five *tan* of rice land exempt from tax) was divided amongst the nine children of the owner, Yamamura Yoshinori. As this attests to the right of women to own property, I will quote it in full (Takeuchi 1974–80:no 1532; see Takie).

There is hardly any difference between the allocation of property rights to the two women in the list, Yamamura's elder daughter (Anenoko) and middle daughter (Nakanoko), and their brothers.[6] But, whereas the other siblings received rice fields in their own respective names, Anenoko and Nakanoko received land in the name of Hando and Kubota. The name of Hando appears in the land register of Kohigashi no shō for the year of 1143 (Takeuchi 1974–80: no 2507), as 'Hando-dono myō'. Hando lay to the south of Tōdaiji, and Kubota was in Ando-mura to the northeast, separated by the Yamato River (Inagaki

1981). Most likely, these are not place names, but, as in the name Hando-dono, the name of a person. We can assume then that the land was received in the name of Anenoko's husband. The document indicates that the name of the person responsible for paying taxes and performing public services was registered as the name of the *myō* (Takeuchi 1974–80:no 3207)· The private owner of these polished rice fields was Yamamura, and his daughters were included in the inheritance of the estate, but the domain owner, the Tōdaiji temple, demanded that the name (*myō*) for delivering taxes and services be that of a man. Presumably this had become the general custom.

This is surely why women do not appear in public registers of land, even though they had the right to own property. Unlike modern times, in pre-modern times land ownership was affected by social status in many ways. People with the status of domain owner could protect their property rights, but for someone like Yamamura, who carried the burden of providing labour and paying taxes, privately inheriting a *myō* did not provide a fully independent right, only an intermediate status with the entitlement to receive annual produce revenue.

Such rights could be strengthened and converted to ownership rights, which were then guaranteed through the right of inheritance, as well as through the supplementary duties of property and authorisation of ownership. The patriarchal attitude was that men should be in charge of tax and service duties, which strengthened this prerogative separately from that of the actual property owners. The converse of this was that, even though women do not appear in land registers, in actuality many *myō* were owned by women. Therefore, there must also have been many cases in which women held the reins of management. Kawane takes the example of a dispute over the Kanshin *myō* in the Tara no shō domain in the province of Wakasa, where Kanshin was the *myōden* (named field) owned by the mother of a boy called Sainen. Since her son was still a child and could not perform labour service, she unofficially borrowed some land for cultivation from her brother Kanshin. To Kawane this shows that there existed a general legal consciousness that a woman did not have the right to receive a *myō* (the right to till land with the incumbent service and tax obligations) (Kawane 1982). This mirrors the case of Yamamura Anenoko. However, I prefer to understand it this way: the official landowners strengthened such a legal consciousness, which was in sharp opposition to the rights of succession for farmers. It indicates that the logic of domain owners won out over the way farmers viewed their *myō* holdings.

I have explained how, despite the fact that women had the right to own property, an officially recognised name (*myō*) was often registered as the name of a husband or other male. In later periods, the name did not represent an actual person, but became a unit that simply indicated the amount of tax that could be taken from a piece of land. Subsequently, the identity of a woman landowner was no longer hidden, as noted in the following cases. Belonging to the Tōji temple was the Tara no shō domain in Wakasa Province, where the Suctakc namc was disputcd bctwccn two women called Nakahara no Uji-me and Fujiwara no Uji-me.[7] In another case, in the Yano no shō domain in Harima Province, also owned by the Tōji temple, the right of ownership of Korefuji-myō was given to a woman called Chiyozuru-me, the daughter of Jōnosaburō Shigesue.[8] As the power of Tōji temple as a domain proprietor declined, its right to make appointments to the *myō* within domains also became less solid, and ownership rights could be inherited or sold without reference to the domain proprietor. As a result, the domain owner had to recognise women's right to own property, which favoured the *myō* owner. This was the case not only with domain owners, but also with farmers' holdings.

The situation outlined above also held for merchants and artisans, as shown by the example of pot makers. Tsude has written in detail about the fact that pottery was chiefly the work of women in the Yayoi period (300BC–300AD) and later (Tsude 1982). In the medieval period, also, pottery was most likely women's work because the Chikuma pot of Ōmi Province was a ceramic dish and was dedicated to the gods by women. The village of Kuzuha was famous for its pottery, as illustrated in the following song from the *Ryōjin hishō*.

By the pasture at Kuzuha
The potter makes earthenware
Ah, but the girl has a lovely face
If only she could ride wedding carts, three or four
Drawn by hand, in procession
As the provincial governor's bride!

The girl is normally interpreted as the daughter of the potter, but, in the light of the foregoing discussion, can we not also see the daughter producing pottery?[9]

When a pottery was formed into a *myō*, it was registered in the name of a male. Fukakusa, near Kyoto, was so famous as a pottery-producing region that its name was given to both pots and potters. There was a concentration of potters patronised by influential families, temples and shrines (Wakita 1969c). Among these groups, one whose situation is known about in detail is the pottery kiln belonging to the Daigoji temple. According to the diary *Daigoji Zasu mihaidō nikki* (Kyōen and Nakajima 1973:v9), in 1179 the names of seven people from Fukakusa are listed: Mitsusato, Koreyuki, Kanesada, Sadatomo, Sadanobu,

Table 2: Chart of Fukakusa potters belonging to Daigoji temple

Estate name	Person (myō)	Field area			Tax and tribute required
		Paddy	**Field**	**Total**	
Fourth ward	Mitsusato	1 tan	5 tan	6 tan	(1) for each tan of land, the equivalent of 4 *to* of rice (for each chō and 7.5 tan)
	Sadatomo	3 tan	0.5 tan	3.5 tan	
	Kanesada	4 tan (small)	1 tan	3 tan (small)	(2) from the group 360 items per month
	Fujiwara	1.5 tan	7 tan	8.5 tan	(720 bundles a year from each person)
	Tokisato	2/3 tan	1 1/3 tan	2 tan	
	Naokane widow*	8 tan	0	8 tan	
	Total	1 chō 7.5 tan	1 chō 4 tan & 2/3 tan	3 chō 3 tan & 1/3 tan	
Maetaki	Koreyuki	1 tan	0	1 tan	Each person to provide 750 bundles of pottery a year
	Sadanobu	1 tan	0	1 tan	
	Sadatoki*	1 tan	0	1 tan	
	Total	3 tan	0	3 tan	

*This name is annotated with the comment, 'has been donated to Muryōju-in temple'.

Source: *Daigo zōji-ki* (*Miscellaneous accounts of Daigo temple*), volume 11.

Kunisue and Tokisato. However, another source from about the same time gives nine names (*myō*) of Fukakusa potters, as is shown in Table 2.

These nine names match closely the previous seven names, except two: Sadatoki who was attached to the Muryōju-in temple and the Naokane widow. The six names in the fourth ward had to provide the equivalent of 4 *to* of rice per *tan*, regardless of whether paddy or field; that is, 360 vessels each month. This is how they were exempted from miscellaneous services. Even the widow was not released from tribute, showing that she too was producing pottery. Each of the three *myō* of Maetaki was given one *tan*, so this paddy was probably supplied by the domain owner, and was exempted from contributing the equivalent of 4 *to* per *tan*; instead providing 750 vessels a year. This example shows that even though women were actually making the pottery, the annual tributes were made in the names of the men, who also attended celebrations in the ritual. It shows that already by this time women's craft and artisan labour functioned within the patriarchal system as domestic labour.

A similar example can be found within sake brewing; in the ancient period this work was done by women. In temples, even in the Heian period, women in the brewing industry carried out miscellaneous tasks such as 'mistress of *hishio*' (soybean or wheat fermenting agent) and 'mistress of vinegar'.[10] Throughout the medieval period, instances can be found of women producing sake, such as in the *kyōgen* play, *Oba ga sake* (*My aunt's sake*) (Koyama 1960): 'I have an aunt living over the mountains. She brews sake every year and sells it.'

The *Shichijūichiban shokunin utaawase* (*Poetry contest by 71 pairs of merchants and artisans*) (Iwasaki et al 1993:misc) also shows a picture of a woman holding a dipper and sake bottle with the caption, 'First, choose pale unrefined sake (*usunigori*), it's very popular. I also carry…'

In the same volume a woman is depicted making *kōji* (malted rice, the agent for fermenting miso bean paste). These examples tell us that women were generally the ones who made and sold fermented products such as sake and *kōji*. However, a list of 347 sake brewers in Kyoto from the years 1425 and 1426 has only three names that might be thought to be women: a nun, and the names Memeko and Hei (Kitano Tenmangū shiryō 1978:Sakaya kyōmyō). Furthermore, there are many names of important samurai and of priests who have landholdings. In 1467, in a list of 22 names of sake makers in Hiyoshi shrine, all but two names (one nun and one lay woman) are men, both lay and priest (*Shinjōin monjo* facsimile).

What is the significance of this? At one time I thought it was a matter of small sake establishments being run by women and large enterprises in the urban centres being managed by men. However, some of the urban ones were quite small, so this theory does not necessarily hold. Rather, just as with potters, it can be surmised that, regardless of who did the actual work, public registers consist of men's names. Thus, only in cases where there was no male householder does the name of the woman householder appear.

Many of the weavers who were the forerunners of the Kyoto Nishijin industry were women. In the *Shichijūichiban shokunin utaawase* women are depicted in the professions of weavers, sash vendors (and makers), tailors and embroiderers, and braiders. The carer of the emperor's wardrobe, Yamashina Noritoki (1507–79), wrote in his diary of the trouble he underwent when he ordered the nun Kakinoki Myōzen to weave his son's costume for his investiture at court, only to have her run away with the money.[11] This confirms that many weavers were women, but the names that appear in official registers are all men's names.[12] In the case of the nun Kakinoki, the business was perhaps registered in the name of her son or son-in-law.

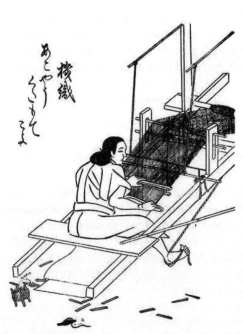

Shichijūichiban shokunin utaawase. High loom (takahata). *Gunshū ruijū* (Hanawa 1933).

The indigo dyer in the *Shichijūichiban shokunin utaawase* is also a woman The ash used as a catalyst in indigo dying came from Tanba Province to Tanba-guchi, one of the entrances to the city of Kyoto, and was the monopoly of four indigo ash dealers. One of these was called Kagame-ryū, who in the early Muromachi period held the right to deal in indigo ash and passed this right on to her daughter. In 1517 there was a dispute concerning this *za* between Sano Matasaburō Shigetaka (founder of the lineage of Haiya Jōeki, 1607–91, a rich business man and cultured person in Kyoto) and Minami-me, the wife of Urai Shin'emon no jō Tomoyoshi. The rights of both sides were recognised in the domain's court of arbitration. This shows Minami-me's direct engagement in the business, and her possession of the right to manage the *za*. However, the *za* regulations were authorised by her husband's signature, as were reports issued to *za* members[13] — even though these members and the central administration of the domain alike were fully aware that the wife was the one doing the work and holding the rights to manage the *za* (Wakita 1969d).

However, there were some instances where a *za* authority was officially recorded under a woman's name. A dispute arose about the succession to one of the six salt guilds in Kyoto, Kimura Yojirō Naonobu. The dispute was between the daughter of Kimura Munenobu Nyūdō and Naonobu's daughter, Goime, who won the case.[14] In another example, the person who possessed the monopoly of the *obi* (sash) business for the whole of Kyoto, a post called Rakuchū obi-za zatō shoku, was a woman called Kameya Goime, who was granted this right in 1528 in a document issued by the Muromachi *bakufu* magistrate (*Tanaka Mitsuji-shi shozō monjo* facsimile). These two women, Kimura Goime and Kameya Goime, are among the few cases where a woman's name was officially recorded as holding the authority of the *za*. Incidentally, the fact that they were both called Goime (meaning women of the fifth rank) indicates that they had received a court rank, and this suggests that even women of court rank could be officially recognised as equal to men. Even if these women belonged to a relatively high social class, why would such mercantile women be granted court rank? It would be interesting to know whether this was because they had served the court as merchant women, or because they had been able to purchase the rank.

Of course, there were women whose names appear as *za* merchants, even without court rank. Kyōto fans, along with swords, were a major export in the trade with Ming China and one of the principal products of Kyōto. The head of Hoteiya, which controlled half of the fan *za* rights, was a nun called Genryōni. She and her daughter and son-in-law were 'folders', responsible for the production of fans, and also engaged in their distribution and sale.[15]

Another example can be seen from the early Kamakura period record 'Rokkaku-chō uo-kugonin'[16] of fish merchants in Kyoto with women's names such as Fukuman-me and Seitoku-me. In the *Shichijūichiban shokunin utaawase* the fish seller is also a woman, and her caption has a poem including the place name of the fish market:

> Fish sold in Rokkaku-chō goes bad as soon as it is sold, just as my beloved
> changes as soon as we get together.

This shows that Rokkaku-chō was always associated with selling fish and that the vendors were women, even though the competition's judge responded

Fish vendor from *Shichijūichiban shokunin utaawase*, Tokyo University Sōgō Toshokan, reproduced in *Gunsho ruijū* (Hanawa 1933).

in this way: 'Fish was sold not only in Rokkaku-chō, but also everywhere else'.

There are many women's names, such as Aguri-me and Tsurumatsu-me, among the vendors of the New Silk Floss Guild belonging to the Gion shrine.[17] The members of this guild were a new type of merchant who emerged in opposition to the Main Silk Floss Guild, which comprised those guilds of the major streets, such as Sanjō-chō and Shichijō-chō, whose representatives were most likely men (Wakita 1969e). Women were frequently involved in newly emerging trades and the extent of their management was wide, but there was a tendency for men's involvement to increase once the new endeavours became established. In the primitive era women traders were common, as is seen in the archaic word *hisagime*. For example, men carried out fishing labour, but women were often the ones who peddled them (Segawa 1971). This may have been a result of the exclusion of women from administrative posts and from sites of basic production, which made them compensate by seeking new areas of activity. The high number of women in businesses such as moneylending[18] and brokering (Iwasaki et al 1993) might also be attributed to the fact that, for those with a little capital, these occupations were accessible regardless of status or class.

In this way, even though women worked and held property rights or authority as heads of a *za*, the position was frequently recorded in a man's name when these rights were overseen by a domain owner. As the whole of society became male-centric, the *miya-za* in the towns and villages came to consist only of men. In this situation it was inevitable that, gradually, women's commercial and craft production and agricultural labour became domestic labour within the patriarchal system. Kagame owned and had probably pioneered the indigo ash business herself, and passed this *za* authority on to her daughter Nene. However, the next owner was Sano Matasaburō, thus establishing a male line of inheritance.[19] The monopoly of the *obi* business for all Kyoto, owned by Kameya Goime, became the subject of a dispute, as a result of which she passed on the right to Yoshida (Suminokura) Munetada; after its acquisition, Munetada obtained the authorisation of the powerful Miyoshi Nagayoshi (1523–64).[20] As commerce became more widespread, it necessitated forging ties with the politically powerful, in the same way that capital is absorbed into the political system today. Although this affected society as a whole, there is no doubt that, with this development, women entrepreneurs lost much of their ability to be commercially active.

In the early Edo period, a biography of the famous artist Honnami Kōetsu depicts Kōetsu's mother as wise and pious (Masaki 1948:Honnami gyōjōki). She was a model woman who helped her husband and a good parent who protected her family. This may be due to the family's occupation of sword-sharpening and connoisseurship. The biography contains some noteworthy remarks: that a bride with a large dowry is not good and neither is a son-in-law from a superior family because he treats his wife as a waiting lady. The portrait is the ideal of a woman in the *ie* system, concentrating on family business. By this time, the medieval woman with her own property and her own occupation has disappeared.

As the medieval period drew to a close, women's industry became domestic labour and was absorbed into the patriarchal system. In the upper echelons of society, women came to work less and less. The values of the Heian aristocracy, which had despised work, gradually filtered through to the middle levels of society. Of course, not all women stopped working. As can be seen in agriculture and in family workshops, the *ie* had become the unit of production, and therefore women's work was an important component of that. *Kyōgen* plays show examples of productive wives and lazy husbands, as expressed in the line, 'My husband even makes me mend the leaking roof'.[21] Because these are comedies, there is an element of paradox in the humour, with a strong wife and a weak husband in a patriarchal *ie* system. The woman in the play, who is able to sustain the household even to the extent of mending a roof, says, 'A man is a man, even if he is wrapped up in straw', and 'A man is a man, even if he is a nose and eyes drawn on a chopstick', indicating that a woman is enclosed in an *ie* represented by a husband with no earning power. There was a couple that worked together in the fields and surveyed the harvest before them. In one scene, the wife congratulates her husband, saying, 'Your fields have borne a plentiful crop right to the edge of the ridges. How auspicious' (*Ukon sakon*). To which the husband replies, 'When I think how this came about because you, my dear, did back-breaking work with me every day, I feel so happy'. A wife's work remains at the level of support for her husband, and the results of the labour are the achievement of the husband—this is the dominant feature of the *ie*. In the early medieval period, this was an outward principle, established in administrative structures, which, over the course of the medieval period, gradually came to regulate real life. Women's labour, roles and rights, which are not easily discerned when buried under those regulations, need to be brought to light.

So did women disappear altogether from outdoor work? As he was travelling to Suruga in 1556, Yamashina Tokitsugu wrote in his diary that when he went over the Ise-Chigusa pass he employed carriers at Nejiro, and that over half of them were women.[22] A typical Kyoto sight from medieval to modern times was of the girls called *ōharame*, who carried loads of charcoal and firewood on their heads. The tradition of girl vendors (*hisagime*) had not died out. However, sake brewing, which had been women's work in the ancient and medieval eras, changed hands by the Edo and modern periods to the extent that women were forbidden to even enter a brewery, since it was believed that their presence would spoil the sake. In the Edo period, the view of women as being polluted reached even the farming villages and was reinforced by economic relations. Spinning and weaving remained as women's domestic labour, but part of the commercialised weaving enterprises of Nishijin became the domain of men in the Meiji period. This tendency had already emerged in the medieval era.

Miko and performers

The world of female shamans and performing artists underwent a similar process to that of artisans and merchants. As already seen, *miko* were the central focus of religious ritual in the primitive age, but by the time of the *ritsuryō* system of power, the erosion of their status had begun—a trend that became even more marked by the medieval period. Local ceremonies were in the grip of local landowners and village community groups, whose members were mostly men. These groups included *miko* and women's guilds, but they were already relegated to a subordinate position.

The world of the itinerant *miko* (*aruki miko*) included male *miko* (shamans); however, women were regarded as the main group, as in the song of the *Ryōjin hishō*:

Are there no women
In the East?
Only male shamans there,
But even so,
The god sweeps down on them
(Kim 1994:148).

In *Shichijūichiban shokunin utaawase*, there is a *miko* called a *jisha* who is, according to Yanagita Kunio, a male shaman dressed as a *miko* (Yanagita 1989b). According to the stories in the *Shaseki-shū* (1279–83), people believed that gods and spirits entered *miko* (*kamioroshi*), hence their status was relatively high. The compiler Mujū Ichien preaches the virtues of Buddhism as superior to these practices, and the *miko* depicted in the stories often changed into syncretic figures with Buddhist elements, like the Kumano *bikuni*.

The decline in women's roles also applied to performers like *kugutsume*, *asobime* and *shirabyōshi*, who had a very close relationship with *miko*. At court, there were professional women performers, called *naikyōbō no gijo*,[23] but it is not certain when their function disappeared.[24]

The court musicians in the imperial palace and the musicians attached to major temples were all men, whereas female artists were itinerant and not attached to any organisation. The *Kairaishi-ki* says that 'they have an easy life because they are not required to perform forced labour or pay taxes'; that is to say, they were a people outside any official system of control. Their speciality was *imayō* (contemporary) songs. The *imayō* anthology *Ryōjin hishō*, compiled by retired Emperor Goshirakawa (1127–1192), was collected from the *kugutsume* community at Aobaka in Mino Province. Already by that time *imayō* had become a classical genre and was in decline. Famous pieces such as *Ashigara* were barely being preserved by a small number of performers and by a handful of the nobility. The *shirabyōshi* entertainers are said to have originated from the *kugutsume*.

Although, like the *miko*, these entertainers were itinerant, they were still not viewed as outcasts in the Heian and Kamakura periods. For example, the lady beloved by retired Emperor Goshirakawa, Lady Tanba, was described in the *Gyokuyō* diary: 'Lady Tanba used to be a lovable courtesan, and now has the title Rokujō-dono.'[25] Her father was the courtier in charge of the emperor's meals, Ki no Takasuke, and it is said both she and her mother were prostitutes from Eguchi. She became the mother of the priest, Prince Shōnin. The favoured lady of retired Emperor Gotoba was Tanba no Tsubone (?–1216), whose real name was Ishi, a *shirabyōshi* whose father was said to have been a bamboo blind weaver. She also became the mother of a princess.[26]

A supplementary law of the *bakufu* proclaimed in 1267 that the estate of a separated wife or concubine became the property of the former husband (Satō et al 1978). Under the earlier *shikimoku* laws, when a wife with property and no blame was divorced, the property given to her by her husband could not be taken back by him, but the new law stated that in the event of the wife's remarriage, property had to be returned to her former husband. However, this only applied in the case of a formal vassal. When a woman not from the vassal class (such as a *kugutsume, shirabyōshi* or other class of ordinary woman) became the wife or concubine of a vassal, in the case of separation and if the wife or widow lived 'chastely', without remarrying, an exception was made and the property could go to her.

Whereas the status of the mother carried considerable weight in the ancient and Heian periods, here there has emerged a stark division between the official wife and the concubine. The social position of the concubine was not an issue, but that of the wife was, which shows the expansion of patriarchal authority. Further, the *kugutsume* and the *asobime* were not yet viewed as outcasts, which would become unthinkable in the late medieval to the early Edo period.

Regarding these groups of entertainers and their close relatives the *miko*, I cannot agree with the view that sees their difference as ethnic (Takigawa 1976). As already discussed, their *hyakujin* cult was shared by the general populace under the *ritsuryō* system. The difference is more a question of lifestyle, and does not mean that the kinship groups of people conducting the primitive gathering economy were maintained (Amino 1984b). It is true that these people did not till fields but, rather, found their livelihoods in a hunter–gatherer economy, entertainment and prostitution. Furthermore, the heads of these groups were women, and the performing arts they practised were passed on from mother to daughter in a matrilineal bloodline. This included the adopted daughter system, which was related to a people trade that was in existence by the Kamakura period and which continued to supply labour for the brothels (with women traded in the guise of family (parent–child) relations) until the modern period.

In the *nō* play *Yuya*, Taira no Munemori's beloved Yuya was head of the station town of Ikeda in Tōtōmi Province. Although an imaginative creation, this tells us that in the medieval period there was a general recognition that the leader of a group of *asobime* at stations would be a woman. A nun called Eiyō-ni was head of the group of *kugutsume* in Imajuku, Suruga Province, and was exempted from general labour tax. She took as her son-in-law the third of four generations of caretakers of the estate. In 1249, she even brought a lawsuit against the *bakufu*.[27] The retired Emperor Goshirakawa's *Ryōjin hishō kuden-shū* (*Secret transmission of the Ryōjin hishō*) says that Nabiki was a renowned singer of *imayō* and was a *kugutsume* of Aobaka in Mino Province. Nabiki's daughter was Shisan, and her daughter was Mei. These and other examples show that the tradition of performing arts was passed on through mother–daughter relations.

Shichijūichiban shokunin utaawase: kusemai performer (left), *shirabyōshi* (right);
Gunsho ruijū (Hanawa 1933).

It is also manifestly clear that through adoption, non-blood relations could play a part in the transmission process. Retired Emperor Goshirakawa's teacher, Otomae, was the adopted daughter of Mei. A criticism of her artistic transmission was that 'Mei also, like a true daughter, did not have to be taught everything'. There is a story about a woman called Sakikusa who became a *kugutsume* after her beautiful voice was 'discovered' as she sang while she did the washing at the river.

In an increasingly competitive environment, the profession required natural endowment of artistic talent and good looks, as well as some commercial ability. It became difficult for mother–daughter relations and other blood-related groups to stay competitive. The groups experienced an influx of refugees from the fixed communities, which brought many changes. Adopted daughter relationships often resulted from human trading, as can be seen from the redemption deed for the *shirabyōshi* Tamaō in 1256 (Takeuchi 1971–89:7992). The document can be interpreted thus: a girl called Tokuishi-me, the adopted daughter of a person called Saishin, was sold elsewhere for the sum of 14 *kanmon*[28] — a sum paid by the *shirabyōshi* Tamaō in order to redeem the girl. It is not clear whether the girl was herself a *shirabyōshi*. In the *nō* play *Hanjo*, an *asobime* of the Nogami station laments, 'I am a piece of bamboo floating in the river'. In the *sekkyō-bushi* narrative *Oguri Hangan*, the phrase 'drifting girl' describes the plight of an *asobime* who is sold from one place to another: the main character Terute is sold for 13 *kanmon* and ends up working at the Aobaka station in Mino Province.

From the 14th century the status of these women started to decline. The communities in which they lived gathered in cities such as Kyoto and in outlying areas and they came to be called *shōmoji*. Among these groups of people was a mixture of male and female performing artists, such as *hōka-sō*, *shirabyōshi*, *kusemai* and *goze*, and also ritual specialists such as *onmyō-ji*, *etoki* and *miko*. They lived on riverbanks (*kawara*) and in areas called *sanjo*. The residents were regarded as beggars, acquiring names like *kojiki hōshi* (beggar priests) from the *sanjo* (Wakita 1987). However, these *sanjo* and riverbank settlements were hothouses of growth for the medieval performing arts: *nō*, *kyōgen* and later *kabuki*—all the major performing arts of the medieval and Edo periods were born from these environments.

Kusemai was not only performed by women (*onna kusemai* or *maimai*), but also, to a lesser extent, by men and boys (*chigo mai*) (Iwahashi 1975). In 1423, *maimai* performers from Ōmi, Kawachi and Mino went to the capital and received lavish praise for their *kanjin* performances at a number of venues. Proper seats cost from 300 to 500 *mon*, and to sit on the grass cost ten *mon*.[29] In 1466, there is a record of a beautiful 19-year-old *onna kusemai* from Mino Province who performed in front of a miscellaneous crowd of four or five thousand: 'her dance is beyond description, superb'.[30] The prime founder of *nō*, Kannami, incorporated *kusemai* into *sarugaku nō*, which was originally simple singing, when he created the play *Shirahige* (*Whitebeard*) and received an ovation from the spectators. His son Zeami wrote, 'Kannami was a great melodist, in the style of Otozuru' (Tanaka 1976b), referring to Kannami's use of the style of the famous *kusemai* performer Otozuru, whose lineage went back to the great *kusemai* performer Hyakuman, who had lived in the *shōmoji* community in Nara.

Zeami was, however, somewhat cold and critical towards *kusemai*. He wrote, 'all they do is go up and down...' (Tanaka 1976b). This probably means that the *kusemai* professional who only used a rising and falling melody was quite different from what was taken into *nō*. Certainly, his comment that '*kusemai* is based on rhythm' (Tanaka 1976a) implies that the *kusemai* simply performed a stomping rhythmic dance, unlike the mimetic dance of *nō*. Therefore, it would seem that the appeal of *kusemai* was often in the physical beauty of the woman or child performer rather than in their specialised skill. Zeami's harsh criticism reaches an extreme in the following passage: 'I feel that the *kusemai Going down to the eastern provinces* is a bad piece, with too much of the same *kakari* melody, alas. However, the melodies are good, although repetitive, which everyone says is typical of *kusemai*' (Tanaka 1976a). The *kusemai* he refers to is a piece with text written by a person called either Gyokurin or Rin'a, with the music by Ebina no Nan'ami, an aristocratic recluse of that time. Zeami is comparing it unfavourably with a piece called *Going down to the western provinces*, whose text was written by the same Gyokurin and the music by Kannami. For Zeami, *onna kusemai* invited ridicule for being repetitive, and yet *nō* developed into a great art by incorporating it.

Other arts from the *sanjo* settlements were absorbed by *nō* and contributed to its formation. The play *Hōka sō* was created around the art of the *hōka*, and the second category *nō* plays (warrior plays) were formed from the *Heike* narrative of the *biwa hōshi*. Plays like *Kosode Soga*, and other plays on the Soga brothers theme, were based on the performance of the blind female *goze* (blind itinerant balladeers) in the *Tale of the Soga Brothers*; *Mochizuki* incorporated the elements of *goze*, *shishimai* lion dance and *kakko* drum. Plays like *Kwagetsu* and *Hyakuman* have artists from the *sanjo* settlements as their main characters, such as the boy who dances with the drum and the *onna kusemai* performer. The main characters of *Makiginu* and *Utaura*, respectively, are a *miko* and a male shaman. Hence, the point of origin of *nō* was the arts of the *sanjo*, which were compiled and synthesised as *nō* drama. Performed within the *nō* plays, they are introduced with the request, 'Please show us your dance'. In this way the *sanjo* arts were appropriated and refined for upper-class tastes. However, for *nō* to succeed, as well as mediating and compiling these *sanjo* arts, it had to be supported by a high level of specialised skills, which it could refine into a sublime art form.

After perfecting the *nō*, the Kanze troupe was linked to the *bakufu*, and was well known for suppressing other *sarugaku nō* troupes such as that of Koinu (Hayashiya 1960). In 1466, it seems that Koinutayū was sued by the *bakufu* for performing while wearing a *nō* mask—a breach of that monopoly.[32] Normally, a *za* commercial monopoly was claimed by supplying materials rooted in a new production technology with which they conquered the market; this became a vested interest, and a claim of monopoly against possible competitors. The way in which the Kanze troupe put pressure on the *sanjo* performers is a clear example of this principle (Wakita 1969e).

In the process of development of *sarugaku nō* into a commercial theatre, the *sanjo* performing arts were left behind and became submerged. Women's performance, as well as men's performance, met the same fate. The *sanjo* arts continued to have their patrons, and arts such as *onna sarugaku* flourished in the Sengoku period; however, eventually women's performance became marginalised on the bypaths of history and was banned. *Kabuki* had its origins in the women's *kabuki* of Okuni and others, but after the ban of 1629 it was transformed into *wakashū* (boy's) *kabuki*, and then into *yarō* (men's) *kabuki*, becoming an exclusively male art. It is worth considering why medieval performance came to be the province only of men, not only in Japan, but also in China and in the West.

The 'women's documents'—nyōbō hōsho

During the period of the Warring States (1467–1568), the imperial institution declined and its administration was sustained solely by women courtiers, or *nyōkan* (*nyōbō*) (Okuno 1942). The hub of this management was a lady-in-waiting with the title *kōtō no naishi* (also called *nagahashi no tsubone*). '*Kōtō*' means someone who takes charge and manages general matters, and originally it was the most senior rank of the *naishi* court ladies. In the period of the Warring States, it seems to have become an official position directly appointed by the emperor.[31] The most important task of the *kōtō no naishi*, as a kind of court officer, was the issuing of documents called *nyōbō hōsho*.

Since the institution of the *ritsuryō* system, the task of issuing petitions (*sōsei*) and decrees (*densen*) had been allocated to female officials (*naishi no tsukasa*—one of the 12 court ranks for women); the *naishi no kami* and the *naishi no suke*; but when the post of *naishi no kami* could no longer be sustained, the task devolved to the *suke* and the *kotō no naishi*.

The oldest extant *nyōbō hōshō* date back to 1263, among documents of the Kamo no Wakeikazuchi shrine (now Kamigamo Jinja) (Satō 1971). Much has been written about *nyōbō hōsho* as old documents (*komonjo*) by Aida Jirō (Aida 1949), Satō Shin'ichi and Iikura Harutake (Iikura 1981), but I wish to consider the significance of these documents for women's history. I will draw on the material offered by the diary of Yamashina Tokitsugu (1507–79) to discuss their scope and efficacy, focusing on actual cases when they were issued as part of daily life at court in the 16th century.

Nyōbō hōsho conveyed imperial commands, agreements and permissions in response to petitions first received via the *kōtō no naishi*. It seems that the number of women's documents far outweighed imperial documents issued by male courtiers, such as *kansenji* (documents conveying the commands of the prime minister), *kuzen'an* (drafts or copies of imperial orders which were orally conveyed) and *rinji* (imperial decrees).

Yamashina Tokitsugu wrote the diary *Tokitsugu kyōki* as his personal daily record of court business. It covers a full two-year period from 1544 to 1545, and all the daily entries relate to his position and responsibilities.[33] Table 3 summarises all the women's documents referred to in the diary.

Table 3: Nyōbō hōsho issued in 1544 and 1545 (compiled from Tokitsugu Kyōki)

	Addressee	Year-month-day
1 Imperial promise of promotion to higher court rank	Tokudaiji family	1545-3-18
2 Imperial decree	the priest Denryū Shōnin	1544-8-29, 9-4, 5
3 Imperial permission to pay musician for kagura music at shrine festival		1544-1-17
4 Letter of appointment of head musician of Sato kagura troupe at Iwashimizu Hachimangū shrine	Ashikaga shōgun	1544-7-19, 7-19
5 Approval to give a hichiriki (double reed instrument) to Iwashimizu Hachimangū		1544-7-8
6 Approval for landholding in Yamashiro Province, Sayama district	Yamanoi Kageo	1545-10-20
7 Territorial dispute between the Yamashina family and Miidera Temple over the Yamashina Nishi no shō estate	Muromachi bakufu	1545-3-15
8 Bird guilds (tori-za) dispute	Mizushi-dokoro and Nagahashi-tsubone	1545-6-7
9 Fish merchants dispute	Takatsukasa Kanpaku-ke (Fujiwara) family and Yamashina family	1545 (see Table 4)
10 Arbitration between temples		1544-11 (intercalary month) -6, 8, 9

The documents issued by male courtiers in the same period provide a means of comparison: a proclamation from the emperor (*senji*) concerning the son of the Kikutei family, who had made application for a change to his name to include a character from the *shōgun's* name; a *kansenji* document regarding the appointment of a priest-examiner to the Hieizan temple; documents declaring imperial authorisation for the promotion and reinstatement of court officers, and the right to carry a sword; and appointments to high priestly rank, and to landlord or governor status. Most of these documents concerned matters of rank. Both priestly and gubernatorial appointments were nominal, and could be purchased. *Rinji* (documents issued by *kurōdo*, male courtiers, by order of the emperor) were issued for the appointment of deputy minister Hirohashi no Dainagon as *densō* to Kamo shrine, for the appointment of the head priest to the Myōshinji temple, for authorisation for the clove-dyed robe of a high-ranking priest for and territorial disputes.

Nyōbō hōsho were issued by the *kōtō no naishi* for official matters other than the documents issued by male courtiers, as well as for private internal matters. For this reason, *nyōbō hōsho* can be said to have transmitted the emperor's personal will. I now look at each item in Table 3 in turn.

1   Imperial promise of promotion to higher court rank

This is a private or unofficial imperial promise (*chokuyaku*) concerning a promotion to a higher court rank. Addressed to the General of the Right, Tokudaiji, who is leaving the capital for his domain in Etchū Province, it promises that after his return he will be promoted to the rank of *shōjō* or minister.

2   Imperial decree

Tokitsugu acted as mediator for the application from the Buddaji temple, which was perplexed because its priest Denryū Shōnin would not return from his stay in Ise Province. The imperial decree urged Denryū's return to the temple, and in this case the personal will of the emperor was also involved.

3   Imperial permission to pay musician at shrine (*beijūdai*)

Beijūdai referred to the hiring of lower-ranking musicians to perform *gagaku* and *kagura* at major shrines such as Kamo Jinja and Iwashimizu Hachiman. Tokitsugu was treasurer (*kura no kami*), and also head of music, so the diary has many entries relating to music administration.

4 Letter of appointment of head musician

This is a guarantee and permission to appoint the musician Yamanoi Aki no Kami Kageo (of the *sato kagura* troupe at Iwashimizu Hachimangū shrine) to head musician, and notification of this to the Ashikaga *shōgun*. For court rank promotion, a *kuzen'an* was issued, but for a lower-ranking bureaucrat a *nyōbō hōsho* was sufficient.

5 Approval for a *hichiriki* oboe to be given to Iwashimizu Hachimangū in *sato kagura*

This is a similar document of appointment of the *hichiriki* player.

6 Approval for landholding in Yamashiro Province

The *nyōbō hōsho* affirmed temporary permission for Yamanoi Kageo to govern the Sayama district in Yamashiro Province.

7 Territorial dispute between the Yamashina family and Miidera temple over the Yamashina Nishi no shō estate

The most serious cases at the time surrounded territorial disputes. This document relates to a dispute between the Yamashina family and the Miidera temple about land under the jurisdiction of the Yamashina West Estate. Through Tokitsugu's petition a *nyōbō hōsho* was issued demanding that an investigation be held and that the decision be made through fair jurisdiction. This document was sent by the imperial representative (Hirohashi no Dainagon) to the *bakufu*.

8 Bird guilds (*tori-za*) dispute

A dispute between two bird guilds, which provided game such as pheasants for the imperial table, one under the jurisdiction of the Yamashina house and one under the jurisdiction of the *kōtō no naishi*. There was an exchange of private letters between Tokitsugu and the *kōtō no naishi*, and in addition a *nyōbō hōsho* was issued to settle the matter. Tokitsugu made a distinction by sending a private letter to the *kōtō no naishi* as the other party in the dispute, and by sending a *nyōbō hōsho* addressed to the *kōtō no naishi* as the lady in waiting (in charge of *nyōbō hōsho*). In this matter, it seems that Tokitsugu gave in easily, based on the petition of the *kōtō no naishi*—with the emperor's official approval he accepted the victory of the *kōtō no naishi*.

9 Fish merchants dispute

Tokitsugu does not give an inch in this dispute between the duties of the fish merchant under the jurisdiction of the Takatsukasa Kanpaku chancellor family and the fish merchants Awazu and Imamachi, who supplied the palace and were under the jurisdiction of the Yamashina family. Allied with the *kōtō no naishi*, Tokitsugu appealed directly to the emperor and pushed his case through. At one point, Awazu was dragged in by Tokitsugu and made to sit down in the courtyard of the *kōtō no naishi*. Evidently, it was preferable for Tokitsugu to make an enemy of the Kanpaku family than of the *kōtō no naishi*. It could also have been because the imperial family, that is, the *kōtō no naishi*, regarded the merchants who supplied their kitchen (*mizushi-dokoro*) and other stores as part of the imperial household management, and as being in opposition to the Kanpaku family.

In order to better understand the role of the *nyōbō hōsho*, the process of this dispute is seen in more detail through the exchange of documents, summarised in Table 4.

In this case, the Takatsukasa Kanpaku family owned the right to tax from all the fishmongers in the capital. The dispute began when, using as agent, the *bushi* Hōkabe, the family demanded payment of tax from the royal fishmongers Imamachi and Awazu, who were appointed to supply the imperial kitchen and who were privileged to be exempt from paying tax.

Through the appeal of Yamashina Tokitsugu, the imperial household promptly inquired about the situation in a *nyōbō hōsho* to the Takatsukasa house, via the Hirohashi no Dainagon. However, as there was no reply forthcoming, the next enquiry was made by the *kōtō no naishi* sending a *nyōbō hōsho* directly to the *senji no tsubone* of the Takatsukasa Kanpaku house. A reply in *nyōbō bumi* was received from them addressed to the *kōtō no naishi*. However, it is interesting to note that, as soon as the Kanpaku decided to appeal to the *shōgun*, he abandoned the *nyōbō bumi* in favour of an *origami no hōsho* letter by his chief secretary, addressed to Hirohashi no Dainagon, the noble who conveyed imperial messages to the *shōgun*. In response, the *bakufu* held a hearing called *sanmon santō* (three questions and three replies), but because it was a matter between two courtiers, any verdict issued by the *bakufu* was not formally recognised. Ultimately the affair had to be settled by an imperial decree (*rinji*). Therefore, when the supplier plaintiffs applied, the *bakufu* governor's document was issued immediately.

In this dispute, the emperor's personal will was announced in a *nyōbō hōsho*, and the official verdict was announced in a *rinji* (issued by male courtiers). This shows that when the *shōgun* house was involved, a clear distinction was made, and a *bakufu* governor's document was issued instead. Formally, women did not have anything to do with the issuing of *rinji*, but when informing the Takatsukasa Kanpaku house that a *rinji* would be issued,

Table 4: Nyōbō hōsho issued on the matter of the fishmongers dispute

Month -day	Content	Addressee
2-5	On the appeal of Yamashina Tokitsugu, two nyōbō hōsho, one each for the suppliers Imamachi and Awazu	Hirohashi no Dainagon, then to Takatsukasa Kanpaku house
2-6	Given no reply from Takatsukasa Kanpaku, a further nyōbō hōsho	Takatsukasa Kanpaku house
2-7	Nyōbō hōsho requesting the Kanpaku's official not to pay tax	Yamashina Chūnagon
2-7	Reply received from Kanpaku's senji no tsubone (in nyōbō bumi or women's style)	Kōtō no naishi
2-10	Nyōbō hōsho sent	Kanpaku house's senji no tsubone
2-11	Kanpaku house senji no tsubone sends reply	Kōtō no naishi
	Tokitsugu sends two letters explaining the situation	Kōtō no naishi and Kanpaku house
2-12	Nyōbō hōsho of 2-7 exempting Awazu supplier from tax re-sent	Yamashina Chūnagon
2-14	Kanpaku house Chūjō hōsho sent	Hirohashi no Dainagon
2-15	Nyōbō hōsho in response	Hirohashi no Dainagon
2-21	Letter from the kitchen (mizushi-dokoro) is shown by Yamashina family to Hirohashi Dainagon	
2-26	Kanpaku petitions the judgment success and failure of military house. Memorandum of the petition sent to the Yamashina family via Hirohashi. Yamashina sent five documents (evidence) and a memo to Hirohashi, then to Kanpaku-ke and Buke. Three questions and answers began.	
5-9	Yamashina family sends three replies	Hirohashi Dainagon
7-25	Nyōbō hōsho requesting a petition to the Muromachi dono (shōgun) that the fish supplier Imamachi's tax exemption be approved	Yamashina no Chūnagon
9-17	Rinji proclaiming tax exemption of fish supplier Imamachi	Takatsukasa Kanpaku house
9-20	Hōsho (official document) from the bakufu governor's office approving tax exemption for the Imamachi supplier of fish to the imperial kitchen	
10-6	Nyōbō hōsho threatening that in the case where the Kanpaku does not provide documentary evidence regarding the Awazu fish supplier, a rinji will be sent to the supplier	
10-10	Urged by the Awazu supplier, Tokitsugu requests kōtō no naishi, and the tsubone promises to issue a rinji	
10-11	Rinji proclaiming full exemption of tax and public service for the Awazu fish supplier. The draft and the (recycled) paper are provided by Yamashina family.	Awazu fish supplier
(undated)	Kanpaku house's tax agent Hōkabe demands an order from the military authorities, the fish supplier applies for a hōsho from the bakufu governor, and this is granted	Yamashina house official

it was done through a *nyōbō hōsho* and, further, it was the *kōtō no naishi* who proposed to Tokitsugu that a *rinji* be issued the next day, Could we not say that the views of the *kōtō no naishi* were most influential here? This is also suggested by the fishmongers lining up in the inner garden of the *kōtō no naishi*, and by the gifts brought by Awazu after victory was achieved and the dispute was settled: he presented to Tokitsugu two barrels of sake and parcels of octopus and snapper; to (*Ō-Sukedono no tsubone*, also two barrels of sake and parcels of octopus and dried kelp; and to the *kōtō no naishi*, he presented fourbarrels of sake and parcels of salmon, octopus and dried kelp. In addition, the sum of 100 *hiki* (one *kanmon*) was presented from the same Awazu fishmonger, but it is not clear whether it all went to the Yamashina family. In the *Oyudono no ue no nikki* entry for the same day, none of these three people are recorded as having presented anything to the emperor. Whether *nyōbō hōsho* or *rinji*, they should both emerge from the emperor's decree, so it is difficult to explain what happened to the gifts.

Satō locates the origin of *nyōbō hōsho* in the Heian period *naishi no sen* (Satō 1971). Furthermore, he claims that in the early days of the *ritsuryō* system, the emperor's will was first communicated to the middle ministry through his female attendants,[34] and that even after the creation of the *kurōdo-dokoro* (male courtiers office), the emperor's will was communicated to the *kurōdo* from the *naishi* in documents called *naishi no sen*.

According to other researchers there is no direct connection between *naishi no sen* and *nyōbō hōsho*. *Naishi no sen* and *kuzen'an* correspond to *senji*, while *nyōbō hōsho* correspond to *rinji*. Both *naishi no sen* and *nyōbō hōsho* show the power of the memoranda of the women (*naishi*) who attended the emperor and, in this sense, they belong to the same category. Moreover, their origins go back to the early *ritsuryō* system, when the *naishi* issued *sōsei* and *densen*. In Tang China, the *Tō Rikuten* (book which details the *ritsuryō* system, revised in 738), on which the Japanese *ritsuryō* system was based, stipulated that the task of writing *sōsei* and *densen* be given to court ladies and eunuchs, but as the Japanese system did not have eunuchs, this role devolved to the court ladies. *Sōsei* and *densen* were the province of the *naishi no kami*; and only when this office disappeared did it become the role of the *naishi no jō*. But for all women at court, even the humblest servants, *senji* existed, showing that women's roles were highly significant (Tsuchida 1959). We can surmise that the role of women at court would have been different under a female emperor.

Regardless of the importance of *naishi no sen* up to the mid-Heian period, it is said that their status dropped after the establishment of the *kurōdo-dokoro* in 810; in addition, the creation of *rinji* hastened this process. However, *rinji* initially served to communicate the emperor's personal interests, via the *naishi*, to the *kurōdo*, who then committed this to writing. They later evolved to official status, leaving *nyōbō hōsho* to fulfill the function of the emperor's private documents.

In the Warring States period, a majority of the documents issuing from the administrative structure of the imperial household were *nyōbō hōsho*. A similar structure existed in the Kanpaku household, where documents issued by the *senji no tsubone* had the same function, as in the case of the fishmongers dispute. The *kōtō no naishi* and the *senji no tsubone*, as managers of the internal running of the households, also had the task of expressing the private wishes of the emperor and the Kanpaku respectively in the form of *hōsho* documents.

Areas of jurisdiction of *kōtō no naishi*

This section continues the analysis of the diary of Yamashina Tokitsugu, *Tokitsugu Kyōki*, this time examining the items on which Tokitsugu negotiated with the *kōtō no naishi*. Table 5 summarises these for the period of 1544 and 1545.

Since the *kōtō no naishi* was basically a secretary to the emperor, she had some say in all business matters. Her position was quite different from the Edo *shōgun's* ladies, who were excluded from official life and limited to the ladies' quarters (*ō-oku*) of the palace. Table 5 may seem unnecessarily detailed, but it demonstrates in concrete terms the extent of the duties carried out by the *kōtō no naishi*.

Takakura Ryōshi (daughter of Susuki Mochiito and adopted daughter of Takakura Nagaie) was appointed *kōtō no naishi* in 1543 and became the mother of an imperial princess, Anzenji no miya.[35] Her primary job was to write and issue *nyōbō hōsho*. All the annual events and ceremonies of the imperial household, such as the new year prayers, burning ritual and incantations, were organised by the *kōtō no naishi*, who gave orders to the courtiers.

Cultural activities, such as 1000-poems parties, *renga* parties, musical performances and *sarugaku nō* performances, were arranged in consultation between the *kōtō no naishi* and the courtiers in charge of each event. Gatherings of courtiers were also arranged by summons from the *kōtō no naishi*. For example, when the father and son named Asukai were summoned to an audience with the emperor, a letter from the *kōtō no naishi* (it is not known whether it was a *nyōbō hōsho* or a private letter) arrived at the Yamashina household and Yamashina Tokitsugu conveyed this to the Asukai family, who were his retainers.

Table 5: Summary of tasks performed by the kōtō no naishi as recorded in Tokitsugu's diary

Category	Item	Year-month-day
Arranging court ceremonies/activities	Sagichō burning ritual	1545-1-14
	Prayers for the New Year	1542-1-26
	Yin–yang incantations for the New Year	1545-1-17 & 3-2
	Mishiho incantations	1544-10-20
	Sarugaku (nō) performance	1544-1-17, 20 & 24
	Senshu—1000 poems party	1542-11-2, 4 & 5
	Renga—linked verse party	1542-2-22
	Arrangements for music performance	1544-3-9
Courtier-related tasks	Summons to attend a gathering	1545-3-17
	Report on absence of a courtier	1544-2-9, 1545-4-29
	Enquiry about a courtier's health	1544-2-14
	Thanks for courtier's promotion	1545-1-16
	Thanks for gift from emperor to courtier	1544-8-1, 1545-1-29
	Record of gift brought to the palace (flowers, chrysanthemums)	1544-7-7, 1544-10-13, 1545-8-1, 1545-9-8
	Gifts of sandals	1544-9-8
Financial and accounting tasks	Contribution of 20 hiki towards 1000 waka party (20 hiki for drinks for courtiers in charge of the poetry gathering)	1542-2-20
	Payment of 800 hiki to Shibuya for the sarugaku nō performance	1544-2-10
	Two eboshi courtier's headgear	1544-12-4, 1545-4-12
	Payment of 30 hiki to the guards for cleaning	1544-12-5
	Two payments of 20 hiki to low-ranking musicians for lesson fees	1545-3-11
Personnel-related tasks	Appointment of court ladies	1542-2-18, 1544-7-24
	Appointment of deputy priest to Kamo shrine	1544-7-14
	Appointment of courtier	1544-8-7
	Imperial rescript authorising clove-dyed robe for a courtier	1544-3-17
	Award of priestly rank of shōnin	1544-6-17
	Imperial decree of appointment of temple examiner to the Hieizan Enryaku-ji	1544-12-19, 20

The *kōtō no naishi* reported any absences from duty of the courtiers, including men in the emperor's inner circle of aides, those in the outer circle and those on overnight duty. When courtiers returned to the capital after travelling to their distant estates, they reported to the *kōtō no naishi.* Any gifts presented to the palace were accompanied by a letter addressed to the *kōtō no naishi.* Similarly, tribute gifts of gratitude from the produce of estates, as well as gifts in appreciation for a promotion to a higher court rank, were delivered to the *kōtō no naishi.* Conversely, the emperor would enquire after the health of a courtier via the *kōtō no naishi.* As a mark of appreciation towards courtiers—even to low-ranking ones—and samurai, the *kōtō no naishi* often served them sake in her quarters.

The *kōtō no naishi* handled requests for offerings to shrines and temples, as well as requests for calligraphy by the emperor, which was a significant source of income for him. An instance is recorded in the diary of Tokitsugu and requests the emperor's handwriting of a poem by Kakinomoto no Hitomaro, two Chinese poems and a copy of the Tendai Buddhist teachings—which he was to collect from the *kōtō no naishi* quarters.

The most important duty of the *kōtō no naishi* was looking after the accounts and treasury of the imperial household. This included collecting banquet fees from courtiers and receiving gifts for the emperor, some of which are recorded in the *Oyudono no ue no nikki* (see Chapter five). The *kōtō no naishi* handled expenses incurred by the emperor, gifts given by the emperor, and she ordered any supplies and commodities. Money to cover a prince's new headgear was sent from the *kōtō no naishi* to Tokitsugu who, as the head of stores, was in charge of the wardrobe. Tokitsugu put in a request to the *kōtō no naishi* for lesson fees for two newly appointed low-ranking musicians, and received permission to give them 20 *hiki* each.

The most amusing case is the documentation about the cleaning of the *seiryōden* hall of the palace at year's end. Two guards were summoned and they presented an invoice of 100 *hiki.* When Tokitsugu presented this to the *kōtō no naishi,* she replied, in a memo rejecting this price, 'Do not respond'. Tokitsugu told the guards, 'I will see if she will agree to 50 *hiki*'; he negotiated with the *kōtō no naishi,* who replied that it had to be reduced to 30 *hiki.* It seems that there had been previous occasions when the price could not be agreed on. Tokitsugu wrote, 'I had to lecture her, saying even though it is a small amount, the emperor is angry about the charges. You have been summoned to work, so get on with it.' In the end, the guards agreed to do the cleaning, which took only one day, for 30 *hiki,* the equivalent of 300 *mon.* A carpenter at that time was paid 100 *mon* for a day's work (Wakita 1969a), so 300 *mon* between two people was a high price. However, Tokitsugu admits that it is a small fee, so perhaps washing the palace involved a team of people led by the two guards. In any case, the way the *kōtō no naishi* managed the accounts was strict.

Tokitsugu's diary shows us the scope of the work of the *kōtō no naishi*. Placed in a pivotal position in the imperial household, she had a substantial say in important business such as personnel matters. Tokitsugu asked her about the appointment of new court ladies and for assistance in appointing an acting chief priest to the important Kamo-sha shrine. The imperial awarding of priestly rank and priestly privilege (such as wearing clove-dyed robes) was done by *rinji*, but often it was the *kōtō no naishi* who submitted these petitions to the emperor, while Tokitsugu received prior consultation about the matters in the quarters of the *kōtō no naishi*. Since the awarding of priestly rank and privilege was a source of income for the imperial household, this was a large part of the work of the *kōtō no naishi* who controlled the accounts. For example, the award of the priestly rank of *shōnin* was normally worth 100 *hiki* (one *kan-mon*); acting as an agent for appointment to a high-ranking office netted an amount of 20 *hiki*.

Negotiations about difficult appointments were often carried out using the *kōtō no naishi* as intermediary. On one occasion, when Tokitsugu was the acting middle minister (*Gon Chūnagon*) and another high-ranking noble wished to be promoted while there was no vacancy, the emperor ordained that the rank be borrowed from Tokitsugu for four or five days, a decision mediated through the *kōtō no naishi*. Such complex unofficial negotiations were a routine part of the *kōtō no naishi's* job. When a *kan-senji* was issued concerning the Hieizan (Enryakuji) temple examiner (*tandai*), it was the *kōtō no naishi* who mediated this.

What can be learned from Tokitsugu's diary is limited to matters in which Tokitsugu was personally involved. Even so, the diary makes it clear that the *kōtō no naishi* presided over all the emperor's affairs. As shown in the previous section, in the dispute between the bird guilds, which was the jurisdiction of the *kōtō no naishi*, and the dispute with the suppliers of fish to the imperial kitchen, Tokitsugu conceded easily; in the argument with the Kanpaku household he used the *kōtō no naishi* as a front and refused to make any concessions. These two instances clearly show the actual power of the *kōtō no naishi*, even though others ranked above her, such as the *ō-suke no tsubone* and *Gon no suke no tsubone*, who often took petitions to the emperor. Towards the end of the Edo period (mid-19th century), the *ō-suke no tsubone* controlled the inner affairs of the court, whereas the *kōtō no naishi* looked after external affairs and exercised the most authority in relation to the outside world (Shimohashi 1979). From the dispute between the Kanpaku household and the fishmongers (who expressed gratitude for the victory by sending gifts to the *kōtō no naishi* and *ō-suke no tsubone*), we can assume that this was the same in the 16th century.

To be appointed to the important position of *kōtō no naishi*, or to have a daughter appointed to that position, brought significant rights and interests. In the late Edo period, it is said that their annual income was 1000 *ryō*, and they were hence nicknamed *sen ryō nagahashi* (Shimohashi 1979). On the sixth day of the ninth month, 1527, when the *kōtō no naishi* Takakura Keishi died, Takakura Norihisa campaigned to appoint a replacement (Okuno 1942) and was reprimanded by Sanjō Nishi Sanetaka, who said that this was 'deplorable, deplorable'.[36] There was a discussion about whether succession should depend on family status or the father's achievement. The emperor ruled that, according to *Kinpishō* (about the ceremonies and customs of the court, written in *kanbun* by Juntoku Tennō, during the Jōkyū period, 1219–22), the *kōtō* appointment should be based on ability, and Ane no kōji Saishi was appointed.[37] Sanetaka's record reads, 'Excellent. This is how it should be.' This shows the seriousness of selecting a *kōtō no naishi*.

Why was so much power concentrated on the office of the *kōtō no naishi*? At this point in history (mid-16th century), there was a clear distinction between the *nyōbō hōsho*, which expressed the personal will of the emperor, and the *rinji*, which declared the emperor's will in his official capacity. The *kōtō no naishi* was in charge of the general and financial management of the emperor's household but, even though she managed negotiations with outside bodies, her authority was strictly limited to internal household (*ie*) matters. However, with the creation of the Muromachi *bakufu* in 1336, the official authority of the emperor became nominal, and by the Warring States period it was confined to court rank and religious appointments (such as appointments to the priestly rank system and high priestly rank; granting permission to wear clove-dyed robes; conducting business relating to imperial temples such as Tōdaiji, which was built to protect the state, and to shrines; the appointment of *Shintō* priests; and appointments of court musicians and artists and governorship titles). In formal terms, these items remained within the emperor's scope because he ruled above the *bakufu* and, in practical terms, they were a principal source of income for the emperor. As with the sale of the emperor's calligraphy, they were part of the task of the *kōtō no naishi* in managing the imperial household finances. The small area of public authority that remained for the emperor was absorbed into the household management and finances of the emperor's *ie*, and hence became part of the jurisdiction of the *kōtō no naishi*. Normally, the establishment of the *ie* is considered synonymous with the establishment of patriarchy; and in the medieval period, too, the *ie* was represented by the male family head. However, I stress that the work and abilities of the *kōtō no naishi*, which are detailed here, demonstrate that women held important roles and authority within the *ie*.

A glimpse at women in other circumstances shows a comparison. In the Muromachi *bakufu*, the court culture penetrated the shogunal and other military houses, including the custom of *nyōbō* functioning as intermediaries. When the young Ashikaga Yoshihisa (ninth Ashikaga *shōgun*, 1465–89; reigned 1473–89; son of Yoshimasa and Hino no Tomiko) was officially made *shōgun*, his father Yoshimasa (1436–1490; reigned 1449–73) was in the position of *Shissei* (regent), but real power was in the hands of his mother, Hino no Tomiko. The imperial ambassador to the shogunal court at the time was Hirohashi no Kaneaki, who had to ask for decisions from Yoshimasa and approvals from Tomiko or the ladies close to her.[38] His diary entries from 1477–79 show that in weighty matters the will of Yoshimasa was communicated by Tomiko, while less important matters were decided in consultation between Tomiko and her chamberlain Ise Sadamune (1444–1509). When a communication arrived for Yoshimasa from the imperial household, it was addressed to the *Buke Densō* with the greeting, 'The emperor says this is to be sent to the *shōgun* (*Muromachi dono ni mōse to te sōrō*)', and was written in a *nyōbō hōsho* using women's language. We have no way of knowing whether a reply was issued from a *nyōbō* close to the *shōgun*. I used to doubt whether *nyōbō hōsho* issued within the *shōgun* household could have had the same impact as documents issued by male officials. However, a letter was located in *nyōbō bumi* that presents the wishes of Yoshimasa to the emperor—a document titled 'Horikawa no Tsubone-bumi' contained in the *Koga-ke monjo* (*Koga-ke monjo* 1982:296). On the back it is signed, 'Written by Horikawa no Tsubone on behalf of the cloistered Lord Yoshimasa Jishōin, 26th day, sixth month, 1486'. The characters, which are illegible, can be reasonably ascribed to Jishō, referring to Yoshimasa by the name of the temple (now Ginkakuji temple) that he built for his own use. From the name of the writer we can judge this to be a *nyōbō bumi* written by Lady Horikawa, conveying the will of Yoshimasa.

The letter concerns a petition that the Koga family sent to Yoshimasa concerning an estate in Ōmi Province called Koga no shō—the land where the temple Hōkyūji used to stand. The petition was shown to Yoshimasa, who acceded to it. He directed that a *bugyōnin hōsho* (magisterial document) concerning the Koga estate be issued, instructing that the lands of the Hōkyūji temple were at the discretion of the Koga family; however, since the incumbent of the Koga estate, the 'Great Nurse', was already well advanced in years, the family was advised to be patient and leave it in her jurisdiction for the duration of her lifetime, after which it would revert to the Koga family. A formal shogunal document was subsequently issued in 1487 affirming that the Great Nurse held the rights or jurisdiction for collecting tribute of this property, and emphasising direct administration of the property (that is, the Hōkyūji temple lands) located in the Koga family's estate in Yamashiro Province.[39] Yoshimasa, in the above mentioned *nyōbō bumi*, consoled the Koga family, who argued on behalf of its steward, by asking them to wait patiently for the present incumbent to die, and promised that it would then be theirs. This shows that the role of the *bugyōnin hōsho* of the *bakufu* was the same as the imperial *rinji*, while the *bakufu's nyōbō bumi*, like the emperor's *nyōbō hōsho*, was used to express a personal undertaking.

In the Edo period, the Tokugawa *bakufu* sequestered their women in the palace quarters, called *Ō-oku*. They had some hidden influence, but they no longer had any relation with official documents and events. In historical research up till now, this situation in the Edo *bakufu* was transferred by analogy to the circumstances of aristocratic women in the medieval era. However, even in the Edo period, in families such as the imperial family and the Sekkanke family, the precedent of the Muromachi-era court lady (*nyōbō*) continued to be followed, as already seen. For example, towards the end of the Edo era, a senior woman of the Konoe family, Muraoka no tsubone (Tsuzaki Noriko), was powerful—most likely because she was in charge of the household affairs of the Konoe family—in a way that corresponded to the *kōtō no naishi* of the imperial family. We can assume that she possessed the same kind of authority as the *senji no tsubone* of the Takatsukasa Kanpaku family in the Tenbun era (1532–55).

Looking further back at the Heian and Kamakura periods, there was a tendency for the responsibilities of the court ladies to shift to the male courtiers (*kurōdo*) following the establishment of the *kurōdo-dokoro* (Haru 1984). That is historical fact. However, while *senji* were now communicated to the *kurōdo*, the *naishi* retained the duty of announcing these and there was no change in the involvement of *naishi* in official documents. At the stage when *rinji* and *nyōbō hōsho* were issued in large numbers, the role of court ladies became increasingly strong. The more despotic an emperor, the more influence was acquired by private documents such as *rinji* and *nyōbō hōsho*. Godaigo (reigned 1318–1339) was one such despotic emperor who issued copious *rinji* and was criticised for the harmful excess of women's influence at court. This was not just a personal characteristic of his, but rather related to the systemic structure of the court in which women held considerable influence. In relations between the imperial family and the court, and between the *shōgun's* household and the *bakufu* (government), there was always a rivalry between the absolute power of emperor and *shōgun* and their respective official administrative structures of ministers and bureaucracy and *bakufu* magistrates (*bugyōnin*). The *ie* of the emperor and *shōgun* lay behind these tensions. As Tsuchida concludes, the *naishi no sen* did not have to pass through the chief minister (*Dajōkan*) and in this they were like the guards (Tsuchida 1959).

In other aristocratic families, such as the Fujiwara Sesshō-Kanpaku family, and in the imperial households of the reigning emperor and the emperor's mother (former empress)—whose household structures were a miniature version of the imperial household—the role of the *senji no tsubone* would have been similar to that of the *kōtō no naishi*. In the period of the retired emperors (11th–13th centuries), the household governance of the retired emperor wielded considerable power—and the influence of Kyō no Nii Kaneko (a lady of second rank) was surely due to this kind of structure. In the Kamakura *bakufu*, the ladies of the shogunal palace held significant positions, and in recognition of their accomplishments they were awarded jurisdiction over large domains.[40]

Many issues remain unexplored, such as the role of the wet nurses (*menoto*), the practical role of women who managed daily affairs in substantial households, and domestic labour in the *ie* of the common people. I have also barely touched on the issue of gender role division in the Warring States era, when the imperial household was in severe decline. During this time, women performed all tasks on a daily basis, whereas in periods when the imperial system was flourishing, the role of men, especially the various levels of vassal in all the major aristocratic families, was much greater.

Aspects of social labour

This section draws on the information provided by the scrolls called *Shokunin utaawase* (poetry competitions by artisans and craftsmen), from which much can be learned about medieval women's social labour (Toyoda 1983; Gorai 1982; Wakita 1982). (*Shokunin utaawase* are a genre of scroll art, which presented pairs of matched occupations, each of which competes with a *waka* poem. Each pair of poems is evaluated in a commentary.) The sex of the original creators of the *waka* poems and the judges who commented on them are not known, but the gendered illustrations are highly informative. I will refer principally to the *Shichijū-ichiban utaawase*, reproduced in *Gunsho ruijū* and elsewhere, not only because of its ready availability, but also because the date of its creation is known and because it shows pictorially very clearly the differences between various occupations.

It is known that the original *Shichijū-ichiban utaawase* was completed in 1500. The inscription at the back of the *Gunsho ruijū* version indicates that

The capital Kyoto had trouble meeting its fuel needs. The female firewood vendors and charcoal vendors from the north of the city walked the streets selling their goods and were indispensable traders for Kyoto's survival. In modern times they also sold simmered peppercorns and *shibazuke* (pickled eggplant and cucumbers), and became a typical sight on Kyoto streets.

From *Shichijūichiban shokunin utaawase*. Firewood vendors (left); charcoal vendor (right). From *Gunsho ruijū* (Hanawa 1933).

this was a copy of a copy of the original and was made in 1520 or 1521, close to the original date of production.

While the scroll reveals something about the situation of artisans in that era, it illustrates 71 pairs, and hence 142 occupations, so there may be cases where the pairing is a little artificial and not all the occupations may be representative of society at that time.[41]

The capital Kyoto had trouble supplying its fuel needs. The female firewood vendors and charcoal vendors from the north of the city walked the streets selling their goods and were indispensable traders for Kyoto's survival. In modern times they also sold simmered peppercorns and *shibazuke* (pickled eggplant and cucumbers) and became a typical sight on Kyoto streets.

Table 6 summarises and classifies the various types of professions illustrated in the *Shichijūichiban shokunin utaawase* scroll. Points to note are, first, that women's occupations concentrated on the making and selling of the necessities of life, such as clothing and food. In this period, a separation between wholesalers and retailers began to appear, but there were still many itinerant

112 WOMEN IN MEDIEVAL JAPAN

Table 6: Gender role division of occupations according to the Shichijūichiban shokunin utaawase scroll (Hanawa 1931–33:v28:464–606).

	Female	Male
Artisans (skilled)	indigo dyer (cloth dyer), weaver, embroiderer, braider	Carpenter, blacksmith, plasterer, thatcher (shingler), sword sharpener, lacquerer, lacquer artist, wooden-container maker, wheelwright, tatami-mat sewer, roof-tile maker, metal etcher, mercury maker
Craftspersons —artistic and military	fan seller, folded paper case seller	Buddha statue carver, scroll mounter, gold, lacquer craftsman, inlaid mother-of-pearl craftsman painter, artist, hatter (court cap maker), ball maker (football maker), court-shoe maker, silversmith, silver/goldleaf artist, needle sharpener, rosary maker, mirror polisher, jeweller (jade polisher), writing-brush maker, inkstone maker, comb maker, pillow vendor, sedge hatter, sword fitter, saddler, wicker-box maker, leather-basket maker, arrow fashioner, quiver fashioner, whistling-arrow maker, hat maker, bow maker, paper maker, umbrella maker, dice maker, armour fashioner, lathe turner, (green) bamboo-blind maker, fusuma-paper maker, stencil artist (motif dyer), leather tanner, bowstring vendor
Manufacture and sale of clothing	obi seller, linen seller, silk-floss seller	formal robe merchant, flax seller, fur leggings maker
Manufacture of household implements	turned wooden bowl seller, match and whisk-broom seller, broom seller, lamp-wick seller, firewood seller	straw-sandal maker, wooden-sandal maker, earthenwares maker, pot seller, rush (straw) mat seller, charcoal maker, hay cutter
Foodstuffs	sake brewer, rice-cake seller, sweet seller, seaweed-jelly seller, fishmonger, rice seller, bean seller, malt seller, beancurd seller, wheat-noodles seller	vinegar brewer, seller of horo miso (bean paste), oil vendor, clam vendor, leek vendor, salt vendor, roadside-tea maker, seller of herbal tea infusions, Chinese chef, ceremonial fish slicer
Medicine and cosmetics	face-powder seller, powdered-rouge maker, incense merchant	medicine seller
Sales and brokering	broker, dealer in used goods	dealer in pawned (used) goods, horse trader, animal-skin dealer
Raw materials		mountain folk (hunter, woodcutter, charcoal burner etc), sea folk (fisherman, salt-maker), woodcutter, ferry raftman

Religion	shrine maiden, shaman, mendicant performer of religious magic, Zen nun, Ritsu nun, mendicant nun,	Zen monk, Ritsu monk, Jōdo monk, Hokke monk, monk from Enryakuji temple on Mt Hiei, monk from Kōfukuji temple in Nara, Kegon monk, Kusha monk, yamabushi, mountain ascetic, shrine official, yin–yang diviner, mendicant ascetic, transvestite shrine maiden, itinerant priest
Performing arts	*goze, shirabyōshi, kusemai*	blind lutenist, itinerant juggler and singer, itinerant dengaku actor, itinerant sarugaku actor, court musician, court dancer, horse-racing company, sumo wrestler, *sōga* singer
Other	streetwalker, prostitute	samurai archer, scholar, interpreter, doctor, linked verse master

women who peddled goods that they had made themselves (vendors called *hisagime* and *ichime*). Second, note that some male occupations also revolved around items such as clothing and food—so, men and women were equally involved in the production and sale of goods relating to basic daily needs.

Men are depicted as vinegar brewers and oil vendors, and women are depicted as sake brewers, fishmongers and rice vendors. Other historical sources show that the imperial fish suppliers from Awazu and from Rokkaku-chō were women. These sources would have been consulted by the creators of this scroll. Salt vendors are drawn as men, yet we know that sellers were both men and women, and this was possibly the case with many other goods for sale. It is unlikely that there was much fixed gender division here. However, in the *Sanjūni-ban shokunin utaawase* (32 pairs of artisans), green vegetable vendors (*nauri*) are depicted as women, and staple foods such as green vegetables, fish, rice and *kōji* (bacteria agent for fermenting rice, wheat and beans in order to make products such as *miso*) are all shown as being sold by women, which indicates that there were considerable numbers of women merchants. However, *chōsai* and cutlers were male. *Chōsai* are depicted with shaved heads, and steaming *manjū* cakes (crusts of dough filled with sweet bean paste), which tells us that they belonged to a profession of cooks originating from China. The *hōchōshi* is wearing a court hat (*eboshi*) and *hitatare* informal court robe and is cutting up fish on a chopping board, which indicates that he is a fish chef of a style of cooking such as *Ikama*—appointed suppliers to the *bakufu*. The tendency in modern Japan for professional chefs to be men dates back to this time. Those who provided for the basic dietary needs of the people in general, however, were more often women merchants; as these occupations became more professional, men took over these roles. This issue is treated in more detail later.

Under occupations listed as 'household goods', earthenware potters and saucepan vendors are men, whereas wood-bowl sellers are women. Although we know that women did make earthenware pots (Tsude 1982; Wakita 1982), and that men turned the lathe for making wooden bowls, these *utaawase* pictures show men as selling earthenware pots and women as selling wooden bowls. Girls (*oharame*) selling firewood are paired with a male charcoal burner, showing that there was little substantial difference between the work of men and women.

In the textile industry, *obi* sellers, sellers of bleached cloth (*shironuno*, or *sarashi*, made from *karamushi* yarn or ramie) and silk floss (*wata*) sellers were all women. Men are depicted as sellers of *hitatare* and *karamushi* yarn (ramie, like linen, was the representative textile before cotton was introduced), and makers of fur leggings (*mukabaki*). In the Nanboku period (1336–1392), there was a dispute in the silk floss guild (*wata za*). Among the village peddlers of silk floss in the famous *Gion wata shinza* guild, almost all those whose names are known were women (Yasaka 1978). It is easy to understand that the merchants who brought in *karamushi* yarn from distant parts such as Echigo Province were men, while it was women who wove it and sold it as *sarashi* cloth. In clothing, also, then, there was not a great difference between men and women, with perhaps a slight tendency for women to dominate.

Also emerging from this data is the clear separation between women's and men's labour in jobs that required special skills. Women only appear in occupations relating to dyeing, fans and *tatōgami* (thick folded paper, used as a folder for clothing, women's cosmetics and tissues or *hanagami*). However, the dearth of women's occupations does not mean that the numbers of women involved in these enterprises were few, or that there were not many women in the workforce. These scrolls were created in Kyoto and the workers reflect the contemporary reality of the capital. Silken textiles, embroidery, braiding and dyed products were Kyoto's principal industries and had a nationwide distribution. As specialty products of Kyoto, fans were equal with swords as major export items. It is therefore no exaggeration to say that women's labour sustained one half of Kyoto's speciality handicraft industries.

Men were evidently the main workers in construction, metalwork, arts and crafts, and military apparatus, which required a high degree of specialisation. The economy—which centred on the domains—fostered the development of highly skilled artisanal industries, which were monopolised by men, with the exception of the textile and fan industries. This is similar to the professionalisation of food production, which led to the specialist occupations of cooks (*chōsai and hōchōshi*), depicted as men's work. This shows that at the fundamental level of the human need for food and clothing there was a relatively equal division of labour between men and women, but the subsequent development of expertise increased the division of labour and men took on the highly skilled jobs. Further, Japanese technological expertise, derived from the introduction of technology from the continent, was developed in the official workshops. The reason for the greater representation of women in the provision of daily essentials could be attributed to the fact that men only carried out the highly specialised tasks—the rest was devolved to women.

The same applied in the fields of religion and the performing arts. At the lowest echelons of these professions there was no differentiation between men and women; if anything, women were dominant in some respects. However, men gained ascendancy in the established Buddhist sects, which towered above folk religion, and also in the performing arts of the elite classes—such as the court musicians and dancers of *gagaku* and *bugaku*, and the newly arisen arts of *sarugaku no nō* and *dengaku no nō*, which became highly systematised. Moreover, this was the world of *nyonin kinsei*, which forbade women from entering sacred Buddhist precincts. Thus, prestigious occupations such as *yumitori* (arrowman = *bushi*), *monja* (literatus), *tsūji* (translator) and *kusushi* (doctor) were for male members of the ruling classes, whereas women could be prostitutes. These professions were closely connected to power and authority and, having grown as part of the ruling classes, that alone was enough to facilitate their sophistication and systematisation. The fact that court bureaucrats and court ladies were not included in this collection is probably because they were central in the song contest itself, and did not consider themselves to be artisans.

Male Buddhist priests of many sects are drawn in pairs, as are nuns (*ni-shu* and *bikuni*). It is well known historically that the first Buddhist practitioner was a nun, but by the Nara and Heian periods nuns had become washerwomen for priests (Katsuura 1984). It was the norm for shrine *miko* to be under the authority of the male *Shintō* priest (*negi*) in the medieval period (Wakita 1982). However, at the bottom of society there was most likely no gender distinction, as in the world of the itinerant *aruki miko* and Kumano *bikuni*, the yin–yang diviners from the *sanjo* districts and the *hachitataki* alms beggars, all of whom can be called *shōmoji* from the *sanjo* districts. It was the same with the performing arts. The four officially patronised Yamato *sarugaku* troupes and the *dengaku Hon shinza* were restricted to men. Yet, the performing arts from which these were born were the *sarugaku* of the *shōmoji* type, including women's *sarugaku*, and were extremely popular.

As a representative of such folk religion practitioners, let us look at the Kumano *bikuni* Ise Shōnin, who came from the tradition of fund-raising

Shichijūichiban shokunin utaawase: Nun (*bikuni*), *Gunshū ruijū* (Hanawa 1933).

nuns from Kumano.[42] The Toyouke Daijingū at Ise (also called Gegū, the outer shrine, dedicated to the god Toyouke Daijin, and part of the Ise shrine) was supposed to be rebuilt every 20 years. In 1563, for the first time in 129 years, there was a ceremony to temporarily remove the deity before reconstruction. In 1549 the head nun of Keikōin temple, Seijun Shōnin, raised money for the rebuilding of the Uji Ōhashi bridge in Ise. In 1551 she undertook fundraising for the new outer shrine. A *rinji* issued by Emperor Gonara (second son of Gokashiwabara, called Tomihito; 1496–1557; reigned 1526–57; coronation 1536) decreed that the newly built living quarters would be called Keikōin, and she was bestowed the title of third generation. Initially, Seijun had planned to rebuild the inner shrine, but permission for this was not granted. Even for the outer shrine, the decree proclaimed: 'From ancient times, such a work has been a public affair, and a nun should not undertake it. There is no exception to this principle. The gods also will not accept such a thing…so it must be stopped.'[43] But evidently she went ahead with it anyway, even though it was made difficult for her.

The works were completed in 1563 (the ritual year for moving the shrine deity), the year when Seijun Shōnin negotiated with the governor of Ise, Kitabatake, to abolish the barrier between Ise and Ōmi provinces. In 1575, her successor, Shūyō Shōnin, carried out the removal of the temporary abode of the inner shrine, and in 1585 she realised the transfer of both shrines. Fundraising was carried out the hard way by collecting small amounts of money from ordinary people but, due to the efforts of both Seijun Shōnin and Shūyō Shōnin, there was substantial support for the rebuilding project from three successive hegemons (Nobunaga, Hideyoshi and Tokugawa Ieyasu), as well as from a number of *daimyō*. As a result, eventually the Keikōin residential quarters were registered in the name of Ise Shōnin, and she and subsequent nuns of this title received the special privilege of a land grant for temples of 100 *koku* from the Edo *bakufu*, and also the right to have a residence in Edo. They went to Edo to receive this title and the official appointment of succession to the property from the *shōgun*. The ceremony of succession involved representatives of families from the court aristocracy, as well as the Kajūji and the Ichijō families, so the title acquired artistocratic cachet despite humble origins.

Nevertheless, Seijun was still a Kumano *bikuni*, and her basic job was fundraising. She acquired influence in this capacity, as had her predecessors in the post at Keikōin. Tradition says that the first generation at Keikōin, Shuetsu, rebuilt the Uji Ōhashi bridge over the Mimosuso-gawa river with funds raised in 1491. The priest of the inner shrine delivered decrees in the first, ninth and the intercalary tenth months in 1498, charging Shuetsu with fundraising for the reconstruction of the bridge, which was commenced in 1504; it was completed in 1506 and the dedication ritual was held in the same year. The letters of Asukai Masatoshi, dating from 1505 and 1506, show that Shuetsu was bestowed with the title of *shōnin* at that time. However, it is not certain that Shuetsu always resided at Ise. She travelled back and forth between Kumano and Ise, and it is said that she trained herself at the granary in Uji Hatachō Bentendō. The second generation Keikōin, Chikei Hōzan, died at Kumano. The third generation Keikōin, Seijun, was most likely based at Kumano, as seen from how she is addressed in the *rinji* with the honorific title for priest or nun (*Keikōin monjo* facsimile). She was given the imperial right of residence in the village Uji Urata-chō, also called Uratazaka, which was on the border between Uji and Yamada. It later became the place where groups of *shōmoji* gathered and settled (Ishimaki 1918). Many Kumano *bikuni* were married to *yamabushi*. In 1497, the *yamabushi* Kan'ami repaired the Kazemiya-bashi bridge in the Ise inner shrine, making the Isuzugawa river his headquarters for fundraising.

The example of Keikōin is somewhat special: using the connections with Ise shrine and the imperial house, and obtaining the support of the Sengoku *daimyō* and the three powerful hegemons that united Japan, the incumbents of Keikōin became members of the nobility. This is not to deny that such a possibility was open to all Kumano *bikuni*; it suggests, however, the kind of fundraising activity that other *kanjin bikuni* of middle and low-rank carried out in medieval society.

This section has used the classification of occupations in the *shokunin utaawase* scrolls as a starting point to discuss women and gender role division. There remain some issues that do not directly emerge from these scrolls.

First is the role of the family. At all levels of society, whether the ruling classes, specialised craftsmen in guilds or rural workers (farmers, wood cutters/ mountain dwellers, beach men/salt makers), most occupations would have been formed around a family, which was sustained by a man and a woman. Manufacturing in a guild organisation was established as a family business, and functioned with the labour of apprentices and servants. The bamboo-blind maker (*sudare-ya*) is depicted as a man, but in another book (*Tsuruoka hōjō-e shokunin utaawase*, Matsushita version) the occupation is shown as the shared labour of man and woman; in contrast, the weaver is depicted as a woman, whereas in the *Tsuruoka* book, the weaver is a man. In the early Edo period *Kita-in shokunin-zukushi-e*, weaving is shown as a shared male–female activity. Paper-making is drawn as a man's work, but we know that at least in the Edo period, and into the present day, the workers were frequently women. Since it was common for one of a couple to produce and the other to sell, either men or women could be depicted as vendors in many cases.

Second, not to be forgotten is the fact that in occupations carried out as family businesses, even if the woman performed the actual work, frequently that work was officially undertaken in the name of the male household head.

The third issue to consider is legal rights. The *utaawase* pictures do not include a moneylender, but many women's names appear as both creditors and debtors in the records. In documents concerning *bakufu* edicts that cancel debts, many cases are brought by women, who apparently possessed equal rights to men for filing suits. Borrowing and lending signifies the carrying out of independent economic activity, which fits in with the overall image of women occupied in various businesses and crafts in this period. The women of Kyoto possessed the right to file civil lawsuits, which presents a different picture of women from that in the Edo period and in the modern period under the Meiji constitution.

Conclusion

This chapter has looked at the activity of women from the early to late medieval period, ranging from women in ritual roles, agriculture and performance to women in the court, and the working women depicted in the *shokunin utaawase* illustrations.

Women working at court might appear to be a special case, but the imperial household was simply the largest household structure. By projecting a concrete image of the *kōtō no naishi* who assumed control of that structure, I have attempted to look at the position of women in similar positions of power in the households of the ruling classes. In aristocratic families such as the Tōgū (imperial princes) and the Sekkanke families, the equivalent of the *kōtō no naishi* was the *senji no tsubone*. All upper-class families, whether imperial or military, large or small, modelled themselves on this structure. The imperial household, although on a larger scale, was typical of aristocratic families in general.

These are all families of the ruling classes: how meaningful is a minute examination of the court women who held power in that exclusive context? If the cause of discrimination against women today, indeed the cause of all kinds of discrimination, ultimately derives from being excluded from power structures, then it is highly significant to distill the essence of the lives of the women who had power in some measure.

The *kōtō no naishi* held such power in the period of the Warring States, an era when the imperial house was in serious decline. Any official authority of the emperor was completely nominal, so basic aspects of daily life became quite prominent. Women were in charge of internal domestic affairs and, furthermore, when they were the emperor's 'wives' it was only natural that they should control imperial household affairs. The situation of these internal domestic affairs, as revealed in Tokitsugu's diary, needs to be looked at closely because such domestic circumstances and the status of those involved normally do not appear in official historical records and documents.

We can state categorically that the indispensable, though monotonous, labour of women, which supported daily life, also supported the development of the highly specialised work of men.

In the primitive clan-system society, the clans, which were units of social life as well as administrative units, were reconstituted into a state based on patriarchy, and their social responsibilities and rights were reorganised into centralised state administrative structures. This process saw the disintegration of the clans and the formation of the *ie*; it also involved a debasement of the roles that women held within the clan system. However, as stated in the introduction to this chapter, the establishment of the patriarchal *ie* was different at various levels of society. In particular, under the so-called 'Asian' mode of production, the dominated community was not broken down and the society ruled as a whole. Therefore, the establishment of the *ie* in the dominated classes had to be delayed. Over the long span of the ancient and medieval periods, it was gradually established, and I would like to posit the early medieval period as a time when village communities were formed by men and marked the new social reality.

Having said that, the medieval period still allowed some scope for women to be active. Whereas in the Edo period, female labour took place as part of the *ie*, in the medieval period there was still some part of female labour that was independent of the *ie*. This chapter has focused on this phase from the point of view of gender role division. In this aspect, as the work of ritual and estate formation and management gradually became a non-domestic matter at the national and social level, women's roles were closed off in the domestic management sphere, and their relative importance was downgraded. Much of the work left for women was small tasks, which were regarded as lowly, so people who engaged in such work came to be similarly regarded, and an attitude towards work as undignified or dirty was formed—so women in the noble ranks no longer wanted to work. The effect was that a new respect for motherhood arose as women's social function narrowed, as seen in Chapter two. This was not the same as the symbol of fertility and prosperity of the primitive period: the respect was for the mother who could bear the successor in the patrilineal system. The status of the mother was paradoxically elevated because of an intensification of patriarchy and the principle of direct inheritance. As part of that ideology, motherhood was venerated, and the ideal of chastity was enforced.

These new customs and ideas penetrated the noble classes, but they only gradually reached the lower echelons of society, so certain groups of women were still able to be socially active in the medieval period. The administrative and political roles centred on men, and the official or public aspects of those roles were often recorded in the name of the father or husband, but the actual rights and activity might have belonged to the woman. Therefore, in the case of the medieval period, it is reasonable and necessary to believe that women's roles and activities were substantial, despite being hidden beneath the surface of official records.

Further, women were suppressed by male overlords and excluded from officially recognised activity, but they were able to take on economic activity and pioneer new areas. For example, commerce was instigated by female vendors, as were newly emerging economic commodities. It was not until the 16th century—when the scope of such business activity widened and linked up with political circles to form a nexus of politics and commerce—that women merchants were eclipsed. This was also the time when small and medium-sized operations of male merchants were absorbed into the dominant system of wholesale warehouse dealers. In this period, women's labour was incorporated into the patriarchal system and assumed the role of 'man's helper'.

Some roles continued to be independent throughout the ancient and medieval periods, and were not slotted into the domination of the *ie*. I have explained how, in ritual and religious practice, which was organised into an official system, women were already relegated to a subsidiary role. However, in the world of the itinerant shamanesses (*aruki miko*) and others like her, female religious practitioners displayed a unique role. In that unchanging climate, their relative status was downgraded; in the medieval period, they formed outlaw-like groups outside the system, and gradually acquired outcast status.

The female performers who had close links with the *miko* went through a similar process. Since physical beauty is the ultimate origin of performance, women and boys are the most likely to be naturally endowed with this attribute. Women were natural candidates for performance, but they also exploited this asset. Male performers who did not have this advantage were required to make special effort to overcome this, as were women who had passed the age of greatest beauty. To take *nō* as an example, Zeami's theoretical writings make it clear that the use of beautiful masks, costumes, vocal techniques and skilful structure of music and drama were strategic devices cultivated in order to bowl over the spectators. It cannot be denied that *nō* drama's monopolistic position in the Muromachi period lies in its success and ingenuity in developing such devices. However, having achieved this success, the privileged *nō* theatre forbade artists of the outcast groups of the *sanjo* area, including women artists, to use the fruits of these developments. Furthermore, *onna sarugaku*, and all women's performance, was eventually banned (in 1629), after which women's performing arts survived only at the very bottom of society, outside the establishment.

At the end of the medieval period, in the 16th century, women's work and general activity was enclosed within the rule of the *ie*, where it was allocated a 'men's helpmate' value. The saying '*gei ga mi o tasukeru hodo no fushiawase*' ('it is a misfortune to have to rely on art for one's livelihood') indicates that a woman in the position of needing to exercise her skills was to be pitied, for the purpose of existence of a woman was constricted to her role as mother. And yet, from the late medieval to the early Edo period, the situation deteriorated further, when the attitude expressed in the phrase 'borrowed womb' came into being. In the Edo period, *all* women were included in the lack of respect accorded to motherhood. This is, however, the topic of another book.

Notes

1   I consider that for the family head of the dominated classes, also, there was the impetus to form an autonomous patriarchal system beside the state system, and that this was based in the ownership of the object of production (land etc) and means of production (Wakita 1983).

2   Here I use the term *ie* in the broader sense, to mean a family that was not thoroughly controlled by the patriarchal head. Of course, the form (*tatemae*) of the patriarchal family system was established with the *ritsuryō* system.

3   Nagaoka Katsue (1958) gives a vivid picture of Edo period itinerant shamanesses
     of the *agata-miko* type, and of the dominance of the *shinjimai tayū*. (*Shinjimai* was
     a sacred dance performed only at festivals that contained the ancient meanings
     of *Shintō*. *Tayū* was the head of a group of performers [trans].)

4   'To the mistress of his west wing (Murasaki) he entrusted...' (Tyler 2003:235).

5   Women who served at court tended to leave after having raised a princess. They
     were well known to many people and were said not to be easy to get into bed.
     This was no doubt true, but it was something of an honour for them to be used
     as messengers to the Kamo festival. Further, having entered a family situation,
     becoming the wife in a respectable domain and producing a daughter who could
     be a *gosechi maihime*, a woman who had the experience of having served at court
     and did not like to ask for information about countrified things.

6   These polished rice fields are not the whole of Yamamura's property—there were
     three other siblings (see Inagaki 1981); therefore, we cannot say that the property
     was equally divided among all the children.

7   Tōji hyakugō monjo, 'Nu' box, a draft petition dated the 26th day of the 5th month,
     1270 (Takeuchi 1974–80), titled Miyakawa Jōren sokujo, Fujiwara no uj-ime
     mōshijō an. Also, in 'A' box of the same, a draft defence, titled Nakahara no
     uji-me jūchinjō an, and a further draft petition titled Fujiwara no uji-me mōshijō
     an, both dated as the intercalary 9th month of the same year.

8   Tōji hyakugō monjo, 'Mi' box, entry for the 21st day of the 12th month, 1336
     (Takeuchi 1974–80), a document of appointment of the Korefuji-myō right of
     ownership to Chiyozuru-me.

9   Kim's (1994:119–20) translation does not allow this interpretation:

     By the imperial pasture at Kusuha / The potter makes earthenware / But his
     daughter has a porcelain face / If only she could ride wedding carts, three or four/
     Drawn by hand, in procession / As the provincial governor's bride! [trans].

10   See Takeuchi (1974–80), no 257, entry for 4th year of Tenryaku (950), 'Tōdaiji
     fūdo shōen Enpeiji yōchō'. For an analysis of this document, see Wakita
     (1969c).

11   *Noritoki kyōki* (1970), entry for the 27th day of the 12th month, 1406.

12   *Tokitsugu kyō-ki* (1965), entry for 16th day, tenth month, 11th year of Eiroku
     (1568); *Koga-ke monjo* (1982:v1 no 592), Ka box for intercalary seventh month,
     15th day, 1546, group petitions from Ōtoneri-za.

13   Kunaichō shoryōbu-zō (Document collection of the Imperial Palace), documents
     concerning taxes from indigo ash, regulations for Indigo ash *za*, petition from
     Sano Matasaburō, Urai Shin'emon no jō and Yagi Joun, 24th day, ninth month,
     1556.

14   Naikaku bunko-zō, 16th year of Tenbun (1532–55), fourth month, 18th day, letter
     on behalf of Goime (Kuwayama 1980; see also Kuwayama 1986).

15   Naikaku bunko-zō, Ninagawa-ke komonjo (Old documents of the Ninagawa
     family), v17.

16 Kunaichō shoryōbu-zō (Document collection of the Imperial Palace), 'Rokkaku-chō kugenin kankei monjo', 24th day, third month, 1323 Kebiishi Bettō no sen (Amino 1984a).

17 Yasaka Jinja kiroku (1978), 'Shake kiroku', entries for 16th day, 11th month, 1343, and for fourth day, 12th month of the same year.

18 It is common to see women's names among those who applied to the *bakufu* for confirmation of credit against debt amnesties. For example, in Kuwayama (1986) the entry entitled 'Senshu fuhikitsuke', 1546–47, lists several women's names. Of course, there were also many women among the borrowers (see Wakita 1981c).

19 See Kunaichō shoryōbu-zō (Document collection of the Imperial Palace), documents concerning taxes from indigo ash, regulations for Indigo ash *za*, petition from Sano Matasaburō, Urai Shin'emon no jō and Yagi Joun, 24th day, ninth month, 1556; see also Wakita (1969d).

20 Documents with the signature of Miyoshi Nagayoshi dated 18th day, 12th month, 1544, relating to these disputes are preserved in the *Tanaka Kōji-shi shozō monjo* facsimile.

21 See the plays 'Kamabara' and 'Ishigami' in Koyama (1960).

22 *Tokitsugu kyōki* (1965), entry for the 15th day, ninth month, 1556.

23 *Murakami Tennō gyoki* (1982), entry for 19th day, 11th month, 957.

24 Tabata Yasuko (1990) points out that again in 1413 there were 38 dancing girls who functioned as *naikyōbō* performers.

25 *Gyokuyō* (1907), entry for 18th day, eighth month, 1183.

26 'Honchō Kōin Shōun-roku' (Hanawa 1959–60). See also Fukiwara (1970), entry for 1205; Kamiyokote (1972:284).

27 'Tōji-hōbodai-in monjo (Documents of the Tōji temple Hō-bodai-in)', document 23rd day, seventh month, 923 quoted in Buraku mondai kenkyūjo (1988b).

28 1 kanmon = 1,000 mon [trans].

29 *Yasutomi-ki*, entry for first day, tenth month, 1396 (Nakahara 1865).

30 Takeuchi (1967a), entry for 16th day, fourth month, 1466.

31 *Oyudono no ue no nikki*, entry for third day, seventh month, 1527 (Hanawa 1958).

32 Bussho kankō-kai (1980), entry for 8th day, 4th month, 1466.

33 In the first month of 1544 Tokitsugu was Sei-sanmi Saemon no suke and was in charge of music, and on the 19th day of the third month he was appointed acting (proxy) middle minister (Gon no Chūnagon). In 1545 he was promoted to sub-second rank, yet the amount of work he took to the *kōtō no naishi* in 1544 was far greater than in 1545. This may have been connected with his rank and his closeness to the emperor as an intimate aide.

34 *Ritsuryō* (1976) tells us in a head note to *kōkyū shokuin-rei* that petitions and decrees were issued for important matters of state, and that for lesser matters this was done by the *shōnagon*. However, in the early Heian period the *naishi-sen* were also involved in important matters.

35 *Tokitsugu kyōki* (1965), entry for 14th day, fourth month, 1554; 'Honchō Kō-ō shōun-roku' (Hanawa 1959–60).

36 *Sanetaka kōki*, the diary of Sanjō Nishi Sanetaka (1455–1537), entry for sixth day, ninth month, 1527 (Hanawa 1958).

37 *Oyudono no ue no nikki*, entry for 13th day, ninth month, 1527 (Hanawa 1958).

38 *Hirohashi Kaneaki kyōki*, entries for 26th day, seventh month; first day, eighth month; and 15th day, tenth month, 1478 (*Dai Nihon Shiryō* 1968–:8/10).

39 *Koga-ke monjo* (1982:303), 22nd day, eighth month, 1487, document in the name of Tomikura Fujihisa, also no. 307: fourth day, 11th intercalary month, 1487, document from Muromachi Bakufu bugyōnin hōsho.

40 'Kōzuke no tsubone was granted the post of Somedono bettō (steward) in Musashi Province' (*Azuma Kagami* 1968–), entry for 13th day, 12th month, 120. Many other instances are also recorded in this book.

41 A comparative look at the arrangement of occupations in various *utaawase* scrolls shows there is no duplication between the *Tōhoku-no-in shokunin utaawase*, the *Tsuruoka hōshō-e shokunin utaawase* and the *Sanjūni-ban shokunin utaawase*, except for the appearance of *katsurame* in both the *Tōhokuin* and the *Sanjūni-ban utaawase* scrolls. Perhaps this lack of duplication came about because the *Tsuruoka* scroll presupposed the existence of the *Tōhokuin* one, and the *Sanjūni-ban* one presupposed the existence of the other two, and chose to include occupations not in the others. Though these three scrolls cover all possible occupations, the *Shichijūichiban* scroll did not try to add to them but to start afresh to cover all occupations. Therefore, there is a good case for using only the *Shichijūichiban* scroll to classify occupations in that period.

42 On *kanjin* in a Buddhist context, see Janet Goodwin (1994); Hirade (1906); Ishimaki (1918); Ōnishi (1952); Kojima (1980); Kuwata (1931); Akihara (1983).

43 'Toyouke Kō-Taijingū sengyo kinrei' (Ōnishi 1952).

The life cycle of housewife, townswoman, nun and itinerant

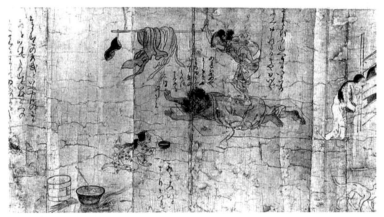

A child is offering to Fukutomi, who is prone in bed, a bowl of what looks like porridge (*zōsui*: rice or millet, probably with vegetables). We can see as cooking utensils an iron cauldron on a tripod and, next to it, a wooden pail, with a bundle of firewood ready for use – the simple kitchen setting of a common family.

Fukutomi sōshi, scroll 2, held by the Shunpoin (Myōshinji) in Kyoto
(Takeuchi & Takayanagi Mitsutoshi 1974:817; Pigeot & Kosugi 2001).

Introduction

The *kyōgen* play *Kawakami*[1] was the source for the Meiji-period Bunraku play *Tsubosaka Kannon Reigenki*, about a blind man, Sawaichi, and his wife Osato, and it praises the virtue of a woman who sacrifices herself for her husband. The *kyōgen* play, however, depicts a brighter love between a married couple. The blind *zatō* and his wife pray to the gods to restore his sight, but as a precondition an oracle demands that he get rid of his bad wife. The wife strongly resists this and the blind man gives up the idea of regaining his sight in favour of keeping his wife—they go on to live happily in a good relationship, with him blind as before. While in other ways this play fits the stereotype of 'husband speaks and wife obeys', the wife also stands up for her rights without taking the easy path of self-sacrifice and devotion: this play depicts a wholesome marriage relationship. Despite having petitioned the gods, when the outcome does not match their common sense, they have no hesitation in sacrilegiously proclaiming that 'even the gods and Buddhas are not always reasonable'. This is a typical portrait of an ordinary married couple in the medieval period.

Social changes in ways of life bring about shifts in the family, in the marriage system and also in ideas about the couple—changes that affect not only wives and mothers but also women who are not in families.

Historical studies of the shifting forms of marriage, of the establishment of the medieval *ie* and of the land ownership system have not always been organically linked. The establishment of the *yometori* type of marriage in the medieval period, regardless of class, signified the establishment of the foundation of medieval society: the patriarchal monogamous family and its symbol, the *ie*. Families in *tsumadoi* and *mukotori*-style marriages basically centered on parent–child relations, whereas the *yometori*-style family had conjugal relations at its base and was a unit represented by the family head as householder. If a woman's husband died and she, as a widow, became family head, she was given the right to represent the household.

In this chapter, I want to demonstrate the establishment of this kind of *ie* in the medieval period from the perspective of changes in the marriage system. Further, the whole lifecycle of women included in the *ie* is examined—wives, concubines and servants—and the concrete detail of their domestic duties and household management are especially compared with the living standards of that time. Many men and women, however, fell outside the *ie* structure. These people mainly resided in the Buddhist monasteries and nunneries, and this is the reason why the role of nunneries is so important in the history of women.

Other groups of women to mention are vendors, artisans and entertainers— groups that sometimes formed *ie* and sometimes did not. I attempt to explain a variety of aspects of the lives of these three groups of women—those in *ie* households, nuns and entertainers—and to look at the relations between the groups and how their work connected with general town life.

The general establishment of yometori marriage

The schema of three types of marriage, *tsumadoi, mukotori* and *yometori,* was conceived by Takamure Itsue and clearly demonstrates the process whereby the high position of Japanese women in the primitive era gradually declined. The schema is largely correct, but only provided that the woman had a certain degree of status and property, or that the man and the woman had equal status and property. In the process of change from ancient to medieval eras, a stark difference appeared between the ruling and ruled classes for both men and women; and whether or not a person had status and property made a great difference to the conditions under which one lived. With this change, the marriage system also altered to include more diversity. In other words, whether *tsumadoi* or *mukotori,* the equality or lack of equality between the sexes was more significant than the type of marriage. The meaning of the two systems would have been quite different in a situation of gender equality from in a patriarchal system.

It is true that in society as a whole the process of change from equality to patriarchy had an enormous impact on individual families, but in pre-modern society, status differences between men and women in individual marriages also had an effect on marriages.

For example, when a man married a woman of higher status who owned more property than him, the woman was unequivocally the dominant partner. By definition, both *tsumadoi* and *mukotori* marriage required a woman with status and property. No man would seek a wife or want to become the son-in-law in a family that had no social pedigree or property, or social influence in general.

Let us recall the fictional portrait of Uemon no jō and his three wives in the book *Shin Sarugō-ki* (circa 1060) (Yamagishi 1979), which gives a thumbnail sketch of three types of wives co-existing in one family: the first wife had parental status and bore many children, the next wife had outstanding ability in household management and the third wife was an attractive playmate. The first marriage was probably *mukotori,* the second was *sue* (see Chapter one), (where the wife was established in the husband's household, the predecessor to the *yometori*-type marriage) and the third was *tsumadoi.*

In the Heian period *tsumadoi* and *mukotori* marriages flourished, and it was an age of polygamous marriages in which one man could have multiple wives; that is, he could have more than one official wife, unlike the system in the following period of *yometori* marriage, which allowed one official wife but several concubines. The Heian period system could more accurately be called a system of one man, multiple wives and multiple concubines. For example, both Kaneie (the husband of the writer of *Kagerō nikki*²) and the fictional Hikaru Genji in the *Tale of Genji* had multiple wives of their own social status, formalised through marriage ceremonies, as well as women to whom they were not formally married. When Kaneie built a palatial mansion for himself and Tokihime, who had borne him three sons and two daughters, their *tsumadoi* marriage shifted to a cohabitation arrangement that was closer to *yometori* marriage. When his achievements became recognised and he rose in status, Genji built the mansion on Rokujō avenue, where he installed all his wives. This indicates that, while *tsumadoi* and *mukotori* marriage depended on the substance of the woman's parents, *yometori* marriage depended on that of the husband.[3]

In *yometori* marriage a man of substance sets up an *ie* and takes a wife, which signifies the establishment of a patriarchal family. It is not true to say that there was no *yometori* marriage in ancient times. In formal terms, the *ritsuryō* system was premised on *yometori* marriage, which was based on the patriarchal system. For example, when governors were appointed to provinces and were accompanied by their wives, the arrangement should properly have been called *yometori* marriage. However, *yometori* did not become the general practice until the medieval period.

Takamure explains the transition from the uxorilocal *tsumadoi* and *mukotori* marriages to the virilocal *yometori* marriage with the following anecdote. After the Genpei Wars (1180–85), Minamoto Yoritomo arranged a marriage between Yoshitsune (1169–1206), the son of the chancellor Kujō Kanezane, and his niece, the daughter of Ichijō Yoshiyasu (1147–97). He had the temerity to suggest that it should be a *yometori* marriage, which infuriated Kanezane, who rejected the proposal (although eventually they did marry).[4] It was rejected because, in the military class, *yometori* marriage was practised when the woman was of lower status; when the woman was higher in status, it was the custom to have a *tsumadoi* or *mukotori* marriage. In the court aristocracy, however, the custom of *tsumadoi* and *mukotori* marriage was still firmly entrenched as the proper way of doing things. Takamure extends this situation to argue that the *yometori* marriage form of the Kantō region military houses (marriage between a lower-status woman and a higher-status man) spread and became the norm for wider society.

Why indeed did *yometori* marriage become so widespread? Women were excluded from bureaucratic society under the *ritsuryō* system and the imperial state, and with few exceptions—the empress, princesses and court ladies—women did not have the opportunity to acquire status and property, and it was difficult for them to maintain property once they possessed it. They depended solely on the protection of their parents and inheritance. Therefore, when their parents died, they had no-one to look after them and were forced into piteous circumstances. There are innumerable stories about such impecunious noblewomen in collections such as the *Konjaku Monogatari*.[5] Such women longed to become a *sue* or 'placed woman' as a wife in a secure marriage. The author of *Kagerō nikki* longed for the security of being taken in by Kaneie. However, although she was a talented poet, and could thus contribute towards Kaneie's strategy of wooing court ladies, he chose to live with the wife he evaluated more highly—the wife who produced two daughters who entered the palace (Shimizu 1982).

Here I want to point out the unbearable insecurity of a wife in a *tsumadoi* marriage—with its loneliness at night and its fretfulness in the daytime, which assailed even the author of the diary—and the treatment of a wife by a self-centred husband on the basis of her relative contribution to his advancement.

There is a clear difference of opinion between Takamure and myself. In reality, a woman who could not have a *tsumadoi* or *mukotori* marriage, with the backing of her parents and its attendant social status and property, would have wished for the security afforded by entering into the protection of a husband who was a patriarchal family head. After *yometori* marriage became the norm, a woman occupied a lower position in the family than her husband, even a woman who had more status and property than her husband. Women's position was not reduced by the marriage system, but the lowered position of women generally caused them to wish for a *yometori*-type marriage before it became the norm.

How did the family differ at the *tsumadoi–mukotori* stage and at the *yometori* stage? First, the former was a system that permitted one man to have multiple wives and concubines, and the family was structured on the principle of parent–child relations. As Takamure argued, the wife–mother–woman had freedom and autonomy, but also undeniable insecurity. By contrast, in the following stage of *yometori* marriage, the patriarchal *ie*—based on the man's property and status—and the principle of monogamy were established. Strictly speaking, this meant monogamy with multiple concubines, but it was a family centered on the marriage relationship: the position of the official wife was assured within the family, and any other woman involved was a concubine or prostitute. The *yometori*-type of marriage went with the establishment of the patriarchal family and the assured position of the wife. A rich patriarchal family included large numbers of male and female servants, and all the female ranks in the court— *nyōkan, nyōbō, menoto, shijo, gejo* (maidservants)—were, in fact, part of a patriarchal family.

At what stage was *yometori* marriage established in the merchant, artisan and agricultural classes, that is, among the common people? In the case of those who had little or no property, the marriage system could be called 'getting-together marriage' (*yoriai-kon*), not *yometori* marriage in the strict sense, since this kind of marriage depended on the earning power and property of the husband. Therefore, for farmers it could only occur with the *myō* system of land management, which gave a certain right over land (the *myōden* right is the right to possess land).[6] It can be thought that the rights and interests towards land as a means of production or as an object of production brought about the establishment of patriarchy. In the medieval period when divided inheritance was carried out, this right of land ownership meant that women also could own land rights; working women could save up their profits and, on occasion, buy land.

However, the right of ownership of land by farmers depended on the approval of the landholder. The principle that a woman could not have rights to a *myōden*, which had to pay taxes and labour, is made clear in the cases of the Tōji temple domains of Tara no shō and the domain of Tōdaiji temple, Kohigashi no shō (Kawane 1982), where the husband's name appeared as the owner (*myōshu*) and the landholder (*ryōshu*) required the contract to be with the husband.

In the case of townspeople—merchants and artisans—it was the same: both in occupations dominated by men and those carried out mainly by women (pottery, sake-brewing, weaving), tribute (in the form of produce) due to an overlord was contracted in the name of the husband who was the householder (Wakita 1988a). For farmers and townspeople, the overlord's control became ever stronger over the householder, those in charge of the *ie* units. This policy for controlling the farmers was imported from China by the *ritsuryō* state, but it did not take full effect until the medieval period.

Upper-level landowners, as well as merchant–artisans and farmers, formed powerful community alliances in order to protect themselves as people who possessed equal official rights and obligations and who performed services to overlords. There were groups of *myōshu* landowners, for example, whose members were all men recognised as *myōshu* by overlords, and each was the head of a specific patriarchal family. Clearly, a system was coming into existence in which both landowner and communities were controlled through the heads of families, as representatives of both the *ie* and the family business (Wakita 1988a).

However, there also existed community groups of women, alongside these men's communities or *za*. In an autonomous village in Ōmi Province there was a *nyōbō-za* in the late medieval period (Tabata 1982). Furthermore, there occurred a transition from *za* for girls (*musume*) to *za* for married women (*nyōbō*)—which, from the case of Kogawa no shō, appears to have occurred in the Nanboku period (14th century) (Katō 1985). However, this transition does not necessarily correspond to a shift from *tsumadoi–mukotori* marriage to *yometori* marriage. In early times, marriage partners were often chosen from within the same village and such a marriage, whether matrilocal or patrilocal, did not affect membership of the village *za*. However, when the selection sphere widened, and girls married into other villages, they started to join the women's *za* of that village, and were not allowed to return to the *za* in their natal villages. Therefore, in these villages the spread of *yometori* marriage must also have begun earlier than the formation of *nyōbō-za*.

The *Shaseki-shū* collection of tales, dating from the mid-Kamakura period, tells what a wife can customarily take with her when she is divorced,[7] presumably in the case of *yometori* marriage. The collection also has a story about a heartless layman, which says that 'it is the husband who divorces the wife' (Morell 1985:205). This is generally taken to mean that only a husband had the right to divorce, but these words are given as the opinion of the land steward, and the story is actually about a woman who filed successfully for divorce. This story can be seen to illustrate the difference between the common wisdom of the steward and of the world of the farmers. I interpret it as the story of divorce in what can be called a *yoriai* (getting-together) type of marriage. Therefore, in the villages, after the establishment of the *myō* system, those in the upper levels of *myōshu* who had land rights and were members of the *za* gradually came to practise *yometori* marriage. As we can see remaining in local folk customs even in the postwar period, *tsumadoi*-type marriage could change to *yometori* only as people attained the status of householder. At the lower levels of village life *yoriai* marriage was practised by those without property or position, and there would probably have been many who could not acquire a husband or a wife at all.

Aristocratic household management and women's life cycle

With the exception of the imperial family and other aristocratic families (such as imperial princes and the five Gosekke Fujiwara families), daughters of the middle and lower ranks of the nobility had three options: going into service at a higher-ranking noble house as *nyōbō*, formally marrying into an *ie* of equal rank, or becoming a nun. The wife of Sanjō Nishi Sanetaka (a member of the middle-ranking nobility known as *daijin-ke* [Shimohashi 1979] ministerial houses) was the daughter of Kajūji Norihide,[8] and both her sisters were in service at the court. The older sister was Shin Dainagon no Suke no tsubone (later called Sanmi no tsubone[9]), in service to the Emperor Gotsuchimikado (1442–1500; reigned 1464–1500). Her younger sister was Shin Dainagon no Suke no tsubone, in service to Emperor Gokashiwabara (1464–1526; reigned 1500–1526, eldest son of Gotsuchimikado). As the birth mother of Emperor Gonara (1496–1557; reigned 1526–1557, first son of Gokashiwabara), she had the title Ju-Sangō Higashi no Tōin dono,[10] and later became Burakumon'in. Highly favourable conditions were created for the Kajūji family, and even Sanetaka, by having relatives who became high-ranking *nyōbō* and mothers of emperors who wielded a lot of power and influence. Whether their daughters went into service as *nyōbō*, or became wives, their work was to preside over domestic affairs and household management. However, medieval domestic affairs were rather different in meaning from how we understand household management today.

Throughout the medieval era in Japan, the imperial household was the biggest of all *ie*, and its domestic affairs and household management were under the control of women. Internal *ie* affairs were always seen to by the *dainagon no suke no tsubone*, whereas dealings with the outside were the domain of the *kōtō no naishi* (Shimohashi 1979). As discussed in Chapter three, the duties of the *kōtō no naishi* included arranging the annual ceremonial events of the court, overseeing the attendance of the courtiers, keeping the accounts and, above all, the right to receive petitions to, and convey decrees from, the emperor. As well as mediating communication from below, they conveyed imperial wishes by issuing documents called *nyōbō hōsho*, which conveyed the emperor's personal will, whereas the *rinji* issued by male courtiers (*kurōdo*) were more official in nature. The personal nature of these women's documents often made them more important.[11] Chapter five looks at the *Oyudono no ue no nikki*—the record of household affairs kept by the ladies-in-waiting, which has been preserved for the years since 1477—and shows the importance of the position occupied by ladies in the emperor's household.

As in the imperial and princely households, in the Fujiwara Sekkanke household there were women officers called *senji no tsubone* who administered business by issuing documents called *nyōbō bumi*[12] (virtually the same as *nyōbō hōsho*). In the Muromachi *bakufu* also, serving women conveyed the will of the *shōgun* in *nyōbō bumi*, while official documents (*bugyōnin hōsho*) were issued by male officers.[13] Thus, both the Sekkanke family and the Ashikaga *shōgun* had similar house administration structures. As the imperial household in the Muromachi and Warring States periods was unable to support a separate household for the empress, it was run solely by female courtiers. The emperor had no official wife, and all women had the status of servants or employees. If there had been an empress, she would have established her own separate household, a unique form not replicated in the Ashikaga shogunate and other households. The wife of Ashikaga Yoshimasa, Tomiko, herself acted as the intermediary when the court's special shogunal envoy (*buke densō*) presented business from the court, and she thereby had direct influence in politics.

The salient characteristic of aristocratic houses, both court and military, is that they were aggregates of the smaller households of the *tsubone*.[14] The *nyōbō* were granted land from which they gained revenue, in return for which they fulfilled the duty of serving in influential noble houses, looking after the annual ceremonial events and the everyday events, and working alongside the male employees. They maintained a separate budget for their work, including their own clothing and food in the *tsubone* quarters. The chief difference between them and the male employees was that they lived in the palace, whereas the men had their *ie* outside.

In the imperial and princely households, also, there was no first wife; the household was run exclusively by the women employees, which led to structurally distorted conjugal relations characterised by female subjugation. Japan has been strongly influenced by the court culture that centred on the emperor, and Japanese culture and sexual mores in general must have been affected by this.

Kanmon nikki (*Dairy of things seen and heard*), the diary of Prince Sadafusa (1372–1456),[15] which relates in detail the circumstances of the Fushiminomiya household, provides material for a case study for understanding the nature of women's life in aristocratic families and the life cycle of women in charge of this kind of work. The family tree of the Fushiminomiya House is extrapolated from the diary.

All the women who are known to have been loved by Prince Hidehito were court employees (*shijo*): Nishi no onkata, Higashi no onkata, Hisashi no onkata, Suke no Zenni and Konoe no tsubone. When the prince died, only Higashi no onkata and Konoe no tsubone remained in the household, and they both became nuns in response to his death. Konoe no tsubone continued to be in charge of the household management after the prince's death, even after the property and inheritance had been passed onto Prince Haruhito and Prince Sadafusa (sons of Hidehito and Haruko). When she became old and ill, she requested retirement and moved to the Kōun'an hermitage in Yamada. The diary

Family tree of the
Fushiminomiya House
(source: Yokoi 1979; Itō 1980)

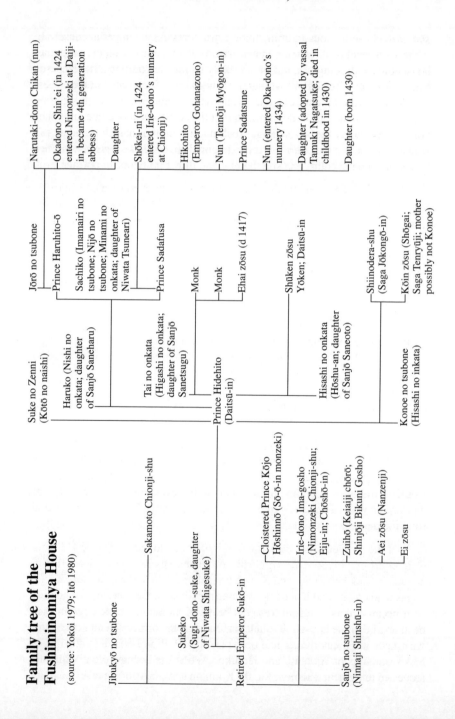

records that Konoe handed over the reins of managing the royal household to Sadafusa's wife Nijō-dono (Sachiko),[16] the daughter of Fushiminomiya retainer Niwata Tsuneari, who bore Sadafusa two sons and five daughters (the eldest son became Emperor Gohanazono (1419–70; reigned 1428–64) and the second son was Prince Fushiminomiya Sadatsune). As far as can be gathered by reading the *Kanmon Nikki*, no other woman bore children to Sadafusa. Although she came into service at the palace, she in effect acquired the status of Sadafusa's official wife and eventually ran the household. Lady Nijō's first *hōsho* since taking charge of administration concerned the allocation of one *tan* of land from the Fushiminomiya family estate, Fushimi no shō.[17] This shows that writing *hōsho* for the prince was part of household administration and infers that the documentation in the princely households was the same model of household management as that of the imperial family.

Konoe no tsubone's duties were probably much the same as those of the *kōtō no naishi* in the imperial household, so her life course can give a picture of a woman serving at court. First of all, she looked after the memorial services (including the costs) for Princes Hidehito and Haruhito-ō.[18] When the two daughters of Haruhito-ō and a daughter of Sadafusa were to be settled in nunneries at the tender ages of seven and nine, she went to the temple with the other companions to see that everything was done properly.[19] These were the grandchildren of her husband Hidehito by Haruko, that is, the two daughters of Haruhito-ō and the only daughter of Sadafusa. She also visited male courtiers and her former fellow ladies-in-waiting when they were sick, arbitrated their quarrels and supervised the arrangements for annual ceremonies according to proper custom.[20] In other words, she capably managed all the affairs of the household. Sadafusa, in recognition of Konoe no tsubone's services in all these respects, bestowed on her the title Hisashi no onkata. Such a title was quite excessive, as Sadafusa writes in the diary in 1419, but he gave it to her in recognition of her long years of service spanning two generations: 'There is no other way to fully thank her for her loyal hard work in working for Fushiminomiya family affairs.'[21] In an era when a woman's name was determined by her father's position in the court, her status as derived from her father's position carried more weight than her own individual achievements. And yet, as head of the family, Sadafusa transcended this convention by writing that it was difficult to keep silent about her contribution.

Konoe no tsubone's son, resident priest of Shiinodera (Jōkongō-in) died of illness in 1420.[22] He and his half-brother Sadafusa had been on good terms with each other. Two years later, in 1423, Konoe no tsubone retired from her official duties, the reason being recorded as old age and beri-beri.[23] She had served in the Fushiminomiya family from the age of 11 for 60 years, making her about 71. With the death of her son, she might have experienced insecurity in her old age, as would have been very common in those days. However, the extremely capable Konoe no tsubone had foreseen and prepared for such a contingency. At Yamada, within the Fushimi domain, there was a hermitage called Kōun-an, whose head resident nun had served in the Hagiwara-no-miya and had a close relationship with the Fushiminomiya family. Konoe no tsubone had looked after this nun when she had been a constant visitor to the family. When her own serving lady retired, she had her taken into the hermitage.[24] She also adopted the new head nun as her daughter. When Konoe herself finally retired from the Fushiminomiya household, she moved to the same hermitage, no doubt secure in the knowledge that she would be surrounded by people with whom she was comfortable.

In addition, when she retired she did not forget to have Sadafusa confirm the arrangement concerning her own landholding, the hermitage estate. She pressed him several times, and eventually received the pronouncement that the land, Ichiyoda in Befu, in Harima Kokuga, would be hers for 13 years after her death, and the Shiozu estate in Ōmi Province would be hers for seven years after her death. The documents of ownership were issued personally by Sadafusa. He wrote: 'Generally speaking, reward for a court lady is lifetime land ownership (or rights to collect tax), but it has been common since ancient times that it be lifetime plus three years. So, lifetime plus 13 years would be excessive, except that her service over a long period was quite extraordinary, and so deserves special terms.'[25]

There are unfortunately too few historical documents to be certain of the content of household duties in the middle and lower ranks of the aristocracy from which court ladies like Konoe no tsubone came. However, looking again at the capable second wife in the *Shin Sarugō-ki*, her household duties included the essentials of food, clothing and lodging, as well as the buying and selling of commodities (probably tribute goods), caring for the armour and managing the servants, which is no different from the work of the *kōtō no naishi* in the imperial household in the Muromachi and Warring States period and the work of Konoe no tsubone in the Fushiminomiya household. The only differences were the scale of the establishment and whether the woman was an employee or a wife. While there were junior female servants in such households, there were no old women (such as mothers-in-law), so the housewife probably had to be fully in charge of household business.

Another household about which we have some information is that of the famous poet and scholar Sanjō Nishi Sanetaka (1455–1537), who left a diary.[26]

At the age of 24, Sanetaka married the daughter of Kajūji Norihide, apparently in a formal marriage. His bride brought with her, as her portion, rights to the landholding of Anashi no gō in Harima Province (about 1000 *hiki* in monetary value). Early in their marriage Sanetaka was dominant and made an effort to educate her by, for example, ordering her to memorise ten poems from the *Kokinshū* every day.[27] However, in her middle age, she became a fearsome wife. This was partially due to the fact that her sisters were active and influential at court, but also because the family was financially insecure, even poor, and she was continually receiving complaints. She took responsibility for the management of the household.

At some point after his son Kin'eda took a wife from the Kanroji family, or perhaps when Sanetaka retired and handed over the family duties to his son, Kin'eda's wife seems to have taken over all the household responsibilities, because Sanetaka handed the food allowance (*hanmai-dai*) over to her.

In 1524, employees of the Sanjō Nishi household consisted of eight men and seven women, and the summer allowance was a total of nine *kan* and 300 *mon*; the winter allowance for the men was a total of 19 *kan* and 200 *mon* (an average of two *kan* and 400 *mon* each); for the women it was eight *kan* and 200 *mon* (an average of one *kan* and 170 *mon* each), a little less than half what men received. (Courtiers were paid twice a year, at *Bon*—in the seventh month—and at the end of the year.) However, averages are not very meaningful, since those with some rank, such as the *shōyū* and *menoto*, would have been paid more, and there was a big differential in salary for both men and women.[28] The cash income alone for the family in 1523 amounted to nearly 200 *kan-mon* (see Haga 1981:Sanjō Sanetaka), which seems like a well-off household budget. This would have come from estates and guilds in the family's jurisdiction; in good, stable times it came in steadily, but in times of disturbance and fighting the flow would immediately cease, so that, for example, in 1527 they had to borrow some money in order to fully pay their employees' end-of-year allowances.

Sanetaka's wife bore him three sons and two daughters. As far as we can tell from the diary, there were no other women he loved. She was therefore the official wife of a ministerial family. In 1526, Sanetaka had a burial ground made for himself and his wife in Nison'in temple. Her life seems to have been reasonably happy. Her elder daughter married into the Kujō family and the second daughter into the Ōgi-machi Sanjō family. At the time of her marriage, the eldest daughter was 16 and her husband Kujō Hisatsune (chancellor, 1501–13) was 28. It would seem to have been a formal marriage, for a bridal palanquin was sent for her from the Kujō house, to where she went in a

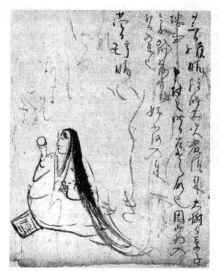

A rough sketch with some scribbling, in the *Sanetaka kōki* entry for 24th day, 9th month, 1480 (Hanawa 1958).

ceremonial manner.[29] The son she bore to Hisatsune, called Tanemichi, later became chancellor (1533–34), and she was given the title Kita no mandokoro. In all, she bore three sons and three daughters. Sanetaka's heir Kin'eda was also formally married, to the eldest daughter of Kanroji Motonaga.

In the imperial and princely households, there was no official 'first' wife, but a court lady whose child became the heir tended to be recognised after the fact as the official wife, whereas in many other aristocratic families, as we have seen, the situation was different and there was a clearly defined official wife. Even in a patriarchal family, where there was a definite official wife, a woman's status was obviously higher and more secure. The *Sanetaka kōki* tells clearly of brides being welcomed and the appropriate ceremony being performed. As a result, because the marriage was formal, the marital relationship was official, which sometimes led to a disadvantage. For example, in 1522, a man called Shodayū no Toshitsune Ason of the Nijō family was accused of dabbling in fox magic and was captured by the *bakufu* police. As a consequence, his sister, who was married to Sesonji Yukitoyo Ason, had the misfortune of being immediately divorced.[30]

Naturally, in addition to the official wife, there are many examples of children being born to serving ladies, and there were many relationships of this kind between male and female employees. There was no end of scandals about relationships between ladies-in-waiting and courtiers in the palace living quarters, and written pledges were sometimes required of courtiers in such cases. For example, in the Fushiminomiya family, the male attendant Tamuki no Nagasuke no Ason had a close relationship with a serving lady called Kaga,[31] which may have been openly recognised since Nagasuke caused his wife and Kaga to have babies alternately, about which Sadafusa wryly comments 'this should be called prosperity'.

Among the aristocracy, there were some similarities with the sexual customs of the imperial and princely houses. Upon the death of the mother of Kikutei Chūnagon, who was a close friend of Fushiminomiya Sadafusa, Sadafusa noted it in his diary as the death of 'Kikutei's serving lady mother'. And the following year, Sadafusa wrote that the woman who served in Kikutei Dainagon's household had died at dawn that day, and that she was the mother of Kikutei's best-loved children. As in the Fushiminomiya family, a serving woman could become the mother of many children but still remain a servant.[32] Wives and concubines lived together in the same establishment, so to what degree did the official wife feel jealousy? An example can be taken from a low-ranking samurai employed in the administration of the Fushimi estate. His name was Ogawa Zenkei and he was also employed by Yamana-uji. His first wife suddenly ran away and became a nun because of 'jealousy of the new wife'[33] — just like a plot from a *kyōgen* play. A totally different example is the case of the chancellor Konoe whose 'beloved wife' died, leaving him in a state of such grief that he declared he would follow her by committing *seppuku*. He was restrained, but instead he cut off his pigtail and became a monk. When recording this incident, Sadafusa writes somewhat coldly, 'Such extreme madness or perhaps extreme grief has never before been seen in the Fujiwara Sekke family — it is inexplicable'.[34] It is interesting for us to note that even in the chancellor's family such conjugal love could be found. Unlike in the *kabuki* play *Yasuna* of the Edo period, in *nō* there is no play in which a husband goes mad grieving for his lost wife, but in reality one such existed.

Life in a nunnery

In 1413, the Korean emissary Song Hui-gyong sailed through the Inland Sea and passed through Nishinomiya and Amagasaki as he travelled overland to Kyoto. He wrote in his journal *Nosongdang Ilbon Haengnok* that, whereas the land was dotted with prosperous villages, in the towns there was a considerable number of beggars, and monks and nuns who raised their voices chanting sutras all over the place (Song 1968). In Japan at that time, unwanted male and female children were put into temples in early childhood, and widows customarily became nuns.

The previous section described how the Lady Konoe no tsubone of the Fushiminomiya household prepared for her own retirement in a hermitage. Prince Sadafusa's diary, *Kanmon nikki*, records another case: the mother of Sadafusa's half-brother Yōken became a nun at the age of 71 at the Tōyō-in temple at Umezu Chōfukuji (the head of the temple must have been a relative, the sister of Sanjō no Sochi no Chūnagon). However, she was without means and had to depend on her son Yōken, who entreated his older brother Sadafusa to let her move to one of the hermitages in the Fushimi domain. It was decided that Sōgyokuan would be suitable, so Sadafusa had talks with the head of the hermitage, who was intractable and set unreasonable conditions. Sadafusa reluctantly accepted the conditions and the old lady was moved.[35] Even though the woman was the daughter of the noble Sanjō Saneoto, and in her service at the Fushiminomiya household she had attained the prestigious title of Hisashi no onkata, in her old age she was left with no means of support.

Indeed, all the children born to Hidehito's serving lady, Higashi no onkata, were sent to temples to be monks, and all died in childhood, but she remained living in her stepson Sadafusa's household. One of her servant women, Bettō (Nikō), followed her mistress and became a nun after Hidehito's death, and was praised by Sadafusa for her loyalty. However, it became financially impossible to retain her service, so she was dismissed and a small hermitage was built for her in a remote part of the Fushimi domain. This nun had previously served Sadafusa's mother (Haruko, also known by the title Nishi no onkata), and was later taken into the service of Higashi no onkata. Sadafusa writes that she was a popular performer at palace banquets, so he took pity on her and could not abandon her in her old age. He looked after her in the same way that he would have looked after a male courtier of the Fushiminomiya household, and arranged for her to be supported from the income of the head of Gyōzō-an hermitage.[36]

In 1509, Sanjō Nishi Sanetaka took similar care of an old woman, Sakyōdayū no tsubone, who had served his family for over 70 years but who had become ill and had no prospect of recovering. He moved her to a small neighbouring hermitage, where he had made prior arrangements.[37] The old woman died 12 days later, and a notice arrived announcing her funeral, for which Sanetaka sent the money. This tells us that there were small hermitages where, for payment, resident nuns would take responsibility for a person near death and take care of all the necessary arrangements after death, including the offering of Buddhist rites. When a serving woman, Umegae, who had been in service for 30 years, was struck with paralysis, Sanetaka simply had her placed on the banks of the Imadegawa river and did not send any funeral expenses. He did express pity for her, but practically threw her away.[38] So, to be sent to a nunnery was preferable treatment.

Nunneries also served as places for women who had spent all their lives serving the aristocracy at court, whether civil or military. After their lords died, they became nuns and could pray for the repose of that man's soul.

For just half a year, a 16-year-old princess from the Kikutei family was the concubine of Prince Ogawanomiya (younger brother of Emperor Shōkō,

1401–1428; reigned 1412–1428); when the prince died, she was obliged to become a nun, as Sadafusa recorded with sympathy.[39] So, nunneries also functioned as refuges for very young widows and it is no wonder that such a large number of hermitages existed.

Even more pitiable were the daughters born into the households of emperors, imperial princes and shogunal courts. In these aristocratic households, both civil and military, there was no longer an official first wife, but principally only relationships with serving women, so for women of these households the opportunity for formal marriage disappeared. As such, the birth of a girl child at the aristocratic level of society was regarded as a nuisance, as Sadafusa writes: 'Too many girls are born and they are disliked.'[40] Therefore, they were sent at the age of seven or eight to live in nunneries as attendants. Why did these families stop making formal marriages? One reason was that the cumulative cost of formal marriage ceremonies was prohibitive. In particular, it became impossible to establish a household for an empress with the necessary large retinue of ladies-in-waiting. Once the basic requirement of producing an heir was fulfilled, other progeny could be settled in nunneries, leaving one in reserve for contingencies.

In the Fushiminomiya household, all the children of Emperor Sukō (1334–98; reigned 1348–51), except for Prince Hidehito, entered priestly orders. Hidehito's children, too, became priests, apart from his successor Haruhito-ō, and Sadafusa who succeeded him. The three surviving children of Haruhito-ō, all girls, were sent to nunneries. Prince Sadafusa had two sons and five daughters. His eldest son Hikohito became Emperor Gohanazono (1419–70; reigned 1428–64), his second son Sadatsune was the next Fushiminomiya prince and, of the five daughters, one was adopted into the household of a courtier-servant and died young, while the other four were placed in nunneries of imperial rank with the guarantee of attaining a high order.

These circumstances are further explained by looking at land inheritance relations in the family. Sanjō no tsubone was the serving lady of Emperor Sukōin (and Sadafusa's step-grandmother), who, having borne him five children, was noted as his most beloved partner, different from the other ladies. In her old age, a small hermitage was built for her at Ninnaji temple and she was given the title Shinshū-in. She was granted two *chō* of rice land at Hōanji and 2000 *hiki* of official tribute land in Harima Province as her income-earning landholding. Land entitlement for a woman was limited to her lifetime, but when Shinshū-in became ill, she requested Prince Hidehito (then household head) to permanently give her land to her daughter, the head (abbess) of Shinjōji (a nunnery with imperial status, whose abbess was always a former imperial princess). In the end, Hidehito issued a document permitting the Hōanji entitlement to go to the imperial nunnery for the abbess's lifetime, and for the income from the tribute land in Harima to go to Shinshū-in for three years after her death.

This issue arose again when the abbess of Shinjōji herself fell ill, and she requested that the Hōanji rice field holdings be changed from hers for life to an endowment to the Shinjōji temple in perpetuity. Sadafusa eventually and reluctantly complied by donating half of the property, but perhaps in compensation he asked that his daughters be accepted into the nunnery as novices.[41] Even if the property was endowed to the temple, by placing the princesses there he could have them cared for, and the income from the property would benefit them and in effect belong to them in the long run. Sadafusa had eight daughters to dispose of, including those surviving of his brother Haruhito-ō, which made this a logical measure to deal with the situation.

Some imperial temples had extensive estates and domains, as well as prestige, so being able to inherit these entitlements was quite a boon. The nun from Shinjōji was ordered by the Muromachi *shōgun* to become the abbess at Keiaiji. This was at first adamantly refused, because of the great expense incurred for the ordination ceremony, but in the end it was accepted. Sadafusa wrote, 'This should be seen as a reward'.[42]

Centuries earlier, Fujiwara Yoshisuke (813–867) had converted his mansion into a temple, called it Sūshin-in, and gathered there all the women in his clan who had no material support, thereby saving them from poverty. There was a long tradition of nunneries as places where women who did not have family position could live together. A similar situation held for men, too. In medieval society, the monasteries and nunneries were in obverse relation to the *ie*. They fulfilled or even surpassed the role of family as a facility for communal mutual help and sustenance. Founders of these institutions established them with huge landholdings, and many of their descendents entered those places. The monks and nuns who served under an abbot or abbess were often connected to the servants and courtiers of the aristocratic households from which the abbot or abbess came.

In the Muromachi period the Fushiminomiya family administered many landholdings and estates, parts of which they could allocate to their sons and daughters and the women who served at court. The rights attached to these lands were often only for the lifetime of the person, and the income was a portion of what was due to the official second-in-charge. The positions of trustee (*azukaridokoro*) or agent (*daikan*) were granted in recognition of services to male courtiers (*keishi*) or to a subsidiary temple (*tatchu*) attached to the Fushiminomiya family in anticipation of the concomitant service and tributary income. In temples and hermitages built by the Fushiminomiya family, an appointment to abbot was also a reward for service. Nunneries, too, were apparently obliged to perform service to overlord headquarters from which they received properties. On the occasion of the Tango Festival on the fifth day of the fifth month, it was customary to present to one's superiors gifts of *kusudama* (decorative balls filled with medicinal herbs and spices, hung in houses to ward off evil spells). The Fushiminomiya family presented theirs to the imperial palace and to the *shōgun*'s palace. The *kusudama* had always been made by the head nun of the hermitage Sōtoku-an, in the grounds of Daikōmyōji temple, but one year she was ill and unable to perform this service, so Sadafusa's daughter Shōkei-ni (now the nun Irie-dono Gokasshiki) was requested to make them instead. On other occasions Sadafusa's niece Narutaki-dono was asked to perform this task.[43] *Kusudama* had to be sent to many places and this work was given to the nuns to do.

Sadafusa wrote:

> The flowers were excellent; the *kusudama* were placed on crimson paper, on which had been laid iris leaves and then they were put into a container, which was placed into a chest. A vassal in a pale pink cloak carried the chest.

It was a most elegant gift, and was presented with a *nyōbō hōsho* attached. It is to be imagined that such a laboriously crafted product was later commodified.

It should not be forgotten that these nunneries constituted centres of industry and business. In Kyoto, an early and well-known example is the fan production called '*ami-ori*' carried out in Mieidō hall of Shin-Zenkōji temple.[44] The *Kefukigusa* (1645/1647, a book on *haikai* poetry edited by Matsue Shigeyori) records references to the nuns Donge-in-dono (Take no Gosho), who produced dried melon, and Irie-dono (Sanji Chion-ji), who made *kazuki-wata* and *omote-zashi no o* (a kind of braid yarn). And Dōmyōji in Kawachi Province produced *hikimeshi* (dried rice), described as the 'great skill of nuns' (Matsue 1943). This type of activity was probably typical also of the medieval period.

A paucity of historical documentation has limited the discussion to the aristocracy, but in the Muromachi and Warring States periods the lower classes were not untouched by these patterns. For example, there is the case of a group of widows who became nuns and were low-class workers attached to shrines, performing miscellaneous tasks and duties. They gained a monopoly over the oil business for all of western Japan, set up a powerful autonomous base in Ōyamazaki, and also built a hermitage for retired nuns (Ōyamazaki-chō-shi Hensan Iinkai 1981–83). These virtuous acts were to be a guarantee of a good afterlife, but can also be seen as having an element of practicality in protecting their rights in this life. This topic is crying out for more research.[45]

Women's life and work in the towns

From the 14th century, the progress of a commodities economy affected life in the towns; this is examined in this section, which largely relies on iconographic evidence and, in particular, looks at how the life and work of women were affected.

The many sets of folding screens painted in the 16th century depicting life in and around the capital—the *Rakuchū rakugai-zu*—show townhouses lined up facing the street, while the area at the back of the houses is a park-like space, in which many daily activities were carried out, including growing things. In a picture scroll, *Naki Fudō Riyaku Engi Emaki* (held by Shōjōge-in temple), this same kind of open space vividly depicts daily life activities: a woman beside a stream is stamping the laundry, with her breasts casually showing; another woman is drying a laundered *kimono* on a pole, while two others are stretching out washed cloth; another woman is drawing water from a well, beside which is a vegetable patch growing the *Kamo nasubi* (round eggplants) for which Kyoto was famous. Between the plants are embedded large pots, probably containing human waste for use as fertiliser, to which anyone could contribute. Each house on the main street had access to a common living space at the back, and it is here that we see women hard at work. Whereas urban communities consisted of district groups formed by male household heads from both sides of a city street—that is, the front part of dwellings (Wakita 1981c)—the back of the houses was women's space.

Naki Fudō riyaku engi emaki (held by Seijōke-in Temple, Kyoto)

However, by the 16th century, such a scene was a conventional pictorial fantasy. I do not know about the edges of the town, but at least in the central sections of Kamigyō and Shimogyō any open space had long been crammed with dwellings. In Tsuchimikado fourth ward, the main street was rented to merchants such as sake dealers, and the Tsuchimikado family itself occupied the land in the middle. The price of land was four or five times that of the rural outskirts or farming villages (Wakita 1981a), so it was no longer possible to use the land at the back of dwellings as commons. Clearly, the space for women's activities was severely constricted. In Shimogyō, rented houses (most likely tenement-style) were erected; their tenants probably paid very little and were not considered as independent townspeople and community members (Kinoshita 1967).

What happened to the living space at the back of the dwellings? On the property of Tōji temple, Yamabuki-chō (in the vicinity of the Kyoto railway station today), there was a disagreement over the use of a well between a wealthy man called Kin'ami and the people of the town. From this, we know that the well was for common use, and that normally it was not at the rear of the dwellings but was in the main street on the roadside in front of a house (Nakamura 1975). In the Edo period, public conveniences were also situated in the street, in the form of containers for collecting human waste for fertilizer (Harada 1980). In Sakai, large containers have been excavated and are thought to have been communal public conveniences used in the 16th century. In Echizen Province, in the Asakura clan's castle town of Ichijōdani, archeological excavation has shown that even the small townhouses of artisans had their own individual toilets, a square framed in stone, which was located in the earthen part of the dwelling (Asakura-uji iseki shōsa-kai 1987).

Dwellings in the vicinity of the Gion shrine in 1378 had a front width (*maguchi*) of either one *jō*, one *jō* and three *shaku*, or two *jō* (one *jō* is equivalent to a little less than three metres), and a depth of seven to nine *jō*. Behind these dwellings were vegetable beds.[46] A warehouse in Hari-kōji (Needle Lane)-Inokuma in the Tōji temple estate in 1395 had a front width of three *jō* and nine *shaku*, and a depth of 20 *jō*—considerably large proportions. Such a mud-wall storehouse would have been comparable to a reinforced concrete apartment building today, and it was also prudent to rent out the land, whose value was very high.[47] Generally, the street was packed with small dwellings of one to two *jō* in width. In the 17th century in Mukō-machi, a semi-rural town outside Kyoto, most shops were two *ken* square (two *ken* by 2.5 *ken*) or three *ken* square (1 *ken* = 1.82 metres), making an area of four to nine *tsubo* (one *tsubo* = 3.3 square metres), which served as both shop and dwelling (Mukō-shi-shi Hensan Iinkai 1985). Presumably the shop-dwellings in Kyoto were

The woman to the left is preparing food in a *suribachi* (mortar).
Yamai no sōshi (*The disease scroll*) (National Treasure, Agency for Cultural Affairs)

of similar proportions. In this cramped space, it would have been impossible
to accommodate parents and children, or extra wives and concubines. In the
Tenbun era (1532–55), a new urban area called Nijō-Reisen-chō was created
in between Kamigyō and Shimogyō, and many sons of townsmen set up
independent houses there (*Reisen-chō kiroku* facsimile; Wakita 1981a). This
indicates that there were many nuclear families living in the normal town
dwellings (*machiya*).

Recent archeological discoveries suggest the kinds of possessions and
implements used in such households (Nihon chūsei doki Kenkyūkai 1985–90),
principally clay containers of various sizes for cooking and storage (clay
cooking pots and saucepans, and pitchers and vats for storing water). These
findings tally with a will leaving the following possessions to a woman:
'*kama, nabe, tsubo, kame, kawago* (leather- or paper-covered basket)', in the
document *Zappitsu yō-shū*, introduced by Gomi Fumihiko (see Gomi 1982).
These would seem to be pots and pans for boiling and simmering, a salt jar
and a water urn.

The illustration above shows the use of a *suribachi*. In the 13th and 14th
centuries, a kneading bowl called *konebachi* (in *sue* ware) was produced in
Uozumi, Harima Province, and became widely used throughout western Japan;
it was replaced by the *suribachi*, a higher-quality striated mortar-type bowl

made in Bizen Province. This change also occurred in Kyoto (Tanji 1985; Morita 1987). The base of some excavated *suribachi* of the Kameyama kilns have burn marks, so Makabe Yoshiko assumes that they were placed on the fire and used as cooking utensils (Makabe 1973). Rotating millstones were not yet in common use, so grains were probably first cooked and then ground in the same *suribachi*. There is evidence of widespread use of terracotta eating bowls called *gaki-wan* in the 12th and 13th centuries, but around Kyoto excavations show that such plates suddenly stopped being used from the 14th century (Hashimoto 1990). This suggests that terracotta bowls were replaced by wooden bowls, which were less likely to be preserved. Further, in Kyoto and all parts of western Japan, examples of Chinese ceramic bowls have been found among local products. The use of wooden bowls and Chinese glazed ceramic bowls, rather than the blackish terracotta bowls, must have aesthetically improved Japanese eating culture (Ono 1985; Kamei 1986).

In Kyoto and other parts of central Japan, not all dwellings had fireplaces. In the 12th and 13th centuries, only earthenware pots with three legs were used (Sugawara 1988). In Awa, on the island of Shikoku, a portable furnace was used in the 14th century (Tokushima-ken Kyōiku Iin-kai 1989)—which suggests only simple cooking such as boiling and simmering. However, in Kyoto in the 15th and 16th centuries, the Nara *hibachi* (portable charcoal fire brazier) was being used. The *hibachi* gave heat and allowed simple grilling, compensating for the lack of a proper fireplace (Tsubonouchi 1988). Excavations show that in the 16th century the Harima *nabe* (iron pan) appeared.[48] The general use of iron pans was actually much earlier, but exact research on this is still lacking. Judging from the size of dwellings, it is not really clear whether a separate kitchen (*daidokoro* in modern Japanese) existed. At that time the word *mi-daidokoro* referred to the official wife of a noble, which suggests that a kitchen was something found only in the palace. At any rate, in the towns—where a separate area for cooking was not readily available, and where fuel was scarce and expensive—cooking was not an integral part of daily life. Most likely, using a three-legged cauldron and small pans, the staple diet was simply cooked grain porridge and vegetables, served in terracotta or wooden bowls (see illustration at beginning of this chapter). As discussed below, women were mostly engaged in some kind of work, which earned them money, and they could not spare a lot of time for housework.

The role of the sales girls or vendors (*hisagime*) dates back at least to the time of the *Konjaku Monogatari*, which contains a story about a woman who chopped up snakes, cooked them and sold them to palace guards. This character had a bad reputation, representing something unsafe (Konno 1993–99:nos 33-33, 32), an attitude that occurred partly because people were not used to buying food from street vendors that was cooked and ready to eat. New things were always viewed suspiciously. However, by the middle-ages such sellers became commonplace and were trusted and, indeed, their trade activity contributed to the diversification of town life as a whole.[49] There were also many male peddlers; the illustrations in the *Shokunin utaawase* scrolls show that both sexes were involved in these street stalls (see Chapter three).

We cannot automatically assume that the *utaawase* illustrations are an exact depiction of gender role division at the time. There are clearly cases when both men and women were engaged in an occupation, but selection of a gender for inclusion in the *utaawase* scroll was more or less arbitrary, especially in the area of food. We know from the documented example of the woman Kimura Goime that both men and women were salt vendors.[50]

By the time of Kimura Goime (1547) there was already a division of labour between production and retailing of daily life necessities through the *za* (Wakita 1969b), but this is not distinguished in the pairs in the *utaawase*, produced in the early 16th century. It is clear that women were engaged in making earthenware vessels, but the figure vending them is male. In contrast, wooden bowls were made by men, so they were presumably often sold by the women of the family. The sake maker and the fish vendor are depicted as women, which is supported by historical records.

The case of partially cooked foodstuffs, such as *tōfu* and *sōmen* noodles, and ready-to-eat snack food such as *mochi* rice cakes, *manju* and seaweed jelly, should be noted. We can imagine that *mochi* and *manju* were made by those who sold them, and that *tokoroten* was also homemade and sold in individual servings with syrup. As with the man selling cups of tea and herbal infusions, people probably ate these in the street. The professional cooks— *chōsai* and *hōchō-shi*—would definitely not have been serving the demands of the common people, but other suppliers of food appear to have done so. Surprisingly, ready-cooked food and partially prepared food was common. The poor quality of cooking implements, combined with the inconvenience of having to purchase wood or charcoal fuel from the *oharame* vendors (see illustration in Chapter three), resulted in a simple rough diet supplemented by 'takeaway' food or by eating at stalls on the street.

Sōmen could not be made without a fine grain stone mill, so at that time it was a Kyoto specialty. In *kyōgen* plays, it is referred to as a rare delicacy of the capital. In the *Tokitsugu Kyōki*, too, often guests were served *nyūmen* (*sōmen* poached in a sauce of soya sauce, miso and condiments) with their sake. *Sōmen* was said to be a specialty of Kenninji temple in Kyoto, but in the *utaawase* picture a common class woman is making it, which shows that

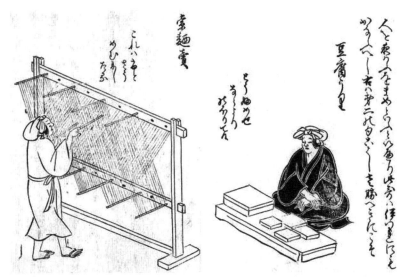

'Shichijūichiban shokunin utaawase': *Sōmen* noodle seller (left) and *tōfu* seller (right).

its production was generalised throughout the city and that it was becoming a popular semi-cooked foodstuff. Miso was also a semi-processed foodstuff and varieties of it (*hōro* and *kuro* miso) were made in Nara and sold by itinerant outcasts. In Kyoto too, miso shops were appearing alongside sake shops, and were attracting tax claims from the *bakufu*. This indicates that there was a high demand for this produce. Other than food, there were also vendors of sulphur, brooms, straw sandals and wooden clogs. Sticks dipped in sulphur were used to start fires conveniently, and brooms had become commodified.

Given the likelihood that little time would have been devoted to cooking, how did people spend their time? The gender division of domestic labour is suggested in a *kyōgen* play in which the wife has to care for the house itself, even mending the roof, while the husband is lazy and does nothing. This is a criticism, indicating that the norm was indeed the other way around, with the wife looking after food and clothing and the husband taking care of the shelter. In another *kyōgen* play, *The boy's mother* (*Hōshi ga haha*), the work of a farmer's wife extends to farm labour and herb gathering, weaving and sewing (Shinma et al 1959); in comparison, the labour in towns was more differentiated between husband and wife. A bad wife is berated with the words: 'At the market she does not even manage to sell a single *shaku* of cloth' (implying she had neither spun nor woven it) (Shinma et al 1959), showing that a woman not only had to weave cloth but also sell it. The time that a farming housewife spent in the fields, the town housewife spent at the market, involved in some kind of production or business.

In the *utaawase* pictures, a large proportion of textile-related occupations are depicted as women's work. In Kyoto, the silk industry was flourishing and was the forerunner of the Nishijin weaving complex. Kyoto silk had an important place in domestic and overseas trade. Chinese raw-silk thread and locally produced thread were bought and woven into high-grade fabric and exported to Korea, Ryūkyū and elsewhere, as well as being sold throughout Japan (Wakita 1988b). Textile jobs represented as women's labour in the *utaawase* illustrations include silk-yarn seller, white-cloth seller, indigo dyer, weaver, embroiderer, braider and *obi* seller.

Fan vendors were also women. The folding screens in the genre *Rakuchū rakugai-zu* always include a fan maker, showing that fans were both made and sold by women. Fans were one of Kyoto's most important specialty products for both overseas and domestic trade. It is said that in Korea, five fans were worth the equivalent of a tiger's skin.

Clearly, the textile and fan industries and their marketing owed a lot to women's labour; hence, in the commercial and production system of the day there were many women who held the rights incumbent on members of za, such as the woman Kameya Goime (who held the merchant rights for the *obi* business in the whole of Kyoto) and the nun Hoteiya Genryō-ni, who held the rights for the fan business in half of Kyoto. However, medieval society was moving towards the *ie* unit represented by the male household head, and so the *ryōshu* in control was not interested in whether the work, called *kashoku* (work of the house), was done principally by women or not, as long as each household was represented by a male (Wakita 1988a). Occupations based on women's productive labour, such as pottery, brewing and weaving, were represented and dealt with at the household level by the male head. Perhaps the names of women such as Kameya Goime and Hoteiya Genryō-ni only appeared on the official documents for tribute and service because they were widows, and thus household heads. It is important that future research uncovers the actual nature of women's labour which was buried inside the *ie* as represented by the *koshu* male household head.

Apart from the occasional appearance of a woman's name in official registers, when the man's name appears it indicates three possible types of cottage industry: woman as principal, supported by the man; man as principal, supported by the wife; and husband and wife collaborating on an equal basis. So far we have discussed the first possibility, yet the second type has been considered the most common. Men's skilled crafts, such as armoury and sword-making, would certainly have been of this second type. The third type of occupation, which required two people, such as bamboo-blind making, are depicted in the *Shichijūichiban utaawase* as the work of a married couple. This work did not necessarily have to be done by a couple, but in a household that could not afford an apprentice this exacting task became a conjugal one. In the 14th to 15th centuries, the silk textile industry was aided by the introduction of the high loom (*takabata*), which required two people to operate: the *orite* (person below, moving the frames) and the *karabiki* (person who passes the shuttle through at the top). Pictures show the loom being operated by a couple, or by two women. In Edo period illustrations, the dominant *orite* role belongs to the man, and the woman has the less-demanding role, showing that women took the assisting role.

Since the Kamakura period, such small businesses began to be controlled by wholesalers (Wakita 1969b). Of the silk yarn sellers attached to the Gion shrine, those whose names we know are practically all women: they were called village traders and sold their wares laden on a yoke. After forming the New Silk Yarn *za*, they challenged the Original Silk Yarn *za*, whose members were the merchants of the main streets in Shimogyō, around Sanjō-machi and Shijō-machi. The Gion shrine became involved and they instigated a court dispute. However, their new *za* was backed by a wholesaler called Harima Ajari Shōzen, who sold them his silk yarn and also supported their case to the Gion shrine: it was this wholesaler who had organised them into the New Silk Yarn *za*.

There were also some women wholesale traders. The indigo ash (*kō no hai*), which was transported from Nagasaka-guchi (Tanba-guchi) to Kyoto, was the catalyst for indigo dying, and there was a high demand for it in Kyoto where the textile trade was flourishing. From early on, there were four wholesale merchants, called the Indigo Ash *za* of Nagasaka-guchi, who had their eye on this *kō no hai* catalyst agent, and they monopolised the purchasing rights. One of these merchants was the woman called Kagame, and later her right was passed on to another woman. The wholesaler Kameya Goime also had a number of *obi*-selling girls working for her.

However, the small businesses of merchants and artisans who were represented by male household heads during the Muromachi and Warring States periods were, in some form or another, under the control of wholesalers— demonstrating that it was a domestic industry in a wholesale system supported by working couples. Otogi no shō domain in Yamato Province was famous for producing *kaya-sudare* (reed blinds), and the farmers of the neighbourhood also took up making them as a side job for extra cash. In Nara and Yamato, they were permitted to sell them directly, but there were two wholesalers who had the monopoly on selling them in Kyoto. They would make down payments to the farmers, take the goods and load them on horses, which then 'formed a continuous line all the way to Kyoto'. Because it took two people to make *sudare*, couples probably made them and gave them to the wholesalers.

In this system of wholesale management of domestic production, the power of the wholesaler was more significant than a gender role division between husband and wife. However, the rights owned by women wholesalers like Kameya Goime and Kagame shifted into the hands of male wholesalers who had extensive rights and were like the merchants who supplied court and *bakufu*. Both men and women's small and medium wholesale businesses could no longer be sustained and gradually disappeared.

Belief and pleasure

Women who were contained in the *ie* (wife, concubine, servant) and women not in the net of the *ie* (those in the nunneries) have been considered as a pair. But there is another pivotal category to consider—*miko*, *kusemai* and *asobime*. We have examined gender role division and aspects of social status, and how these affected the lives of these groups of women (see Wakita 2002b), but here I consider the issue from the perspective of their relation to the *ie* in general and to the community.

The *nō* play *Aoi no ue* (*Lady Aoi*) is based on an episode of the *Tale of Genji*, where Lady Rokujō's spirit possesses both Lady Aoi and her companions. In the *nō* play, a specialist woman shaman, an *azusa no miko*, summons the spirit by plucking her catalpa bow, but it is actually exorcised by a male *yamabushi* (Buddhist mountain ascetic). This illustrates how healing practices in the Nanboku and Muromachi periods were carried out in urban life. In the Heian period, also, specialist women shamans called *monotsuki miko* were possessed by random spirits rather than specific ones. In the *Konjaku Monogatari*, the *miko* is a highly respected *uchifushi no miko* (thought to have been possessed by the deity of the Kamo no Wakamiya shrine) and is said to have been patronised by the chancellor Fujiwara Kaneie (Konno 1993–99:31-26). There must have been an intrinsic difference between a *miko* who was attached to a highly reputable shrine and a common *monotsuki miko*, who was possessed by just any spirit. A picture scroll from the late Heian period, *Nenchū gyōji emaki*, which depicts the annual ceremonies and events of the court, has an illustration of the Gion Goryō-e festival, where a *miko* is riding on horseback next to the portable shrine (*mikoshi*) as part of the procession. This probably expresses the role of the *miko* as conveying messages from the gods after being possessed by them. However, by the 14th century, the *miko* had certainly lost these powers of divine communication and were only entrusted with performing the sacred *kagura* dances. When an official of the Gion shrine went to seek a cure for a sick relative, the shrine summoned a reputable *monotsuki miko* from the *sanjo* area (where *shōmoji* religious practitioners lived) and had her perform a divination.[51] Compared with earlier stages when shamanistic behaviour could be expected from almost any woman, there was a separation into the *miko* attached to a shrine who later only performed *kagura* and the *monotsuki miko* who operated independently as diviners and summoners of spirits of the living and the dead.

In the previously mentioned Ōyamazaki *miya-za*, the daughter of one of the members belonged to a *miko-za*[52] — perhaps a vestige of the early medieval form of *miko*. In Wakide no miya (in Yamashiro Province Sōraku county), where a *nyōbō-za* survives to the present day, girls of 15 to 16 years of age who are members of the *miya-za* offer *kagura* performances in a *miko*-like role.[53] Generally, however, an increasing proportion of *miko* were becoming professional in towns and villages in the central (Kinai) region in the late medieval period — although occasionally ordinary housewives suddenly became possessed and went into a trance (*kamigakari*). In Ishii village on the Fushimi estate there was a god (Ubusuna no kami), called Gokōnomiya, who functioned to unite a community of several villages. The lively scene of its festival is described in detail in the *Kanmon Nikki*. The position of *kannushi* (shrine head priest) for Gokōnomiya shrine was a hereditary right, and was owned by a local samurai family called Sōgi. Apart from this, there was a fulltime permanent *miko* at the shrine who still had powers of divination. The *miko* perform a divination for Sadafusa after a bird flew into his palace living quarters and left droppings. The *miko* divined, 'nothing unusual, but droppings can signal some bad incident', and a purification ritual was performed.[54] Even for sore eyes, a *miko* would be called, and in a ritual called *fujō make* (overcoming pollution after contact with filth) the god of Gokōnomiya was prayed to.[55] The *miko* was only expected to divine whether an omen would be good or bad, not to perform the necessary prayers in response to the omen. It was the task of the *yamabushi* to overcome any spirit and they often worked in tandem with the *miko*, as in the example from the *nō* play *Aoi no ue*.

Another type of religious practitioner was the Kumano *bikuni* who, unlike the *miko*, performed exorcism and prayers. Originally a Kumano *bikuni*, Ise Shōnin conducted *kanjin* fundraising campaigns and thereby achieved the rebuilding of the Ise shrine (both inner and outer shrines), as already seen (see Chapter three). The fourth generation Ise Shōnin, called Shuetsu, divined that the child of Princess Sen (Sen-hime, 1597–1666) had died because of a curse from the vengeful spirit of her dead former husband Toyotomi Hideyori (1593–1615), and performed placatory prayers for her (Kuwata 1931). This surely suggests that earlier in the middle-ages, also, illness was attributed to the curse of malevolent spirits, and that Kumano *bikuni* were relied on to cure it through their incantations.

The *Katsura-me* was a type of *miko* who lived in the Katsura area and performed prayers for safe childbirth (Amino 1984b; Natori 1938). From the Heian period, they are documented as having sold sweetfish (*ayu*) and as being similar to the *asobime*. In the Muromachi and Warring States periods, they served in the battle camps of generals: there is a reference to Lord Hatakeyama's Katsura, indicating that they had free access to the innermost areas of these camps, including the women's quarters. This suggests that their role was more like midwife (providing prayers for safe delivery) than prostitute. At a time when curing illness was a matter of overcoming malevolent spirits, those who performed prayers for safe delivery may well have also served as midwives, but unfortunately there is no historical documentation of this.

There were also the *shirabyōshi* and *kusemai* performers, who did not go into trance as often as *miko* but shared many similarities with them. In a Gion shrine festival procession (*mikoshi togyo*—*mikoshi* dedicated to the god) in the 14th century there was a float that included *kusemai-guruma*. This means that a wealthy person who wanted prayers offered from Gion paid the shrine and hired *kusemai* dancers to perform on the float as an offering.[56] These dancers came from the *sanjo* settlements of *shōmoji*, a part of Nara called 'five places, ten *za*'. They were in the tradition of the *kusemai* woman dancer Hyakuman, who was reputed to be a superb artist and was mentioned by Zeami in his treatise *Go-on*.

Zeami's father, Kannami, learned *kusemai* from Otozuru—who came from the lineage of Hyakuman—and introduced this art into *nō*, a major factor in its development as an art form (Omote & Katō 1974). One of Kannami's successful plays was *Saga monogurui* (*The mad woman of Saga*), which was rewritten by Zeami as *Hyakuman*. The great *kusemai* performer loses her child and becomes crazed, later reuniting with the child at the Hyakumanben Dainenbutsu ceremony at Seiryūji temple in Saga. The play's highlight is the great Hyakuman dancing *kusemai*. Zeami probably also had in mind the link with Dōgo Shōnin, founder of the Hyakumanben Dainenbutsu ceremony, who was said to have been an abandoned child (Hosokawa 1989c).

In times of famine, separation from children was a daily occurrence, whether because the parent abandoned or sold the child, or because the child was kidnapped and then sold. Hence, there were many mothers who hoped and prayed to find their children again. Hyakuman is a representative of such mothers as she offers her *kusemai* dance at the temple and, through the intervention of the gods in the play, her prayers are answered and she is granted her wish to reunite with her child again. Plays about mad women form a whole genre in *nō* and can also be called mother plays (*hahamono*). They have the following typical plot: a mother searching for her estranged child loses her mind and, in this state, performs a dance and prays to the gods (and/or Buddha) for the child's protection. Through the mercy of the gods, she finds the child. One of these plays is *Sumidagawa*, in which the searched-for child is dead by the time he is found—a variant of the usual plot. To oversimplify, in order to reunite with the lost child the mother must go mad and then please the gods by dancing for them in that state. Because the normal mother cannot, in such a crazed state, perform such a beautiful and efficacious dance, the professional *kusemai* dancer undertakes this on her behalf. The *nō* mad-woman plays are a dramatisation of such a belief. Drama always reflects the real world of its time to some degree, and the fact that we have so many mad-woman plays in *nō* surely reflects the high incidence of child separation in the medieval period (see Chapter two).

The book *Mineai-ki*, which was written towards the end of the Kamakura period (early 14th century), tells about the vigorous growth of a cult at the Minodera temple in Harima Province, where huge crowds of all classes of people gathered to see performances by *kugutsu* and *kusemai*. The reason why this temple attracted large numbers of these performers is that, in order to have their prayers answered, people paid to offer dances to the deities and this encouraged the development of these performing arts. A bit later, in the Nanboku and Muromachi periods, performing arts like *nō* and *kusemai* developed into the *kanjin* (subscription, donation for charity) mode, with large paying audiences and an increase in the entertainment aspect. Even so, as is suggested by the term *kanjin* (donation), their main purpose was still to make an offering to the deities.

The earlier practice had been for individuals and communities to hire performers of *sarugaku*, *dengaku* and *kusemai* to perform at shrines—as an offering to the gods and also as entertainment for an audience. With the change to the *kanjin* style, performances were arranged for an unspecified number of spectators, putting performing arts in a much wider context, and a process of weeding out occurred because of competition. In each region devotional performances were supported but, as competition became more fierce, artistic excellence came to be questioned intently. In 1423 *kusemai* was being performed throughout the capital, by troupes from Ōmi, Mino and

Kawachi,[57] and in 1471, in the Fukudera temple in Nara, there was a *kusemai kanjin* performance.[58]

By the Nanboku period, as Zeami writes, *kusemai* was in decline and was already restricted to the family of the woman Kaga. This lineage can be traced through Hyakuman–Otozuru–Kaga and was the same family as the dancers on the *kusemai-guruma* in the Gion festival (Omote & Katō 1974). This decline was also noticeable in changes occurring in regional festivals. As mentioned, at the Minodera temple in Harima, at the end of the Kamakura period, many different troupes of *kugutsu* and *kusemai* gathered;[59] but in the Gokōnomiya festival, recorded in the *Kanmon Nikki* (1420s), the focus was specialist *sarugaku* performers, hired by a local samurai as an offering to the gods, and the *furyū*-type colourful folk performances from local villages—there was no *kusemai* by this time.[60] There was a strong cult around the Katsura Jizō, which attracted adherents from local villages and samurai serving in the palace. Together they formed a group performing *furyū*, a processional dance, dressed in fancy decorative attire and beating gongs.[61] Nothing, however, is mentioned of either *kugutsu* or *kusemai*, which was said to be sedate and lacking in colour. It was no longer very popular by this time, it seems.

With the rising prosperity of *sarugaku*, *onna* (women's) *sarugaku* also flourished and, with many *kanjin* performances, became very fashionable. However, for community festivals in towns and villages, it was men's *sarugaku* and *dengaku* that was offered at shrines and temples, and it seems that women performers were not used. This is probably because there was a growing tendency for women to be excluded from such rituals, since it was a society that abhorred those who were defiled by either contact with the dead or by blood—and in a society in which community groups were formed by men.

Last but not least is the category of *asobime* (prostitute). It is hard to say that *asobime* were completely divorced from the groups we have just been discussing: *miko*, *kusemai*, *shirabyōshi*, *kugutsu*, Kumano *bikuni*, *Katsura-me*. In Emperor Gotsuchimikado's court there was an attendant called Shinzen who was a nun but had formerly been a *yūjo*. Occasionally the emperor had her perform *kusemai* song and dance.[62] *Shirabyōshi* and *kusemai* could be called the arts of the *asobime*. Amino distinguishes the early medieval *asobime*, *kugutsu* and *shirabyōshi*—who were not despised as outcast and practised prostitution of their own volition—from those in the later medieval period whose social status was very low and for whom prostitution had become a kind of slavery (Amino 1984b). As I have argued elsewhere, *shirabyōshi* and *asobime* were traded even in the early medieval period (in 1256, the *shirabyōshi* Tamaō was sold to the woman Tokuishi for the high sum of 14 *kanmon*).[63] The *kugutsu*

Gojō no Otomae, who taught *imayō* dancing to retired Emperor Goshirakawa, was the adopted daughter of a *kugutsu* of Aobaka in Mino, called Mei (Takagi et al 1965). This practice, in which a girl could become an adopted daughter through a contract, creating fictive family ties, was seen from the late Heian period.

Viewing people as outcast was not completely unknown in the early medieval period, but, compared to the later period, this prejudice was slight. As the status system was reinforced, so was the attitude of viewing certain people as pariahs. However, the saying, 'even without a good family, a woman can marry well (*Uji nakushite tama no koshi*)', shows that as the patriarchal system became stronger the social origin of a concubine, unlike that of a wife, was not regarded as important, and so the issue is a complex one.

In the Heian period, the family provenance of a wife or mother carried weight, so in a polygamous situation it was unusual for an *asobime* or *shirabyōshi* to become a wife. The 10th century book *Yūjo no ki* shows in detail that many emperors and chancellors had concubines who were *asobime* (Yamagishi et al 1979: *Yūjo no ki*).

However, instances of *asobime* or *shirabyōshi* becoming wives occur only after the time of Goshirakawa (1127–92; reigned 1155–58) and Gotoba-in (1180–1239; reigned 1183–98; retirement 1198–1221), when the retired emperors could exercise despotic power. In the court of the Kamakura period (late 13th century), the daughter of a *dengaku hōshi* performer was chosen to enter the palace women's quarters (see Perkins 1998). My interpretation of this is that, rather than a change in the status of the *asobime* and *shirabyōshi*, it was a direct result of the changed family system as patriarchy became stronger. As the status difference between the official wife and the concubine became clearly delineated, it became less crucial to question the social origins of concubines.

In the *bushi* class the custom of married cohabitation with a clearly fixed official wife began early, so relations of a concubinal nature with *asobime* and *shirabyōshi* were common. For example, the official wife of Minamoto Yoshitomo (1123–60, member of the Seiwa Genji) was the daughter of the head priest of the Atsuta shrine, and their children were Yoritomo (1147–99), later *shōgun*, and Mareyoshi. By the *asobime* from Hashimoto, Yoshitomo's son was Akugenta Yoshihira; and by the Kaba-*asobime*, he had a son called Kaba no Kanja Noriyori (*Sonpi bunmyaku* 2001). He also had relations with Ōi, the head of the *asobime* in Aobaka station in Mino.[64] With Tokiwa, whose status was court servant (*zōshi*) and concubine, he also had three children, including Yoshitsune. There is a record from 1249, concerning the nun Eiyō-ni of Imajuku in Utsunoya, Suruga Province, who filed a legal suit to the *bakufu* to be exempted from labour and won an official guarantee (see Chapter three).[65] Eiyō-ni was the head of a group of *kugutsu* women performers and, according to the record, she became the mother-in-law of a land steward in this same village. This account has given rise to the interpretation that there was no discrimination against such women at the time. However, it is important to note that this steward visited the area from the capital, and the woman was not necessarily his official wife.

In an additional law of the Kamakura *bakufu*, in 1267, concerning the settlement of property rights of a divorced woman (wife or concubine), 'non-*bushi* women (such as merchants or farmers), *kugutsu*, *shirabyōshi* and all other low class women' are stipulated. This law, which makes no distinction between wives and concubines, aimed to prevent a woman from cheating her husband of property, and concerned the return of property in case of divorce—suggesting that the emphasis is on concubines. In the case of *bushi*, also, the marriage was the monogamous *yometori*-type, where the official wife's position was secure and there was a clear distinction between wife and concubine.

In an *otogi zōshi* from the Muromachi period, called 'Saru Genji no sōshi', a sardine seller is in love with an *asobime* called Keiga. He consults a recluse, who advises him that if he has enough money he can have the daughter of a noble or a high-ranking prelate for his wife, but an *asobime* would not make an appearance for anyone but a *daimyō* or a high-ranking aristocrat.

This vividly shows how the nobles and *bushi* had assured status lineages but were poor in real economic terms and, also, how the *asobime* were completely outside the status system. In the brothel quarters—a space quite cut off from the social status establishment—a separate ranking was created. A woman at the top of that ranking would not consider selling herself to someone as lowly as a sardine seller. This status gulf between normal society and the world of the *asobime* became more marked as time went on. In the Edo period, prostitution quarters were completely isolated in certain parts of the city, forming (with the theatres) 'bad places on the margins', a trend that was already apparent and growing in the medieval period. In the Muromachi period, there were a number of *asobime* establishments scattered throughout most towns. As neighbourhood community groups were set up in the cities, these *yūjo-ya* were pushed to the outskirts, where they tended to cluster. In Kyoto, Nijō-Yanagi-machi and Rokujō-Misuji-machi, which had formerly been at the edge of the city, were such places. One can see how the city expanded over time, by following the trajectory of these quarters as they were pushed further and further out. Before the Edo *bakufu* created formal prostitution quarters (*yūkaku*) and public prostitutes (*kōshō*), the separation of these quarters was already being carried out by the community groups in the towns.

Women were divided into two categories. Wives, who gave birth to the heirs of the *ie* and protected the household through their management skills, were the personification of good morals and manners: *asobime*, the playful ones, were immoral but enjoyable. Both categories of women had to sacrifice themselves in the service of men, yet they were two conflicting categories and each regarded the other with hostility. The jealousy of wives in a polygamous marriage (one husband, many wives) and the antagonism of women in a polygamous domestic situation (one husband, one main wife and multiple concubines) eventually led to the social and geographical isolation of women (in the licensed prostitution quarters of the Edo period), which was officially sanctioned. This was the inevitable outcome in a society in which women existed only for men.

Notes

1   A play in the extant repertoire of the Izumi school of *kyōgen*. It can be found with the title 'Kawakami Zatō' in Furukawa (1954).

2   Fujiwara Kaneie, Sesshō Dajō Daijin.

3   After *yometori* marriage became the norm, it was often dependent on the substance of the husband's parents.

4   *Gyokuyō* (1907), entry for second day, sixth month, 1191.

5   See for example the story 'Nakatsukasa no Taifu no Musume' in Yamada (1959).

6   In the post-*ritsuryō* era, that is, in the late Heian and medieval periods, *myōden* was a unit of land used to calculate tax and service due to landholders (Takeuchi & Takayanagi 1974:924) [trans].

7   'Two whose hearts were free of envy', *Shaseki-shū* 7(1), see Morell (1985:196–7).

8   *Sanetaka kōki* (Hanawa 1958).

9   *Sanetaka kōki* (Hanawa 1958), entries for third day, fifth month, 1499, and 13th day, fifth month, 1485. See also Okuno (1942).

10 *Sanetaka kōki* (Hanawa 1958), entries for sixth day, ninth month, 1484, fourth day, third month, 1532. See also Okuno (1942).

11 In the Sengoku period, there were cases when *nyōbō hōsho* documents overode the *rinji*. In other cases they shared responsibility of issuing *rinji* with the *kurōdo*, and they mediated imperial views on whether a *rinji* should or should not be issued, while the *kurōdo* merely wrote the *rinji* (see also Chapter five).

12   In the Takatsukasa Sekkanke household there were *senji no tsubone* and they issued *nyōbō-bumi*, as can be seen in *Tokitsugu kyōki*, entries for seventh, tenth and 11th days, second month, 1482 (see Chapter five).

13   *Koga-ke monjo* (1982:296), the document dated 26th day, sixth month, 1486, is signed by female courtier Horikawa no tsubone, servant of Cloistered Shōgun Yoshimasa. See also Chapter three.

14   The *nyōbō* were given living quarters called *tsubone*. They also had their own homes in their home villages, where they often had family establishments (see Chapter five).

15   *Kanmon nikki* (Hanawa 1958). This journal was written by Fushiminomiya Sadafusa, later given the title Gosukō-in. It covers the years 1416–48, in addition to a separate account of 13 volumes for an imperial journey in 1408. Total of 55 volumes. Also called *Kanmon gyoki*.

16   *Kanmon nikki* (Hanawa 1958), entry for second day, intercalary sixth month, 1425. For the principal research on this journal, see Yokoi (1979); Shimofusa (1968); Itō (1980); Ichino (1982).

17   *Kanmon nikki* (Hanawa 1958), entry for 25th day, seventh month, 1425.

18   *Kanmon nikki* (Hanawa 1958), entries for 26th day, 11th month, 1416, and 18th day, fifth month, 1417. On this latter occasion, Konoe was sick and could not attend.

19   *Kanmon nikki* (Hanawa 1958), 16th day, 11th month, 1416, ordination of Narutaki dono. Also, in the entry for 19th day, fourth month, 1424, Sadafusa's daughter Irie-dono entered a nunnery. On the 30th day, ninth month, 1424, Haruhito-ō's daughter Oka-dono did the same.

20   The *Kanmon nikki*, entry for 18th day, eighth month, 1424, records that Konoe visited a former fellow lady Suke no Zenni who was sick. The entry for the seventh day, first month, 1420, records that through the mediation of Konoe the territorial dispute of three years between a vassal of Sadafusa (Saki no Minamoto no Saishō) and Sanmi was conciliated. The entry for the eighth day, first month, 1424, records that Konoe no tsubone was asked about the customary ritual of demon-bean throwing, and the ritual was carried out by both the *nyōbō* and some servants from the palace (Hanawa 1958).

21   *Kanmon nikki* (Hanawa 1958), entry for tenth day, first month, 1419.

22   *Kanmon nikki* (Hanawa 1958), entries for 11th, 13th and 14th days, ninth month, 1423.

23   *Kanmon nikki* (Hanawa 1958), second day, sixth month, 1425.

24   *Kanmon nikki* (Hanawa 1958), entries for 26th day, third month, 1419, 16th day, second month, and 29th day, fourth month, 1424, and fourth day, eighth month, 1424.

25   *Kanmon nikki* (Hanawa 1958), fifth day, tenth month, 1425.

26   *Sanetaka kōki* (Hanawa 1958) covers 63 years (1474–1536): 158 scrolls in Sanetaka's own hand are extant. This diary by Sanjō Nishi Sanetaka is a valuable record of the politics, society and culture of the unsettled times following the Onin

Disturbance (1467–77). Written in *kanbun*, 158 volumes are extant in Sanetaka's own hand [trans].

27   *Sanetaka kōki* (Hanawa 1958), third day, third month, and ninth day, ninth month, 1479, and others. Principal research based on *Sanetaka Kōki* can be found in Hara (1929); Haga (1981; 1960). .

28   *Sanetaka kōki* (Hanawa 1958), entries for 17th day, sixth month, and 26th day, 11th month, 1524.

29   *Sanetaka kōki* (Hanawa 1958), entry for 25th day, seventh month, 1495.

30   *Kanmon nikki* (Hanawa 1958), entry for 14th day, ninth month, 1430.

31   *Kanmon nikki* (Hanawa 1958), entry for ninth day, second month, 1423.

32   *Kanmon nikki* (Hanawa 1958), entry for 26th day, 10th month, and 1st day, 11th month, 1418, and 12th day, 9th month, 1419.

33   *Kanmon nikki* (Hanawa 1958), entry for 1st day, 2nd month, 1425.

34   *Kanmon nikki* (Hanawa 1958), entry for 23rd day, intercalary 10th month, 1422.

35   *Kanmon nikki* (Hanawa 1958), entry for 16th day, 2nd month, 1420.

36   *Kanmon nikki* (Hanawa 1958), entries for 11th day, 11th month, 1417, 22nd day, fifth month, 1421.

37   *Sanetaka kōki* (Hanawa 1958), entry for 28th day, first month, 1509.

38   *Sanetaka kōki* (Hanawa 1958), entries for sixth and seventh days, 11th month, 1505.

39   *Kanmon nikki* (Hanawa 1958), entry for 15th day, second month, 1425.

40   *Kanmon nikki* (Hanawa 1958), entry for 15th day, 11th month, 1395.

41   *Kanmon nikki* (Hanawa 1958), entries for 20th day, seveth month, and 27th day, ninth month of 1416; fifth day, fifth month, 1417; and 13th and 16th days, fifth month, 1421.

42   *Kanmon nikki* (Hanawa 1958), entry for 25th day, tenth month, 1417.

43   *Kanmon nikki* (Hanawa 1958), entries for fourth day, fifth month, 1422; and third day, fifth month, 1425.

44   Yōshū fu-shi (old name for Yamashiro Province) (*Yōshū fu-shi* 1984–89).

45   Research is beginning to appear on the state of nuns in the medieval period. See for example Ushiyama (1989).

46   Yasaka (1994), Part II, no 2128, dated fifth day, 12th month, fourth year of Eiwa (1375–78, so fourth year should be 1378, but would have been 1379 in Gregorian calendar), and a draft of an order for renting land to build on (*chishi*).

47   *Dai Nihon shiryō* (1968–:v2), So, 1-61, 24th day, 12th month, 1395 (Ōei 2), guarantee for a mud-wall storehouse in Hari-kōji.

48   The documents of the Akuta family of iron casters (*imono-shi*) in Harima show that they established monopolies in local markets, and among the goods they sold there were many pots and pans (Wakita 1990a; Wakita Osamu 1985).

49   In documents (*fuhikitsuke*) relating to the *bakufu* courts, we find many cases of actions filed by women merchants (Kuwayama 1980).

50   'Fuhikitsuke' for 18th day, fourth month, 1547 (Kuwayama 1980).

51   'Shake kiroku' (Yasaka 1978), entry for 29th day, third month, 1350; 13th day, fourth month.

52   'Dōshi shutsusen no nikki' and 'yorozu no kiroku' (Shimamoto-chō-shi 1976).

53   Based on my fieldwork at the festival at the Wakide no miya kagura-za (*nyōbō-za*). See also Kyoto-furitsu Yamashiro Kyōdo Shiryōkan (1984).

54   *Kanmon nikki* (Hanawa 1958), entry for tenth day, 12th month, 1425.

55   *Kanmon nikki* (Hanawa 1958), entry for ninth day, 12th month, 1423.

56   In the *Shichijūichiban shokunin utaawase* there is a poem about this *kusemai-guruma*: On the float, 'Kuruma ni te, kami uchifuruu, maihime kakaru, koisu to hito wa, shiriki ya' (Iwasaki et al 1993).

57   *Yasutomi-ki* (Nakahara 1965), entry for first day, tenth month, 1423.

58   *Daijōin jisha zatsujiki* (1968), entry for fifth day, eighth month, 1471.

59   *Mineai-ki* (Hanawa 1982:part 1).

60   *Kanmon nikki* (Hanawa 1958), entry for ninth day, ninth month, 1416, and eighth and ninth days, ninth month, 1417, and 14th day, fourth month, 1417, and tenth day, ninth month, 1419.

61   *Kanmon nikki* (Hanawa 1958), entry for ninth day, eighth month, 1416.

62   *Oyudono no ue no nikki* (Hanawa 1958), , entry for 12th day, first month, 1477.

63   *Kamakura ibun*, no 799 (Takeuchi 1971–89), 'Shinpukuji Hon'wa myōsho ura monjo', dated 25th day, fourth month, 1256; and Buraku Mondai Kenkyū-jo 1988a. See also Chapter three, and Wakita (1985).

64   *Azuma Kagami* (1968), entry for 29th day, tenth month, 1190.

65   'Tōji Hōbodai-in monjo', 23rd day, seventh month, 1249, *Kantō gechi-jō*, in Buraku Mondai Kenkyū-jo (1988b).

Court ladies and the emperor, as seen in the Oyudono no ue diaries

Towards the end of the first month of the year, on the first day of the mouse (*ne no hi*), a palace banquet for the nobles was held in the palace. This picture shows the scene after the poems presented to the Emperor have been read out. The Emperor's face can be glimpsed above the folding screen at the front. The seated lady in the middle is a *baizen no suke* (senior court lady who served food), attending to the Emperor's needs, formally dressed in splendid 12-layer robes. The nobles are all seated together on an enclosed dais; and in the top right, the ladies are bringing out more food.

From the *Nenchū gyōji emaki* scroll (possession of the Tanaka family)

Introduction

When the Portugese missionary Luis Frois wrote in the 16th century about differences between Japan and the West, he remarked on the widespread literacy in Japan and that upper class women's rank depended on their ability to write (Matsuda & Jorissen 1983).

The central material for this chapter is the communal diary of several generations of court women.[1] This diary, called the *Oyudono no ue no nikki*, was written continuously by the women who directly served the emperor, using *nyōbō kotoba*, the special women's language of the court. The fact that the official diary of the imperial household was written by women, in *kana* mixed with *kanji*, challenges the idea that official records were written by men in Chinese and surely is most unusual for anywhere in the world.

Several extant *nikki*—daily records of events, not edited accounts—remain as official documents of public institutions. They include the Heian period *Denjō nikki*, written by male courtiers (*kurōdo*) of the sixth rank as a record of their duties, and the *Geki nikki*, a diary written by the secretariat to the chief minister of state (*dajōkan*). Both were gradually discontinued towards the end of the Heian period. It has been suggested that this was because they overlapped with the private diaries of high-ranking courtiers (Hashimoto 1976). After the demise of these male official diaries, women courtiers' official diaries came into existence, and it is interesting to note that they continued right through to the 19th century.

This chapter explores why these official records written by women have come down to us, and what they tell us about the roles of women at court, their subjectivity and their life strategies.

Chapter one showed how court women's literature occupied the mainstream of Japanese classical literature. Shimizu argues that it was the private nature of Heian women's diaries, which are characterised by not being dated, which led to their literary achievements (Shimizu 1966). Matsumoto states that in the medieval period, women's diary-writing took on the public character of record-taking and lacked the depth of self-reflection of the earlier period, reflecting the change in the position of women at court (Matsumoto 1983).

The *Oyudono no ue no nikki* is an extreme example of this change, as the entries throughout offer nothing but business and work-related records, showing absolutely no trace of literary quality or subjectivity. As noblemen's diaries became private diaries kept for the sake of their *ie*, women's diaries became official records written in *kana*.

It is necessary to question the validity of the set schemata of *kanbun*–men–official versus *kana*–women–private before talking about its apparent reversal. Consider, for example, that after the Tentoku court poetry competition in 960, *waka* became part of official court events; also that Lady Murasaki Shikibu's diary (circa 1008–10) was written in large part in order to eulogise the glory and prosperity of Fujiwara Michinaga's house: it is then more realistic to conceive that Japanese writing had already acquired a place in the official world of *kanbun*, rather than seeing it as the reversal of a previous order. In the medieval period, this led first to an intermingling of public and private, and then to the prioritisation of the private. The existence of the *Oyudono no ue no nikki* and the role of the women who wrote it not only shows that women had an important function, but also points to a key feature of a medieval society in which the *ie* had become the basic social unit.

The *Oyudono no ue no nikki* can be called the housekeeping diary of the emperor's private household. The reason why it acquired an official character was rooted in the special nature of the imperial household, whose private matters took on universal significance. Another reason is the specifically medieval characteristic that political structures became fused with the ruler's power over his own private *ie*. This applied also to the relation between the *bakufu* and the *shōgun*, as we saw in Chapter two.

The *Oyudono no ue no nikki* records are extant from 1477 to 1826, leaving a large gap in the earlier medieval era. What do we know about official documents written by women earlier than this?

In the early to mid-Heian period there was the *Ōkisaki no nikki* (*Dowager empress diary*); in the early Heian period the *naishi no sen* documents bear witness to the authority of the *naishi* at court; and the *nyōbō hōsho* go back to the early Kamakura period (Gomi 1990) — all suggesting that it is not unreasonable to assume that women's court diaries existed from the Heian period.

Abe has pointed out that in the *Ben no naishi nikki* entry for the 19th day, first month, 1247, the words, 'At the time of the *Ōdairi*, three volumes of diary were entrusted to *Chūnagon no sukedono*', show that in the early Kamakura period something akin to a diary by women courtiers existed. The same entry says there was a meeting with the alternative *sesshō* (regent) and the *shōshō no naishi* wrote down all the names of the attendees in the margin of 'the upper notebook (*kami no sōshi*)'. Was this 'upper notebook' perhaps not similar to the *Oyudono no ue no nikki*?

It is remarkable that as the official diaries written by male courtiers disappeared, the only official records that continued to be written for the imperial household were the women's diaries. In the Kamakura period, daily records were kept by officials and court scribes, but these were the diaries of individuals in houses whose official posts were hereditary; they were not shared communal diaries, which recorded the daily minutiae of the job, written by rostered personnel, as was the *Oyudono no ue no nikki*. Even if other work-related diaries existed, they may not have survived because they did not belong to an *ie*.

The *Oyudono no ue no nikki* was written in women's language—*nyōbō kotoba*; therefore, it has been researched extensively by historical linguists as a linguistic resource (Kunida 1964; 1977; Inokuchi & Horii 1974; Matsui 1968; Odaka 1985). It has not, however, been treated for its value as a record of women's lives and as women's diary literature. Historians have quoted from parts of it for its value in providing historical realities but have not dealt with it systematically. Only Koresawa has considered basic aspects of its character as a diary (Koresawa 1944; 1951; 1952; 1957–59; Oyudono no ue no nikki Kenkyū-kai 1973), and I would like to acknowledge my indebtedness to his work. From the perspective of women's history, Jugaku and Matsui's work is significant (Jugaku 1982; Matsui 1979). I, too, will analyse the diary from this perspective.

When I first read this diary I viewed its special women's language negatively, as a form of linguistic discrimination in contrast with men's language—influenced as I was by the then-current view that any distinction was discrimination and that equality of the sexes meant that women had to be the same as men. Of course, there is an element of discrimination in *nyōbō kotoba*, but it is also true that the phenomenon cannot be fully understood on that basis. *Nyōbō kotoba* is, above all, a form of self-expression for women, as well as being the result of oppression. Jugaku argues that it is full of self-respect and pride. It certainly asserts a dignified sense of existence. When we consider the related 'palace language' (*gosho kotoba*), which was used by male courtiers, we cannot view women's language merely as a form of discrimination, but neither can we say categorically that there was no discrimination in the circumstances of the court women. I explore this complexity in the following pages.

Since I am neither a linguist nor a literary specialist, I am being ambitious. However, I hope to explain to some degree the background to Japan's particular women's language— *nyōbō kotoba*.

Overview of the Oyudono no ue no nikki

The writers of the diary

The *oyudono no ue* (literally 'above the bathroom') was a room in the imperial palace, close to both the emperor's quarters and the bathroom. It was the quarters of the women who attended to the emperor's bathing needs; hence, it was the chamber of the court ladies (*suke* and *naishi*) who waited on and served the emperor. It was sometimes simply called the *oyudono* (Koresawa 1951).

The *Oyudono no ue no nikki* was the daily record written by the women who resided in these quarters and who were on duty for that day. Koresawa made a thorough study of the various women in this category of diary contributors[2] There was the group loosely called *suke*, including *jōrō no tsubone, dainagon no suke no tsubone* (also called *ōsumoji*), *gon no dainagon suke no tsubone* (also called *gon no ōsumoji*) and *shin dainagon no suke no tsubone*. Another group, lower in rank, were the *naishi* (or *naishi no jō*). We know from a part of the diary written in the hand of Dowager Empress Mibu that the emperor's natural mother was included in this group (Koresawa 1954). The *kōtō no naishi*, as the most senior of the *naishi*, had her own official diary to keep (Koresawa 1944) and would not have contributed to the *Oyudono no ue no nikki*. Koresawa's detailed research has made it clear that occasionally the emperor's own hand can be detected in the diary, giving rise to the theory that the emperor originally used *nyōbō kotoba* when writing; however, even if the emperor contributed on odd occasions, it was in principle the writing of the court women.

As noted, during the Muromachi and Warring States periods it was not possible to set up a household for an empress; neither could the women's position of *naishi no kami* be sustained—this left only *naishi no suke* and *naishi no jō*. The reason that it was not possible to have an establishment for an empress is not completely clear, but certainly financial reasons were important, since for many years it was impossible to afford the enthronement and abdication ceremonies. Perhaps it was also for political reasons, because of the relationship with the Ashikaga *shōgun* family, which was more highly ranked than the Fujiwara family. At any rate, there was no empress for 300 years—from the time of Emperor Godaigo (1288–1339; reigned 1318–39) until the time of Emperor Gomino-o (1596–1680; reigned 1611–1629), who set up Tokugawa Kazuko as his empress. The situation in families of the princely households was the same. In the Fushiminomiya household, as far as we can tell from the *Kanmon nikki*, Prince Sadafusa referred to the court women as 'servants' (*shijo*), though they were de facto wives.

Nyōbo kotoba — women's language

The *Oyudono no ue no nikki* was written in *nyōbō kotoba*, the language used by the high-ranking court women and also by equivalent women who served in the princely families, other noble families and imperial nunneries. It was not simply a jargon or private language used by groups of women—the official nature of the *Oyudono no ue no nikki* shows that it can be considered the official language of the court's women officers. In the long historical development of Japanese court life since the ancient period, it can also be called the professional language of the court ladies, which was cultivated in the women's quarters.[3]

Today, discussions of *nyōbō kotoba* focus on the Muromachi period, because the language of the *Oyudono no ue no nikki* forms the standard by which it is understood, but in fact much of this language dates further back to the previous era. The Kamakura shogunal household had active contact and even intermarriage with noble court families. At times, a *shōgun* was appointed from the Fujiwara Sekke (regent) family and became the Sekke *shōgun*, and at other times an imperial prince was appointed as *shōgun* (the 'prince *shōgun*'); hence, the shogunal court absorbed a strong influence from imperial court culture, including *nyōbō kotoba*. The Ashikaga *shōgun* family (Muromachi period) took as official wives women from the aristocratic Hino family, leading to a vigorous exchange between the women of the imperial palace and those of the shogunal palace,[4] so that the culture and fashions of the latter came to be based on those of the former. It is natural to assume that *nyōbō kotoba* was used in both contexts equally; and, indeed, the *nyōbō bumi* (women's documents) of the Ashikaga *shōguns* were written exclusively in *nyōbō kotoba*.[5] No doubt *nyōbō kotoba* was used even in the ladies quarters (*ō-oku*) of the Tokugawa shogunate (1603–1867), since the official wife of the *shōgun* was often chosen from the Fujiwara (regent) and similar families.[6] Furthermore, *nyōbō kotoba* became more popular and began to influence the speech of upper-class women, forming the foundation of contemporary women's speech. I personally remember that many women born in the Meiji period (1868–1911) used a variety of speech called *moji kotoba*, where *sushi*, for example, was called *osumoji*. For better or worse, *nyōbō kotoba* set the tone for women's speech, which, in turn, set the tone for women's culture.

The high status accorded to women's literature in Japan must be due in large part to the existence of a strong women's language. A careful study of this language is crucial for women's history and, in the case of these diaries, will not only reveal the nature of the duties of the women court officials but also, by extension, will contribute to our understanding of the lived experience of all Japanese women, since women's language was influenced by *nyōbō kotoba*. Such a task cannot be carried out by historical investigation alone, but needs the help of linguistics, and I look forward to such research being done. However, here I rely on existing research to outline the structure of *nyōbō kotoba*.

There is a vast body of nouns relating to food and drink, clothing, cooking implements, uncleanness and fire. Another body of vocabulary relates to personnel, human relations and annual ceremonies. Then there is a separate vocabulary of modifying words (verbs, adjectives and adverbs) to denote actions and states.

Table 1: Example of nyōbō kotoba

Category	Normal Japanese and meaning	Nyōbō kotoba
nouns referring to food	sake (rice wine)	kukon, sasa, yamabuki
and drink, clothing,	obi (sash)	omiobi
cooking implements,	nabe, kama (pan)	kuromono
uncleanness and fire	(uncleanness)	sashiai
	(fire)	akagoto
personnel, human relations	nagon (rank)	namoji
and annual ceremonies	haha (mother)	kaka, fukuro
	(tenth month Inoko	otsukutsuku no oiwai
	celebration)	
modifying words to denote	naku (weep)	mutsukaru
actions and states	okiru (get up)	ohirunaru
	sukimanaku	onhishihishi to
	(continuously)	
	todokōrinaku	onsurusuru to

A key feature is the tendency to use euphemistic terms to express things that are vulgar or not nice. This was the case also with language used by male aristocrats, and still characterises Kyoto speech today.

Jugaku argues that *nyōbō kotoba* was the language of a clearly defined world of the court, enabling it to remain unmoved regardless of what happened in the outside world. She says it cannot be seen as a secret language (like that of the *yakuza* underworld) because, rather than having a defensive function, it was redolent of a sense of superiority. Although it might at times have been derided as quaint, there was a pride felt in being able to use it; because of its association with the power and authority of the court women (Jugaku 1982), it conveyed a strong sense of upward social mobility. Upper-class customs were rapidly disseminated throughout Japanese society, and the influence of this language eventually permeated all classes of women.

Women's diaries: lineage and types

Diaries written by women courtiers and other aristocratic women exist in great number from the Heian period right through to the Meiji period, probably including many that have not yet been made public.

Among the oldest is the partially preserved *Ōkisaki nikki*. This diary of Empress Onshi, the consort of Emperor Daigo (885–930), survives in a Chinese version (*manabon*) and a *kana* version, with some believing that the latter is in her own hand, although it may have been written by her women attendants (*shijo*) (Tokoro 1978). Either way, it shows conclusively that from the early 10th century, women's diaries were being written in the court, and that these were no doubt the forerunners of subsequent women's diaries.

The extant portions of the *Oyudono no ue no nikki* cover the period from 1477 to 1826, but it is uncertain whether such a diary by women serving at court was kept in the preceding six centuries. Analogous diaries are *Sendō Oyudono no ue no nikki* (for retired emperors), *Nyōin Oyudono no ue no nikki* (for dowager empresses) and *Tōgū Oyudono no ue no nikki* (for a prince), all of which are based on the conventions of the court. Princess Seikan-in no miya left a diary in her own hand, and one of her *jijo*, Niwata Tsuguko, also wrote a diary called *Seikan-in no miya osoba nikki* (1847–77), which can be viewed in a similar way. Even in the women's quarters in the modern period (since Meiji), the head of the *suke* wrote an official women courtiers' diary, and middle-ranking court women (*myōbu*) kept records of storeroom holdings in which concubines recorded *oaisomono* (gifts given and received by the emperor).[7] In the period covered by the *Oyudono no ue no nikki*, *kōtō no naishi* apparently also kept separate diaries, which were records of their official business, although the nature of their work differed, as discussed below.

The personal diary of imperial Princess Kazunomiya (1846–1877), *Seikan-in no miya no-nikki*, is extant for the period January 1868 to December 1873. It seems that a diary is preserved in the Mitsui family and was written by a young lady from the Maeda *daimyō* clan who married into the family.[8] It is highly likely that the aristocratic custom of women's diaries extended to women in the warrior class. In the Edo period, there are many travel diaries written by women in Confucian scholar families, and also in the commoner class,[9] which shows us that the custom of diary writing was truly widespread throughout all levels of society.

Literary diaries are of two types. The first records, fairly faithfully and in a celebratory way, events at court, such as nuptials and Buddhist and other ceremonies, and makes them elegant works of literary interest from the perspective of court attendants about their overlords. A prime example is *Murasaki Shikibu nikki* (extant for the years 1008–10), and probably also *Sanuki no suke nikki* (by Fujiwara Chōshi; 1108–09) and *Ben no naishi nikki*. The latter records dates in detail, giving a strong impression of being an accurate record, but it also has a highly personal flavour with its use of *waka* poems to express the writer's own feelings about events. This places it between the *Oyudono no ue no nikki* and the personal diaries. The second type of literary diary is represented by *Kagerō nikki*, which creatively uses the writer's personal experience as a vehicle for her literary talent. Other examples of this type include *Izumi Shikibu nikki* (1007?) and *Towazu-gatari* (1313–24).

All these types of diaries can be found in men's writing also, with the exception of the last-mentioned, the personal literary diary. The main difference is that men wrote in Chinese (*kanbun*), whereas women wrote in *kana* with a few *kanji*, using *nyōbō kotoba*. This suggests that the literary diaries of Heian court women are a significant feature of Japanese women's writing and history. (The *Tosa nikki*, written by the male courtier Ki no Tsurayuki using a female persona, is an exception and is discussed in the introductory chapter.) So, by the Kamakura period, there was a narrowing of the gender gap, at least in regard to diary writing, and men's diaries were written in Japanese *kana*, sometimes using a female persona as narrator.[10] Women's diaries in this period, however, tend to be of the work-related, record-keeping type. If this is so, in order to discern the characteristics of medieval women, we need to ask why women's literary diaries emerged in the Heian period—a golden age of women's literature in Japan, yet a time when the authority of court women was not obvious in comparison with the Kamakura and Muromachi periods. The *naishi no sen* documents had died out, and *nyōbō hōsho* had not yet appeared, so it was a low period for women's power. Perhaps women turned to literature as an outlet for their energies and creativity because their authority was weak, or perhaps their literary output demonstrates that their authority was, in fact, strong. This is an issue that requires further consideration.

At any rate, my point is that women wrote the same non-literary type of diary as men. There exists a large number of women's diaries, both official and private, some written by attendants, some by rulers. This is surely a symptom of women having lived lives full of tension, which could only find an outlet in writing diaries. This perspective was not recognised until the broader development of women's history.

In the following pages, I examine the *Oyudono no ue no nikki*, exploring its official character, what it tells us about the differences between men and women, and the position of the women who made the entries.

The character of the Oyudono no ue no nikki

Naishi formed the largest group of the 12 offices of female courtiers in the *ritsuryō* system. They waited on the emperor, performed the administrative tasks of writing petitions and decrees, and were in charge of the daily running of the inner palace. According to the *Kinpishō*, a manual of protocol issued by Emperor Juntoku around 1220 (*Kinpishō* 1983), already by the Kamakura period 'there are no *naishi* in the *naishi-dokoro*' — the *naishi-dokoro* being the quarters of the *naishi* in attendance; by this time *naishi* worked from the general women's quarters. Later still, in the Muromachi–Warring States periods, there was no *naishi no kami*, and one of the *naishi no suke* had become the head of the women officials, running the court together with the *naishi*, who were next in rank. These women were really divided into two groups: those on whom the emperor bestowed his favours, and the others. The appointment of a *naishi* to the senior position of *kōtō no naishi* is as prescribed in the *Kinpishō*—in order of seniority—but in the Warring States period it was a direct appointment by the emperor.[11] By the Edo period, it is legendary that such positions were available for purchase (Shimohashi 1979).

Chapter three examined the role of the *kōtō no naishi*, especially their issuing of *nyōbō hōsho*, using the information afforded by the diary of Yamashina Tokitsugu. These documents differed in character from the *rinji* issued by male courtiers, and by the 15th century women's documents had assumed major importance in the court because they directly expressed the emperor's will. This section establishes the position of the *Oyudono no ue* diary in the court.

The primary function of the *Oyudono no ue no nikki* was as a record of the emperor's closest aides and of their household administration. In the Edo period, imperial household internal matters were run by the *Ōsumoji* (*dainagon no suke no tsubone*) and external matters by the *kōtō no naishi* (Shimohashi 1979). The *Oyudono no ue no nikki* shows that the same kind of division of labour applied in the Warring States era. Since a separate diary was kept by the *kōtō no naishi*, this means that the *Oyudono no ue no nikki* was a record of the internal affairs of the court by the *Ōsumoji*, pertaining solely to the emperor's personal affairs. On the occasion of the 13th memorial service for Karakumon-in in 1500, only a list of those who attended is recorded in the *Oyudono no ue no nikki*[12] (this is similar to the already-mentioned *Ben no naishi nikki*, which recorded those present in the 'upper diary'). The most important function of the diary was to record the work done by those serving at court. The expenses incurred for the Buddhist ceremony in this case were probably recorded in the *kōtō no naishi*'s diary (which we do not have). Matters relating directly to outsiders do not appear at all in the *Oyudono no ue no nikki* and this helps to define the nature of this diary.

A major feature of the diary is that there is no mention of the issuing of *rinji* or even of *nyōbō hōsho*—which were written by *kōtō no naishi*, as well as occasionally by the *suke* class of women. The absence of such records indicates clearly that the task of issuing *rinji* and *nyōbō hōsho* was outside the jurisdiction of the writers of the *Oyudono no ue no nikki*. In other words, such tasks were to do with public relations and formed a different category of work.

For example, on the 23rd day of the eighth month, 1473, *Shōgun* Ashikaga Yoshimasa (1436–93; reigned 1449–73) presented a petition (*shissō*) to have a *rinji* issued authorising an attack (hunt down and kill) on Hatakeyama Yoshinari (?–1493).[13] However, in the *Oyudono no ue no nikki* entry for the 22nd day the only items recorded are the return of the *Eiga Monogatari*,[14] which had been borrowed from Yoshimasa, and the *Ōkagami*,[15] which had been borrowed from the *shōgun*'s wife, Hino no Tomiko. On the 23rd, the day on which the *rinji* was issued, it was noted that the *daimyō* Takeda had presented an offering of the first geese of the season from his domain. This does not reflect the personal interests of the women, but the area of their jurisdiction.

A second example is the case recorded in Emperor Gonara's journal *Gonara Tennō Shin-ki*, entry for 20th day, ninth month, 1536, concerning Tōdaiji temple's application for permission to carry out a fundraising campaign for repairs to Hachimangū. This case shows the difference between *rinji* and *nyōbō hōsho*. The diary quotes both the *rinji* and the *nyōbō hōsho*, and sometimes even quotes the draft documents. Another entry in the emperor's journal for the 19th day, tenth month, in the same year, records that a *nyōbō hōsho* was issued concerning the Kamo Jinja shrine. However, none of these issues are alluded to in the *Oyudono no ue no nikki*. What is more, fixed types or amounts of payment would have been required from those in whose interest *rinji* or *nyōbō hōsho* were issued, but the *Oyudono no ue no nikki* does not mention anything of this nature.

Similarly, there is no mention in the *Oyudono no ue no nikki* of incidents that required the active involvement of the court women and the issuing of a *nyōbō hōsho* for their settlement. This can be seen by referring again to the fishmongers dispute of 1545, detailed in Chapter three. The royal supplier of fish was under the jurisdiction of the Yamashina family. When they won the case, the fishmongers lined up in front of the quarters of the *kōtō no naishi* and presented lavish gifts not only to Tokitsugu but also to the *dainagon no suke no tsubone* and the *kōtō no naishi*—this shows that the input of the women was substantial. However, there are no entries about this in the *Oyudono no ue no nikki* for this period, nor even a mention of any portion of the gifts being offered to the emperor.

Such examples demonstrate conclusively that work relating to public relations and the issuing of *rinji* and *nyōbō hōsho* from the emperor had no place in the *Oyudono no ue no nikki*. We can conclude that the Edo era arrangement of *dainagon no suke no tsubone* handling intimate personal affairs of the emperor and of *kōtō no naishi* handling public relations holds also for the medieval period, which explains why the work of the *kōtō no naishi* was not set down in the *Oyudono no ue no nikki*. However, the fact that *rinji* and *nyōbō hōsho* are recorded in Emperor Gonara's journal demonstrates that a chain of administrative responsibility existed from the emperor to the *kōtō no naishi* to the *kurōdo*.[16] Such administrative and clerical matters were presumably recorded in a journal kept by the *kōtō no naishi*. Such a clear demarcation of tasks confirms that the *Oyudono no ue no nikki* was a list of the responsibilities of the *dainagon no suke no tsubone* and, as such, was the daily record of routine domestic matters by the women who attended the emperor, at the same time as being the official record of the emperor's personal life.

The following summarises the type of items recorded in the *Oyudono no ue no nikki*.

• Gifts to the emperor, both public and private

• Tribute (income in kind from estates): if large, the amount is specified

• Names of the men and women on duty at court (including night duty)

• Annual events and ceremonies: exorcisms, incantations, visits to shrines and temples (performed by court women on behalf of the emperor), offerings and donations to temples

• Gatherings featuring *waka*, *renga*, explication of sutras, *gagaku*, other performances

• Appreciations of sake, food etc.

Gifts included souvenirs (*miyage*) from people who paid visits to court, articles presented in gratitude for promotion or bestowing of titles, thanks for a successful lawsuit after a dispute, seasonal greetings and first things of the season. These items are recorded in great detail and form the core of the diary, since there was the need to reciprocate with a certain portion of the value. For example, there are many gifts received from the *shōgun's* household: that is, from Ashikaga Yoshimasa and his wife Tomiko, and the next *shōgun*, Yoshihisa. However, in the case of Tomiko, it is impossible to say whether

Table 2: Examples of gifts received in the imperial household in 1482

Place	Giver	Gift	Date
Nagahashi	Ushikai	1 basket of melon (there were a large number of other things presented from the *nagahashi*)	22nd day, 7th month
Sue	Takeda	2 kinds of shells, seaweed	29th day, 7th month
Sue	Takeda	goose	21st day, 8th month
Sue	Takeda	cod	16th day, 10th month

these were personal gifts or tribute from the estates over which she had the rights as representative of the imperial family.[17] Similarly, there are many gifts such as souvenirs from courtiers. There must, for example, have been many goods that were tribute from the jurisdictions of Kura no kami, belonging to the Yamashina family, but there is no mention of this. Perhaps they went straight to the *kōtō no naishi*, whereas the *Oyudono no ue no nikki* records only concerned personal gifts. This disctinction is difficult to make with certainty.

However, the diary records partially the tribute goods from the emperor's estates. Presumably income of this kind, which went towards defraying the emperor's private domestic expenses, was handled by the *dainagon no suke no tsubone*, and thus was recorded in the *Oyudono no ue no nikki*. This included gifts distributed to the women, of which Yoshino has made a detailed table (Yoshino 1982), but it does not show everything received from the land over which the women had jurisdiction. In *Daijō-in jisha zatsujiki*, for the 20th day, second month, 1480, it says that because tribute had not been presented by the Kurima no shō of the imperial domain in Ise Province there was some hardship experienced by the women courtiers, which suggests without a doubt that their income included a large part of the tribute allotted to them from the emperor's holdings.

There were many reception points in the imperial household for gifts received. There are records of what was presented directly to the *Oyudono no ue* quarters and of items that were first presented from the *nagahashi* (*kōtō no naishi's* quarters), and yet others from the scullery (*sue*, the low status women's room in the palace). Examples are shown in Table 2.

Therefore, it seems that for financial purposes the *oyudono* was seen quite separately from the *nagahashi* and the *sue*. The *kōtō no naishi* kept a separate record of income and expenditure for matters that she dealt with, which concerned the imperial annual events and ceremonies. The money for these activities was probably disbursed directly to the *kōtō no naishi*. There may also have been a separate journal for the scullery, like the *Storeroom Diary* (*onando nikki*) that was kept in the *shōgun's* family in the Edo period. This can be surmised because one woman, with the title *Iyo*, the head of the middle-ranking court women, had a large number of responsibilities and would have handled a lot of expenses.

Looking only at the financial aspect of this task, an example can be seen in the second day, second month, 1481, when there was a 13-item program of *sarugaku* in the palace. The *Oyudono no ue no nikki* records that various courtiers contributed money and summoned a *te-sarugaku* (not one of the officially patronised troupes) performer, Shibuya. Yamashina Tokitsugu was in charge of payment, and had to get 200 *hiki* of the total cost of 800 *hiki* from the *kōtō no naishi*, and the remaining 600 *hiki* from Hirohashi.[18] It is not clear how much Hirohashi and the *kōtō no naishi* paid personally. However, since both male and female courtiers contributed money, possibly each simply collected from their respective groups.

As for the expenses of the imperial household itself, the drama of the end-of-year cleaning of the imperial palace for 1481 has already been discussed. The cleaning was to be done by guards called *eji*, who requested a fee of 100 *hiki*. Tokitsugu intervened and made it 50 *hiki*, but the *kōtō no naishi* cut it down further to 30 *hiki*.[19] However, the *Oyudono no ue no nikki* only notes that 'Today the exterior cleaning took place'.[20]

Table 3: Structure of the imperial household in the late Muromachi and Warring States periods

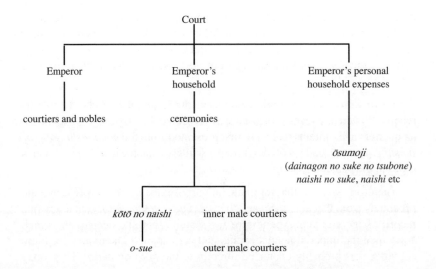

The above tells that there was a separation between the finances handled by the *kōtō no naishi* relating to the court as a whole and the personal expenses relating to the emperor. It is not clear which part of annual tribute from estates went to the *nagahashi no tsubone* and which to the *oyudono no ue*.

The structure of the court in the late Muromachi and Warring States periods, as seen in the *Oyudono no ue no nikki*, can be summarised in Table 3.

The life of women at court: service and reward

The public duties of the *kōtō no naishi* do not appear much in the *Oyudono no ue no nikki*. Only the aspects of her direct attendance on the emperor are recorded, as for the *naishi no suke*. The records in the diary focus, above all, on the personal needs of the emperor, such as meals, bathing and grooming, and letter-writing, and on recording gifts given and received. There is an absence of a grammatical subject in the entries because everything refers to the emperor and revolves around him.

The prime task of the women was to look after the emperor's basic needs of shelter, food and clothing. Serving the emperor's meals was called *gobaizen* and seems to have been done only by the *naishi no suke*. On New Year's Day, 'Gobaizen, as every year, was brought by the ōsumoji',[21] which indicates that this task always went to the *dainagon no suke no tsubone* at New Year, whereas it was normally the daily task of the *naishi no suke*. This can be confirmed by an entry concerning the concubine of Emperor Gotsuchimikado, Higashi no Onkata (Kazan-in Kenshi, the mother of cloistered Prince Enman-in Jingo): 'Lady Higashi is of *jōrō* rank (upper class of courtier). She should not be asked to serve the emperor's meal, so the *densō* was asked.' Even though Higashi no Onkata was a *gon no suke*, not an *ōsumoji* (*suke*), she was a special concubine of the emperor who had borne him princes and princesses and so she seems to have received special privileges.

It appears that meals were not served by menstruating women: 'The *jōrō* for the day refrained from serving the meal. She came in (or served) at the beginning, but did not serve the dinner. She took part in [illegible] after the banquet.'[22] This might have been because it was the New Year celebration. What is worth noting is that menstruating women were not required to leave the palace altogether.

Of course, women, probably *naishi no suke*, served the emperor's sake. On occasion they also served sake to courtiers in different rooms, according to their rank. For example, it was customary for Ichijō Sadaishō (Fuyura 1464–1514) to be served sake ceremonially (twice the three-cup routine) in an 'unglazed cup' by *jōrō* or *ōsumoji* in the conference room. People of lesser rank were served sake in the *sue* scullery: for example, the lower court musician Tominaka was received in the 'third room', and afterward was served sake in the men's scullery by the *kōtō no naishi*. Even someone of high rank, if dressed informally, was entertained by the women in the lower rooms. These conventions were prescribed in great detail.

The *nyōbō* mixed with courtiers in functions such as banquets and poetry parties on an equal basis, including drinking practices such as 'ten rounds' (*jūdo nomi*). It is amazing to note how much the women drank. They were adept at poetry too. In one *waka* party held by Emperor Gotsuchimikado, a *kōtō no naishi* called Yotsutsuji no Shunshi was given the same points as the emperor by the referee, Asukai Nyūdō (Masachika, 1417–93), which was such an embarrassing honour for her that she playfully presented the emperor with a barrel of sake as a consolation prize.[23] Especially in the Heian period, and still in the Kamakura period, there were many women at court who could play *gagaku* instruments proficiently, but in the *Oyudono no ue no nikki* of the 15th century such skills are not apparent.

The diary records in detail the service of washing and bathing the emperor—both *oyukake* (washing outside the tub, pouring on water) and *oyu suru* (getting into the bathtub)—and washing his hair, which was done by *naishi no suke* rank women. Dressing the emperor's hair (*okezuri, okushi*) was sometimes done by *naishi no suke* or by *kōtō no naishi*, but mostly it was the task of *naka no naishi* and *shin naishi* (see Table 4). This shows that bathing the emperor was considered a very important service and was only permitted to the *suke*. This accounts for the name of this *oyudono no ue* office and its diary *Oyudono no ue no nikki*, literally *Diary of the bathroom*.

Incidentally, the bathing and hairdressing is recorded as taking place on average only about twice a month, although it is possible that on some occasions the record was not made.

The *dainagon no suke no tsubone* had the secretarial function of writing letters for the emperor. The *kōtō no naishi* was thus not the only one who wrote *nyōbō hōsho*, although hers were more likely to have an official character. The *rinji* were, of course, the official documents from the emperor, and the *kōtō no naishi's* documents were mainly personal, but they had more official status as conveying the emperor's will in comparison with the letters written by the *dainagon no suke no tsubone*, which revealed the more intimate feelings of the emperor. For example, in the case of a fire in 1477, Hino no Tomiko arranged for the imperial household to move temporarily to the residence of her mother, Hino Naeko. A special guestroom was made available for the

Table 4: Service register for the oyudono for 1483 (15th year of Bunmei era)

Month-day	Duty	Person entrusted with the task
1-12	Oyudono e, okezuri	Ōsumoji, Shin-ōsumoji
2-2	Okezuri, okushi	Shin-naishi
2-18	Okezuri, oyu mo mesu	Ōsumoji
3-2	Okezuri	Naka-naishi
3-16	Oyu mesu	Jōrō
3-17	Okezuri, okushi	Naka-naishi
5-5	Oyu mesu	(no name)
5-6	Okezuri, okushi	Naka-naishi
5-24	Okezuri, okushi	Naka-naishi
6-30	Oyu mesu, on-sata	Jōrō, Ōsumoji
7-10	Okezuri, okushi	Naka-naishi
7-24	Okezuri, okushi	Naka-naishi
8-28	Okezuri, okushi	Shin-naishi
9-12	Okezuri, okushi	Shin-naishi
9-30	Oyu mesu	Ōsumoji
10-26	Okezuri, okushi	Kōtō no naishi
10-29	Oyu mesu	Naka-naishi
11-14	Okezuri, okushi	Shin-naishi
11-29	Okezuri, okushi	Naka-naishi
12-13	Okushiage	Jōrō
12-16	Okezuri, okushi	Shin-naishi
12-24	Oyu mesu	Meme sumoji

Key:

Oyudono e	going to the bath
Okezuri	dressing the hair
Okushi	doing the hair
Oyu mesu	bathing

emperor and princes Ichinomiya and Ninomiya. A letter of thanks to Tomiko was written by a *dainagon no suke no tsubone*. Before that, in the same year (27th day, fourth month), a *sukedono* (which *suke* is not specified) wrote a thank-you letter to Tomiko and her son Yoshihisa for visiting the imperial palace.[24] Because Tomiko was of the first (women's) rank, one might expect that the rank of the woman who wrote the letter was correspondingly high; however, as in the exchange with Takatsukasa Sekkanke over the fishmonger dispute, this could be left to an exchange of letters between the *senji no tsubone* in each household, while a letter written by the *Ōsumoji* expressed both extra politeness and at the same time intimacy, or a personal touch.

Another of the women's tasks was making visits to shrines and temples on behalf of the emperor. On the 18th day of the first month, 1483, the emperor had a slight cold, and on the next day one of the emperor's nurses went to the Hachiman shrine to have an incantation performed (Asai 1985:O-ochi)· On the way back she was delighted to pick up a fan with the auspicious hammer and magic jewel design, which would grant all wishes.

From the 1470s to the 1680s, the monthly shrine visits to Kiyoshi shrine and Kuramadera temple were made on behalf of the emperor, normally by members of the *naishi no suke* class (*kōtō no naishi* and other *naishi*).

In addition, a large part of the service of the women took the form of material gifts to the emperor. These were in such quantity that it would seem that all the emperor's needs could be met from this source. On the first day of the first, fourth and ninth months—the occasion of changing to new season's clothes—entries such as 'From today wearing silk from *Shinsuke-dono*'[25] mention the woman whose duty it was to supply the emperor's clothing for that day. These, too, were duties of the *naishi no suke* class. Whether they actually presented the emperor with the silk for his robes is not clear. In addition, the women on duty for the *ushi* (cow) and *hitsuji* (sheep) days of each month[26] were required to present gifts: rice cakes (*mochi* or *kachin*) on *ushi* days and considerable quantities of various kinds of paper, such as thick *danshi* paper (made from *mayumi* tree fibre), on *hitsuji* days (perhaps because sheep eat paper). This cycle of 12 days meant that such gifts were presented

Table 5: Register of gifts received on cow (ushi) and sheep (hitsuji) days in 1477

Donor / Month	1	1a	2	3	4	5	6	7	8	9	10	11	12
Wet nurse		c		s	s	c		s			s		
Jōrō	c			c	s		c	s		c	c		c
Higashi no onkata	s			c		s	c		s		c	s	
Ōsumoji			c		c			c	s				
Sukedono (sumōji)							c,s					c	s
Shinsumoji		s	s				s	c	c		s		
Shinsukedono						s			s				c
Kōtō no naishi		c				s		s	c		s	c	s
Iyodono					c	s		c		s	c	s	

Key: c = cow day; s = sheep day; 1a = intercalary 1st month

two or three times a month by the women on duty, including *naishi no suke*, *kōtō no naishi* and the *Iyo-dono* type.[27] This is summarised in Table 5.

On top of that, the women worked with the male aides (*nainai no otokotachi*—inside men) to organise *sarugaku* performances and offerings of sake and tidbits to the emperor, as well as to bring back considerable quantities of local goods after they had visited their homes. In particular, the women who had borne princes and princesses had an obligation to present lavish offerings from themselves and their fathers.

In return for these services, the women were granted the privilege of receiving the income from various estates (Okuno 1942).

Table 6: Offerings for the year 1477

Month/Day	Donor
1.5	Nyōbō women offered sake drinks according to the customary auspicious ceremony
1.9	Ōsumoji offered the usual drinks
1.17	Nyōbō women offered the young crown prince annual sake drinks
1a.11	Suke-dono graciously offered gifts of sake from her family
3.22	Ōsuke returned from home, and offered three gifts in unglazed containers, a shallow dish (of cooked food – nimono), and also a barrel (of sake). The Emperor was most appreciative.
4.5	Gon no suke returned from home
4.22	Nagahashi presented two barrels (of sake), and a shallow dish (of snapper)
4.25	Lady Higashi offered sake at dinner
4.28	Shin sumoji offered sake at dinner
6.6	The nagahashi had the same number of poems as the Emperor, so she presented him with a barrel (of sake) to make up for this.
6.11	The woman (suke dono) on duty for the day (On-hitsuji), whose duty it was to present paper, also offered melon and a barrel (of sake) while the Emperor was dining
6.16	Today was the celebration of the Katsū festival/ceremony, and the women presented sake to the Emperor.
8.17	The nurse came and offered sweets
8.3	The nurse offered a basket of persimmons
9.10	Lady Higashi sent mochi
9.27	Ōsumoji offered chrysanthemums
10.8	Shinsumoji offered mandarin oranges
10.11	The nurse offered annual red salmon
11.17	Lady Higashi offered yam potato on the lid of an inkwell

Further, they were in a position to redistribute to the male courtiers the articles presented to the emperor, as well as allocating themselves a share. The Yamaguni no shō domain was an estate that belonged directly to the emperor. In 1483, the direct rights for managing this estate were transferred to the Jōshōkōji temple and the annual tribute came to the palace. The monthly income was allocated to Shin-ōsuke,[28] who in gratitude and delight presented a simple meal of rice and soup to the emperor, as well as tidbits and four barrels of sake. Another woman who was allotted some of the tribute from the Yamaguni estate, in return presented the emperor with sake and tidbits. Yoshino made a chart based on the *Oyudono no ue no nikki*, demonstrating that the women received plenty of income from estates as a reward for their services (Yoshino 1982).

This section has shown how the relation between the emperor and the women who attended him was one of unqualified favour and service — to send one's daughter into such service could amount to a great deal of unending expense. A woman was given a place to live, with maidservants, and ran an independent household. Women of the third rank and above were expected to set up a full household administration. It is hard to say how much real capacity the court women had for running such an independent household structure by the Warring States period, but at least they did have separate homes and were able to present gifts from their establishments.[29] When they were given leave, they returned to their own family homes. Some of the high-ranking (second and third rank) women are known to have had their own mansions. For example, the sister of Sanjō Nishi Sanetaka's wife, Kajūji Tōshi, was a *shin dainagon no suke no tsubone*[30] and she had her own mansion next to Sanetaka's establishment.[31]

How court women viewed their lives

Uppermost in the minds of all the women was a focus on the emperor in all things. This focus is vividly realised in the style of the diary, which usually has no grammatical subject: it is taken for granted that the emperor is the subject of all the entries. For example, on New Year's Day it says, 'On the first day, had a bath, went to the seat, had sticky rice to celebrate New Year as usual'.

The only time a subject is specified is when the action refers to someone other than the emperor,[32] as in '(the emperor and empress) are both fine. The mother of the emperor is also in good spirits, so it is something to celebrate. Lady So-and-so is…'

At the risk of oversimplification, before the Meiji period, *nyokan* were a group of secretaries, of whom a small number performed the extra role of concubine (unofficial wife). This is the same structure as the Edo period *shōgun's* court, where certain favourite young men became bedroom companions. It differs, however, in that it was the officially recognised system. As is well known, in China the eunuchs replaced female courtiers as clerks. Japan adopted the *ritsuryō* system in its entirety, with the exception of having eunuchs. At the beginning, the roles of female clerk (*nyōkan*) and concubine or unofficial wife (*sokushitsu*) were clearly demarcated, but by the Heian period this distinction had blurred, with the *naishi no kami* becoming concubines. By the Muromachi period, there were no longer the resources to establish an empress (*chūgū*), or even a *nyōgo* (next in line of seniority to *chūgū*), so only *suke* and *naishi* acted as consorts.

There were two groups of men serving the emperor: those who served as his closest aides, called *nainai no otokotachi* (inside men), who did rostered night duty, and those who served outside, called *tozama no otokotachi* (outside men). These men were in a personal relationship of service and favour with the emperor and, within some degree of court ranking, the emperor's favourites were chosen as aides. The earlier *kurōdo-dokoro* office, with its male courtier-clerks (*kurōdo*) who were official scribes for the imperial household or the court, was no longer functioning by the Muromachi and Warring States periods: the system had changed to one where the women performed all clerical tasks.. This is shown by the case of the fishmongers' dispute, which Yamashina Tokitsugu could only settle by going through the *kōtō no naishi*.[33]

Among these women, there were some who had sexual relations with the emperor (*otetsuki*, touched) and others who did not, making this a group of women who were both concubines and clerks. The fact that they continued to be active in court administration, even if they had borne heirs, distinguishes them from the harem-like *oheyasama* of the Edo period *bakufu*, where women did not have that clerical function. This same pattern could be observed in the Fushiminomiya household.

So, with what kind of awareness did these women view their lives? If the main feature of the diary is that it centres on the emperor, the second feature is that there is no personal perspective, no subjectivity, and that it is always written positively—glossing over complications without complaint. The *Oyudono no ue no nikki* is an official log written according to a prescribed form, and therefore it does not directly reflect the women's lives, as would a literary diary. Of course, there is a great gap between this record and their private lives, but it is still necessary to make clear the attitude that the women courtiers adopted in this diary. It seems to me that the women's bureaucratic position is clear. Such a conscientious attitude of presenting things favourably would also have been more or less required of the men attendants who kept public records.[34]

This point can be seen by inspecting a few relevant entries. On the first day, seventh month, 1479, the emperor was using the mansion of Hino Naeko (Hino no Tomiko's mother) in Kita no kōji as his temporary palace and, while there, the mansion caught on fire. The emperor was put in a palanquin and transferred to his sister Anzenji-dono's place (Shōjuji). Because it was too confined there, the *bakufu* was asked to help find a better place, and by the tenth he was settled at the mansion of Hino Masasuke.

In the *Oyudono no ue no nikki*, these events were recorded neutrally:

> In a palanquin, went to Anzenji-dono. The court ladies went in a cart. Because the shogunal deputies (*kwanrei*) guarded the procession so loyally, when they arrived at the temple the emperor gave them a gift of swords.

However, according to the diaries of some noblemen it was not such a simple matter. First, on the night of the first day, seventh month, when the fire broke out, the emperor first stopped by the ruins of the Hanagosho and requested the *bakufu* find him a temporary refuge.[35] The Tsuchimikado palace had not been destroyed, so why did the emperor need to be living outside the palace anyway? In the Ōnin-Bunmei disturbance (1467–77), the *bakufu* and the *shōgun's* eastern army wanted to secure the emperor and be recognised as the official imperial army, and in order to achieve this they took the emperor away from the Tsuchimikado palace (Momose 1976). Therefore, the emperor's point of view would surely have been that it was up to the *bakufu* to decide where he should go and to provide a refuge. The *bakufu* nominated either the Hino Masasuke mansion or Anzenji temple, and the temple was settled on. The *Oyudono no ue no nikki* entries for the second and third days simply record the visitors and gifts of sympathy received by the emperor, and nothing else; but in the *Chikanaga kyōki* entry for the third, Chikanaga recorded that the *bakufu* did not send any help and urged it to hurry and decide on what to do to settle the emperor. There was still no response by the sixth day. Finally, on the tenth day it was arranged that he should move to Hino Masasuke's place.[36] On the tenth day, the *Oyudono no ue no nikki* notes the auspicious and successful relocation of the emperor: 'This evening, even the palanquin bearers put on their best official dress and the male attendants were all there.' The *Nagaoki Sukene-ki* says, 'The attendants were not formal at all. All were in unofficial (not proper) court code.'[37] In *Daijō-in jisha zatsujiki*, it was rumoured that the retinue for the emperor's removal consisted of 17 or 18 formally dressed attendants, as well as several dressed informally, and that this was deplorable.[38] Furthermore, during the move, there was a strike by the palanquin bearers, who demanded that they be exempted from separate fees for delivering to each wing of the palace now under repair. The aides had to persuade them to drop their demands on this occasion (Koresawa 1944). When they finally arrived at the Hino mansion, Masasuke pleaded severe inconvenience and petitioned that a new place of refuge be found as soon as possible (Jugaku 1982). This temporary removal was arranged by Tomiko's hand, and Yoshimasa had nothing to do with it. Even the repairs of the Tsuchimikado inner palace started with Tomiko supplying the funds for laying the floorboards.[39]

As a further complexity of the situation, the emperor was severely displeased that the *bakufu* could not respond appropriately in this situation in which he was homeless, and on the second day of the month threatened to abdicate. Yoshimasa tried desperately to persuade him to stay in office; however, Tomiko seems to have seized on this as a good opportunity to have him resign, and apparently schemed to overthrow him.[40]

Yoshimasa supposedly joined with her, but because an abdication would require more expense in the form of building a *Sentō gosho* (palace of the retired emperor), he eventually asked the emperor to become a monk. The palace fell into panic. There were all sorts of rumours circulating, such as that there was a ghost in the palace, that strange smoke was seen billowing and that a giant woman had threatened the emperor in a dream.[41] In the end, the noble Machi no Hiromitsu, who had tried to engineer the abdication, was censured; his sister, who was one of Tomiko's court ladies, was made to cut her hair and become a nun, and the matter was settled. Tomiko was not worried: '(during this altercation between the emperor and the *bakufu*) the *Midai* (Tomiko) adopted her usual policy of hushing things up (*kusai mono ni futa*)'.[42]

All these records show that the women diarists wished to present everything in a respectable light and did not want to mention bothersome things. Probably they knew too much about everything, and felt obliged not to write about it in detail. A similar attitude is found in the famous passage in the *Ben no naishi nikki*, which, on the day of the enthronement of Emperor Gofukakusa, has the record, 'A spring day, particularly mild and lovely, all the ceremonies went beautifully, a most auspicious occasion'; whereas, in fact, on that day it poured with rain and thunderstorms, and was altogether terrible weather (Kobayashi 1974).[43] It seems that the attitude of the court women was that, even if they had to call black white, they had to create an auspicious reign for the emperor; therefore, to put into words anything that would disturb the peace augured ill. For example, the record for the 23rd day of the first month, 1483, comments on the rumour that Hatakeyama Yoshinari (?–1490) had brought his army to Yawata and had pulled down the Ujihashi bridge: 'This must be a false report.'

No doubt it was the desire to maintain peace and calm in a small universe and not face reality that lead to this kind of writing.

There is another entry, quite different in nature, on the 23rd day of the third month, 1480.

> In the *naishi-dokoro* this evening there was a performance of *kagura*. All day the weather was changeable (it rained since dawn); but it cleared late in the afternoon. Tōchū no Shō Nobuchika (Nakayama), who was in charge, came late. The *kōtō no naishi* had already sent him a message, after which he presented himself.

This censures Nobuchika for being late. Furthermore, he willfully changed the performance to wet weather mode, even though the emperor had decreed an extraordinary *kagura* because of the fine weather.

> In the last few hours it rained, so the ceremony was changed into rainy mode. Basically the weather was fine, but without asking, Nobuchika made the decision to alter the program. Nothing has been more outrageous than this recently. It is understandable that he is not used to this, nevertheless it is extraordinary.

The tone of this entry in the diary is very high-handed, quite different from the usual style of the women's entries. As well as stating, *Chikagoro no kusegoto nari* (a very strong expression), the women officials are referred to in Chinese titles (*naishi, tenji*). This contrasts with the entry for the 30th day of the third month, 1483, which records a similar *kagura* performance in a more characteristically neutral way: 'The sword bearer was the treasurer; with him were *Osumoji* and *Shin-naishi*.' This is the normal writing style of the women officials, which makes the previous entry look as if it was written by a man using *nyōbō kotoba*. Since the only man with access to the diary was the emperor, we can surmise that this part is in the emperor's hand.[44] In length, too, it is about six times longer than comparable entries about *kagura* in the *naishi-dokoro* in other years. This was the first *kagura* performance in the *naishi-dokoro* since his return to the Tsuchimikado palace[45] and the emperor probably made a special effort to write it himself.[46]

If this is indeed the emperor's own writing, the difference between the two styles should be attributed to the lord–servant relationship rather than to gender differences. The expression 'Nobuchika did a terrible thing tonight' could only be written by someone of very high standing.

In order to compare lord–servant relations in the case of men's diaries, a suitable example is the Yamashina household butler's journal, a diary that was written over several generations of Yamashina lords and which has been preserved. This is also nothing but a record of the daily running of the Yamashina household, but occasionally reference is made to local gossip, and criticisms are expressed. For example, a section written by Ōsawa Nagato no Kami criticises *Shōgun* Ashikaga Yoshihisa (1465–89; reigned 1473–89) for taking advantage of a rebellion by farmers in order to reclaim his mortgages: 'Then he took back the mortgages during the farmers rebellion. This is unfair.'[47] There is another entry deploring the re-dyeing of the emperor's clothes: 'The emperor's summer costumes were dyed and today they were presented. The cost was 100 *hiki*. It is unjust and miserly.'[48]

In comparison, the *Oyudono no ue no nikki* style of the women courtiers shows how they strove to make everything appear respectable. What is the reason for this difference? The Yamashina household record written by Ōsawa Hisamori, as a vassal, is an official record; at the same time it is the record of the private housekeeping of the Yamashina family and cannot compare with a diary kept at the imperial court. The journal covers successive heads of the Yamashina family—Noritoki (1328–1409), Tokikuni (1452–1503), Tokitsugu 1507–79) and Tokitsune (1543–1611)—who intended the record for successive generations, although it was not a public diary. It shows a reversal of the situation in the Heian period, when Chinese letters and the Chinese language were adopted for use by men as the official language. In contrast, women were able to express themselves using *kana* in something close to everyday language, whereby they secured an advantageous position for developing literary writing. However, their official position at court was gradually displaced by the *kurōdo* and they were pushed into the background. The peak period of private women's literature written in *kana* lasted until around 1220, the time of retired Emperor Gotoba (1180–1239; reigned 1183–98; retired emperor 1198–1221). *Naishi no sen* written in *kanbun* were then replaced by the *nyōbō hōsho* written in *kana*, which reappeared in this era. Compared with the official records kept by men, the diaries written by women with a personal perspective are of literary merit. The interest of the *Kagerō nikki* (974) derives from the individuality of the writer, whose free position allowed her a rich creativity. Although both Murasaki Shikibu and Sei Shōnagon were women serving in the 10th century court and were thus close to those who wielded power, the strength of their writing came from the fact that they were on the fringes of that power, not assimilated with it, and so could retain objectivity in their writing. And yet Murasaki's diary, the *Murasaki Shikibu Nikki*, had the function of commemorating the glory of Fujiwara Michinaga and his daughter Shōshi (988–1074), who became an imperial consort. While achieving literary brilliance, it required also that the work celebrate their flourishing. Subsequent women's diaries were always aware of Murasaki's legacy, and this created the tradition that a diary should be premised on the centrality of one's lord.

In comparison, the *Oyudono no ue no nikki* is an official logbook. It is different both from the Heian period women's diaries, which were interesting because they were written from a highly personal viewpoint, and from women's court diaries, like Murasaki's, which celebrated the achievements of their superiors in great literary style. The *Oyudono no ue no nikki* is a diary that women had to write as an official record, not as something interesting to read.

On the contrary, men kept a household diary for the sake of the *ie* and its descendents. Thus, the *Oyudono no ue no nikki* ironically represents a reversal of the earlier situation.

The entries in the *Oyudono no ue no nikki* are written by women in their official capacity, and therefore there is no question of presenting the individuality of any of the women who contributed each day; it is a matter of being part of a group situated within an administrative system—trained and perfected through the imperative that women courtiers conduct themselves in a particular way. To put it another way, they embodied an idealised image of how women should control a household. *Nyōbō kotoba* became a model for upper-class women; and then, because it was respected and admired by people, it formed the origin of contemporary women's language. This pride distinguishes *nyōbō kotoba* from other secret languages for in-groups.

What was the idealised image of court women? As already seen, the *Menoto no fumi* (*Niwa no oshie*), attributed to the nun Abutsu-ni (formerly a court lady), was a guidebook for women courtiers. Nothing is left unexplained regarding the progress of a woman at court and the skills and tactics required for success. There are things in common between this and the women who created the *Oyudono no ue no nikki*.

One extant copy of the *Menoto no fumi* has an inscription at the back (quoted earlier) which shows that the book was written for her daughter Ki no Naishi to guide her in the ways of serving as a woman at court. The circumstantial evidence is strong that Abutsu-ni is the author:[49] the work contains an extract from her essay 'Yoru no tsuru', her daughter was employed at court, and her granddaughter became one of the wives of the Kamakura *shōgun* Prince Hisaaki (reigned 1289–1308) and bore the Prince Hisayoshi.

Menoto no fumi begins with the teaching that by the age of 30 a woman at court has acquired wisdom and understanding, but at the age of 20 she is full of unsettled thoughts; even a peerless beauty without a clear mind will lose her way by thinking foolish things. However much she might want to do something that will be rebuked when it is known, she should avoid being the object of slander. Indeed, it is always bad to act according to one's wishes. She should not show on her face either pain or pleasure. She should not talk loosely about her own feelings, her situation or about others.

It is unseemly to act too grand, so she should show discretion in such areas and must be mindful of these things in her behaviour: 'Whether in public or in private, be prompt and speedy when necessary, and when asked to do something, carry it out properly till it is finished.'

This is surely excellent advice for women whose roles as intermediaries formed the core of their duties. However, it was not good to promote oneself and stand out:

> Be calm and beautiful, refrain from judging things as good or bad. Foster younger colleagues; do not to join in with gossiping and criticising others. Servants should not be treated too casually. When burning incense, do not use an over-strong, vulgar fragrance, nor one that fades too quickly—it should be an attractive scent, which expresses your character. To dress and behave in an eye-catching way, to appear knowledgeable, to behave brightly and charmingly is all right once, but a second time it fades and is less attractive.

Human relationships are given detailed attention: 'It is bad to laugh and talk about things that can only be appreciated by a closed circle. Act older than your years, but do not go too far with this.'

On poetry, the reader is advised that a woman should not write overdone, exaggerated poetry and should use correct diction:

> Your poetry should be attractive, serene and bright. Take an interest in poetry and try to get your poems into the imperial anthology. In that way, your name will be remembered by later generations. Work hard at your calligraphy. Women do not like writing *kanji*, but it is important to be able to do so, because it is required, for example, in the titles of poems. Study the poems of Akahito [early Nara court poet] and Murasaki Shikibu [mid-Heian]; you should be familiar with the *Tale of Genji* [early 11th century], and you should also memorise all the poems of the great anthologies such as the *Kokinshū* [905] and the *Shin-kokinshū* [1205].

The writer advises:

> As for music, you should acquire the basic skills in *koto*, *biwa* and *wagon*. You learnt the *shō* and *koto* from the age of five, and when you made your first appearance at court at the age of seven, you played in front of the retired emperor; at eight you had enough skill to play a duet with the crown prince. You must continue to work hard to acquire skill and fame.

In this way, she instructs young women to acquire skills in poetry, calligraphy and music; to take great care with incense-burning and clothing; to take pains to not incur displeasure in human relations; and to develop a sweet refined character. The goal of such behaviour was to become the mother of an emperor—'My heart, I have such a silly ambition.' Her ambition as a mother was for her daughter to bear an imperial prince and thereby become the mother of the nation (*kokumo*). Without such a memory, a mother's experience in the afterlife would be bad.

The author writes that the god of the Kasuga shrine appeared to her while she was pregnant: 'I had a strange and trustworthy dream, in which I was told that my baby would be a girl. The god showed me that she would rise to the supreme rank, and shine on the world.'

She teaches that there is no point to living if things do not turn out as one wished, and the best option is to become a nun—to find salvation and find the true way. If, on the other hand, the ultimate reward is unexpectedly achieved, detailed instructions are given on the best way to behave.

This is a bare outline of *Menoto no fumi*. In reality, a large number of women actually did leave court life to become nuns and spend their days in religious practice (Hosokawa 1989a).

It was common wisdom amongst nobles in the Heian period that the best way to rise in the world was to have one's daughter become the consort of the emperor and to grasp power when she bore the heir to the throne. This is surely what is behind the Akashi episode in *The Tale of Genji*. It is noteworthy that it is the mother who has this ambition for her daughter: the father presumably would also have wished for such success, but it is the mother who actively participates in the struggle for her daughter's advancement.

The distaste with which men viewed the rivalry between women who wanted such status has been seen; their perceived selfishness led to the creation of *setsuwa* tales about mothers going to hell for wanting only their child to prosper.[50] The *Menoto no fumi*, however, does not show a mother who is condemned to hell for her selfish ambition for her child; rather, she finds consolation in expectation of her child's worldly success. She believes that if one's expectation is not fulfilled, one's lot is to end up in hell anyway, so it would be sad to wander a path of darkness without any memories of one's daughter's success. This is quite different from the era in which womanly virtue was defined as living submissively. Certainly it was ambitious and career-oriented to aim to obtain the favour of the emperor and become the mother of an imperial prince (nation's mother), but it is thrilling to read about this clear ambition. It is similar to the phenomenon of the 'education mama' in postwar Japan.

For aristocratic women, to serve at court and perhaps obtain the favour of the emperor was the only possible way to advance in the world. It is therefore hard to blame them for devoting themselves thoroughly to achieving this. Rather, we should blame the society of the time, in which men blatantly wished for promotion and competed for court positions, while women were exclusively educated not to expect such advancement and to be subservient to authority and to men.

The exhortations of *Menoto no fumi* were brilliantly realised in the lives of the court women who wrote the *Oyudono no ue no nikki*. It is as if they read it and tried to put its lessons into practice: being skilful at poetry, calligraphy and music; not drawing attention to oneself; behaving modestly, so as to develop a fragrant character; neither dissembling nor embellishing the facts; being straightforward when making requests — precisely the accumulated wisdom of the court *nyōbō*. Furthermore, by following the dictum to promptly carry out the tasks that they were called on to perform, or when acting in the interests of others, they fulfilled their duties as court women.

This was in many aspects no different from what was expected of male courtiers (except for those women who became *otetsuki* and bore children). In the *bushi* manual *Hagakure* (1716), also, there are many tactful hints on how to behave successfully in samurai society, such as 'it is bad to show off one's ability' — the wisdom of subservience applied to both men and women who were in a master–servant relationship at any social level. According to a popular saying, to be in service at court always involved hardship and unpleasantness, even humiliation. In order to keep afloat in such an environment, it was wise to heed this advice not to overstep the mark.

However, it is a peculiar way of thinking, given that the ultimate goal was not to stay in employment for the rest of one's life but to obtain the favour of the emperor and bear a child, realise the enthronement of that child, and rise to the position of 'nation's mother'. This ambition was general, whether it applied to the emperor or to one's overlord, and women trapped in a situation where motherhood was the only way for their existence to be valued defied their circumstances and acted positively.

There were cases, however, like in the *Tale of Genji*, where, through adultery, a man became the father of the emperor and obtained power. Also, from the Heian to the Edo periods, examples of men gaining advantage through homosexual liaisons are too numerous to mention. The difference was that in a man's society such behaviour, which everyone knew took place, was officially condemned. In the case of women, who were prevented from using the normal channels to achieve social elevation, the most highly regarded path was to bear a child who could climb to a high position, and to be respected as his mother. Women who were forced into such a situation made this their ultimate goal, and who could blame them? Whether or not *Menoto no fumi* was written by Abutsu-ni, its contents match her life closely: in order to get to the top, a woman full of energy and vitality had to use a woman's charms and native intelligence, had to be crafty enough to get a powerful man to love her, and had to bear his child and fight to protect the interests of that child. We might say that such a woman's talent was buried in motherhood. But, was her behaviour purely motivated by love for her child? Rather, this behaviour used motherhood as a cover for self-realisation. Unlike today, at that time any course of action was permitted to a woman on the condition that it was out of self-sacrifice for her child: a woman could not admit that she might be acting for her own sake.

I believe that we must investigate the significance for women's history of competent women who wielded power, such as Hino no Tomiko and Ano no Renshi (1311–59; wife of Emperor Godaigo, mother of Emperor Gomurakami). Hino no Tomiko's son, *Shōgun* Ashikaga Yoshihisa, found his mother's political interference a nuisance, so in this case it seems she acted for her own sake, not for her son's. Hōjō Masako (1157–1225; wife of *Shōgun* Minamoto Yoshitomo, mother of *shōguns* Yoriie and Sanetomo — known as the Nun *shōgun*) held onto power, even after her two sons had died, possibly for the sake of her own Hōjō family, rather than for the sake of her children. For a woman to hold power, it had to be the manifestation of the spirit of self-sacrifice, whether for her child, her husband or her natal family. The only way a woman could be recognised as acting for her own sake, or on behalf of society as a whole, was by taking religious orders as a nun.

Women were limited to using the label of motherhood, and immersing themselves in motherhood. Yet, to be critical of this is to be critical of the male-led society, which locked women into the role of motherhood. The more that women tried to claim a value for their existence in such a society, the more they had to find a way to take advantage of it, as did court women like Abutsu-ni: it is impossible to condemn them for that.

The desire to advance in the world was not limited to men; however, the available means to achieve this differed, because each gender's starting position was different. As has been shown, the heart that desired only the advancement of one's own child was doomed to hell. This warning became the guiding norm of a male-dominated society, which imprisoned women's ambition in motherhood, forcing them to turn frustration into an advantage.

Conclusion

The *Oyudono no ue no nikki*, the official record of the imperial court, shows the lives of the only elite professional women of the pre-modern era. Speaking and writing in the unique language of *nyōbō kotoba* created a distinctive culture, which should be called women's court culture. It influenced the *gosho kotoba* used by male courtiers and nobles and, as the origin of Japanese women's language, it also had an impact on ordinary women. In this sense, the study of the *Oyudono no ue no nikki* is highly significant for women's history.

Women in the court performed both social labour and domestic labour, but it was actually the same for men in service to an overlord. In the medieval period, when the *ie* was an administrative structure and a production site, there was not a great difference between women and men courtiers. What has magnified the difference is the male-centric view of history by historians of the modern period.

After the decline of the *ritsuryō* bureaucratic system, which derived from the patriarchal Chinese bureaucracy, the *ie* became the government's unit of control and household structures became the core of society. The gender role division in this period needs to be investigated further. Unfortunately, the household structures themselves have been interpreted as leading to the decline of the *ritsuryō* system, and have not been dealt with directly. The role of the women officials who worked in these structures has been considered even less. My decision to tackle the difficult *Oyudono no ue no nikki* was in order to lay a foundation for future research in this area.

As both social and domestic labour, the meaning of being in service was the same for men and women. But there was a very clear difference between the nature of this service for men and women as evidenced by the fact that the term *kōtō no naishi*—as a woman 'touched' by the emperor—became a codeword for concubine. As far as can be seen from the *Oyudono no ue no nikki*, women who had relations with the emperor were expected to perform the same duties and were treated no differently from those who did not. Treatment did change, however, if her child ascended the throne, or when this was anticipated, because her status as the emperor's mother rose. At the same time, the birth mother of the retiring emperor became a nun, and could not continue to wield power in the court. Just occasionally, she might have some say in promotions of court rank. A woman's position as a *nyōbō* and her court rank were determined by her father's status. With a few exceptions, it was the same in the case of male courtiers, as the highest position was also fixed by family status. Real, secular power was in the hands of the *kōtō no naishi*, who was like a secretary-general (in charge of clerical and secretarial matters),

rather than the *dainagon no suke no tsubone*, who ruled over internal matters
of the court; a different principle from that of status was at work here. Those
closest to the person of the emperor had the highest status, especially those who
supervised the emperor's daily bathing and toilet. In comparison with this, the
work of the *kōtō no naishi* seems like general administrative tasks. There was
a unique status principle in the structure of the medieval court, within which
we must place both male and female courtiers.

It must be admitted that the records in the *Oyudono no ue no nikki* do not
make interesting reading. What is to be made of this in comparison to the
present day, when often women's diaries are far more interesting than men's?
Contemporary women's diaries are interesting because the writers are private
individuals. Whether male or female, the sensibilities of a writer who becomes
a public figure are suppressed and do not appear on the surface. The private
diaries of men in the medieval period were written in large part for their
descendents, so they had to reveal the goings-on behind the scenes. By contrast,
ironically, women left us with the official *Oyudono no ue no nikki* diary. Behind
these records, beyond a doubt, there were acts of concealment—incidents
where the women had to grit their teeth and cover up their own feelings and
impulses. The only other recourse was to become a nun or to write a radical
work of fiction that exposed the ego.

The *Oyudono no ue no nikki* does not show us this aspect of the women's
lives, but women's history has since progressed and provided many case studies
to fill this gap: Ano no Renshi, whose child rose to become emperor, just as
prescribed by Abutsu-ni (Wakita 1977); the mothers of generations of emperors
in the Muromachi period (in the main, these were women in the *suke* class[51]);
nuns, such as Shinnyo-ni, who began by serving in the court but later took
orders and led lives of faith (Hosokawa 1989b; Abe 1987); and the consort of
retired Emperor Gofukakusa-in, Lady Nijō, who sought her self-expression in
literary creativity by writing the *Towazugatari*. Comparable with the *kōtō no
naishi* was Konoe no tsubone in the Fushiminomiya family, who was in charge
of the household and prepared in advance a suitable situation for herself after
her retirement in old age (see Chapter one). All these women are situated on
the obverse of the *Oyudono no ue no nikki*, with its demure and prim accounts.
It is surely impossible to properly apprehend the world of the court women
without steadily fixing our gaze on both sides of the picture.

Notes

1   The term *nyōbō* in this context refers to the high-ranking women who served at court in an administrative capacity [trans].

2   There is no need to assume that women's official diaries were modelled on those of the male courtiers, because women's diaries existed from the early Heian period, given that Fujiwara Onshi or perhaps other court ladies wrote the *Ōkisaki no nikki*.

3   *Nyōbō kotoba* was not only the language of women at court, it was also the language used by nuns in high-ranking monasteries, and it exercised a strong influence on the *gosho kotoba* language used by male courtiers at the imperial palace (see Inokuchi & Horii 1974).

4   For example, the young concubine (Waka-jōrō, also called Higashi no Onkata), Kazan'in Kenshi (the mother of Prince Enman'in Jingō and Princess Anzenji-no-miya) of Emperor Gotsuchimikado (1442–1500; reigned 1464–1500) used to be a lady-in-waiting to the *shōgun's* wife (*sokushitsu*), Hino no Tomiko, but she was called back to the imperial palace at the emperor's personal wish, according to the *Chikanaga kyōki*, entry for 22nd day, tenth month, 1473. (This is the diary of Kanroji Chikanaga [1424–1500], 40 volumes covering the years 1466–98.) Another example is Made no kōji Meishi , a lady serving Gon Dainagon *suke no tsubone* of the Emperor Gotsuchimikado; because her father committed an offence, she had to leave her post and later became a wife (*sokushitsu*) of the *shōgun* Ashikaga Yoshihisa (1465–89; reigned 1473–89). (*Daijō-in jisha zatsujiki*, 18th day, 11th month, 1482.)

5   *Koga-ke monjo* (1982:no296), 26th day, sixth month, 1486. 'Retired *shōgun* (Jishō)'s decree, original (not draft) written and certified by Lady Horikawa (see Chapter two).

6   An example can be found in a diary such as Ōgimachi Machiko's *Matsukage no nikki*. She was the wife (*sokushitsu*) of Yanagisawa Yoshiyasu (1658–1714), secretary to the *shōgun* Tsunayoshi.

7   Personal communication from a court woman serving Empress Teimei (wife of Emperor Tennō, 1884–1951), Tsuzaki Noriko. In 1980, Jugaku Akiko and I interviewed this lady and Akazawa Fukuko concerning the life of a woman serving in the Ōmiya Gosho Palace (residence of the emperor's mother). Although there are obviously big differences between the modern situation and that of the medieval imperial palace, it gave us the opportunity to gain a sense of the atmosphere of that experience. I would like to express here my gratitude to Ms Jugaku, and to the two ladies for graciously responding to my impertinent questions.

8   Personal communication from Hayashi Reiko.

9   It is well known that many women from the warrior and merchant class wrote diaries, such as the famous *Koume nikki* and *Nitchi-roku*, but it is amazing to learn that many women wrote travel diaries (see Maeda 1977).

10 Examples of diaries written by men in *kana* are *Minamoto no Ienaga nikki* (1198–1207; he lived 1170?–1234); *Minamoto no Michichika nikki* (he lived 1149–1202). Several possible people have been suggested as the author of the

Mumyō sōshi, including Shunzei (1114–1204), Shunzei's daughter, imperial Princess Shikishi (?–1201), and Jōgaku (see Suzuki 1981). More recently, it has been suggested that the author was Fujiwara Takanobu (1142–1205), the portrait painter (see Gomi 1991).

11   *Sanetaka kōki* (Hanawa 1958), entry for sixth and 13th days, ninth month, 1527. *Oyudono no ue no nikki* (Hanawa 1958), 13th day, ninth month, 1527.

12   *Oyudono no ue no nikki* (Hanawa 1958), entry for 28th day, fourth month, 1500.

13   *Nochi no Hōkō-in no ki* (Takeuchi 1967b), entry for 25th day, eighth month, 1482.

14   Historical tale covering the reigns of Emperor Uda, 887–897, and Emperor Horikawa, 1086–1107, focusing on the achievements of Fujiwara Michinaga [trans].

15   Historical tale covering the period 850–1025 [trans].

16   The *Tokitsugu kyōki,* tells that, in the dispute of 1545, the *kōtō no naishi* made a promise to Tokitsugu to have a *rinji* issued.

17   Tomiko had the rights to administer the imperial estate of Kurima no shō, in Ise Province, which she divided between her vassals.

18   *Tokitsugu kyōki* (1965), entries for 17th, 20th, 24th, 27th days of the first month, and first, second and tenth days of the second month, 1481.

19   *Tokitsugu kyōki* (1965), entries for fifth and sixth days, 12th month, 1481.

20   The money for the *kagura* payment was supplied by Hirohashi. Some was also paid from the emperor's treasury. In these times of extreme financial hardship for the imperial household, money had to be scraped together from various sources, therefore it is difficult to classify all these payments systematically.

21   *Oyudono no ue no nikki* (Hanawa 1958), entry for first day, first month, 1477.

22   *Oyudono no ue no nikki* (Hanawa 1958), entry for seventh day, first month, 1483.

23   *Oyudono no ue no nikki* (Hanawa 1958), entry for sixth day, sixth month, 1477.

24   *Oyudono no ue no nikki* (Hanawa 1958), entry for second day, sixth month.

25   *Oyudono no ue no nikki* (Hanawa 1958), entry for first day, fourth month, 1477.

26   The zodiac calendar numbered the days in groups of 12, the same as the 12 zodiac signs [trans].

27   This probably refers to *chūrō,* also called *myōbu.* In the Bakumatsu period, the head of the *myōbu* was called *Iyo.* The mention of *Iyo-dono* in just one place in the *Oyudono no ue no nikki* suggests that this was the case from the 15th century.

28   Niwata Chōshi, the mother of Kōtaishi Katsuhito = Emperor Gokashiwabara.

29   In recent excavations of Osaka Castle, remains of rice were discovered in many different locations, which seems to indicate this kind of separate hearth and home within one complex.

30 The mother of Emperor Gonara, Higashi no Tō-in-dono, was also known affectionately as Oachacha.

31 *Sanetaka kōki* (Hanawa 1958), entry for fourth day, third month, 1532.

32 This attitude continued to the attendants of the Meiji period, as I have affirmed through interviewing two women who served the Empress Teimei (1885–1951), the consort of Emperor Taishō. I interviewed Tsuzaki Noriko, and another of her *nyokan*, Shirafuji Naishi's niece, Akazawa Fukuko, who was a serving lady.

33 *Tokitsugu kyōki* (1965), entry for tenth, 11th, 12th and 18th days, tenth month, 1545.

34 See Wilson (2002), where the wisdom of the follower is also emphasised.

35 *Harutomi sukune-ki* (Otsuki 1971), entry for second day, seventh month, 1479, et passim.

36 *Chikanaga kyōki* (Fujiwara 1965a), entries for first to 11th days, seventh month, 1479.

37 *Nagaoki Sukene-ki* (*Dai Nihon shiryō* 1968:8-11), entry for 11th day, seventh month, 1479.

38 *Daijō-in jisha zatsujiki* (*Dai Nihon shiryō* 1968:8-11), entry for 13th day, seventh month, 1479.

39 *Daijō-in jisha zatsujiki* (*Dai Nihon shiryō* 1968:8-11), entry for 14th day, seventh month, 1479, the letter 'Zuishin-in Genpō shojō '.

40 *Jūrin-in Naifu-ki* (*Dai Nihon shiryō* 1968:8-11), entries for first, third, fifth days, seventh month, 1479.

41 *Harutomi sukune-ki* (Otsuki 1971), entry for 18th day, seventh month, 1479.

42 *Daijō-in jisha zatsujiki* (*Dai Nihon shiryō* 1968:8-11), supplementary documents, 'Genpō shojō ' (*Dai Nihon shiryō*, 8-11, entry for 16th day, seventh month.)

43 Kobayashi (1974) connects this with the Buddhist Way, but Matsumoto Yasushi (1983) interprets this as showing that the *naishi's* role was to write only positive, auspicious things.

44 Koresawa Kyōzō (1944) has pointed out that from time to time the emperor's brush writing can be detected in the *Oyudono no ue no nikki*. However, he does not mention this passage.

45 *Nobutane kyō-ki* (Fujiwara 1965b), entry for 23rd day, third month, 1480.

46 The entry for the 26th day of the same month seems to be by the emperor.

47 *Yamashina-ke Raiki* (1967–2002), entry for 29th day, ninth month, 1480.

48 *Yamashina-ke Raiki* (1967–2002), entry for fifth day, fourth month, 1480.

49 For a case arguing against her authorship see Fukuda (1972), while Matsumoto (1983) is an example of the argument for her authorship.

50 The example of 'Mokuren no sōshi' is discussed in Chapter two.

51 Emperor Gokashibara's mother was Niwata Tomoko, later Shindainagon no suke. Emperor Gonara's mother was Kajūji Tōshi, Shindainagon no suke .

Bibliography

Abe Yasurō 1987, 'Chūsei Nanto no shūkyō no geinō: Shinnyo-ni to Wakamiya Haiden miko o megutte', *Kokugo to Kokubungaku* 64–65.

—— 1989, 'Nyonin kinsei to suisan' in *Shiriizu Josei to bukkyō 4: miko to megami*, Heibonsha, Tokyo.

—— 1991, 'Yama ni okonau hijiri to nyonin: Shigi-san engi emaki to Tōdaiji, Zenkōji' in *Taikei Nihon rekishi to geinō*, volume 3: *Seihō no haru: shushō-e, shuni-e*, Heibonsha, Tokyo.

Adachi Kuwatarō 1931, *Imagawa Ujichika to Jukei-ni*, Yajima-ya, Shizuoka.

Aida Jirō (ed) 1949, *Nihon no komonjo*, Volume 1, Iwanami shoten, Tokyo.

Akihara Tatsuo 1983, *Miko to bukkyō-shi*, Yoshikawa kōbunkan, Tokyo.

Amino Yoshihiko 1984a, 'Tennō no shihaiken to kugonin and tsukute', in *Nihon chūsei no hi-nōgyōmin to tennō*, Iwanami Shoten.

—— 1984b, *Nihon chūsei no hi-nōgyōmin to tennō*, 'Chūsei ni okeru ukai no sonzai keitai', Iwanami shoten, Tokyo.

Arntzen, Sonja (trans) 1997, *The Kagero diary : a woman's autobiographical text from tenth-century Japan* [by Michitsuna no Haha], Center for Japanese Studies, University of Michigan, Ann Arbor.

Asai Torao 1985, *Nyokan tsūkai*, Kōdansha, Tokyo.

Asakura-uji iseki chōsa-kai (ed) 1987, *Ichijōtani*, Asakura-uji Iseki Shiryōkan, Fukui.

Aston, WG (trans) 1956, *Nihongi: Chronicles of Japan from the earliest times to AD 697*, George Allen & Unwin, London.

Azuma Kagami 1968-, Volume 32 of *Shintei zōho Kokushi taikei*, Yoshikawa kōbunkan, Tokyo.

Brazell, Karen (trans) 1976 [1973], *The confessions of Lady Nijo*, Stanford University Press, Stanford.

Brown, Delmer M and Ichiro Ishida 1979, *The future and the past: a translation and study of the Gukanshō, an interpretative history of Japan written in 1219*, University of California Press, Berkeley.

Buraku Mondai Kenkyū-jo (ed) 1988a, 'Shirabyōshi Tamaō seimon' in *Buraku-shi shiryō senshū: kodai-chūsei,* Buraku Mondai Kenkyū-jo, Kyoto.

—— 1988b, *Buraku-shi shiryō senshū: kodai chūsei hen,* Buraku Mondai Kenkyū-jo, Kyoto.

Bussho kankō-kai (ed) 1980, *Inryōken nichimoku,* Meicho Fukyū-kai, Tokyo.

Chūsei Eikoku Romansu Kenkyūkai (ed) 1986, *Chūsei Eikoku Romansu-shū (Anthology of medieval English romances),* volume 2, Shinozaki shorin, Tokyo.

Dai Nihon shiryō 1968-, Tokyo Daigaku Shiryo Hensan-jo, Tokyo.

*Daijō-in Jisha zatsujiki (zōjiki)*1968-, supplementary documents, 'Genpō shojō' in *Dai Nihon shiryō,* 8-11, Tokyo Daigaku Shiryo Hensan-jo, Tokyo.

Frois, Luis 1977–78 [1583–1597], *Nihonshi [Historia de Japam],* Chūō kōron-sha, Tokyo.

Fujiwara Chikanaga 1965a [1470–98], *Chikanaga kyōki,* Rinsen shoten, Kyoto.

—— 1965b [1480–1522], *Nobutane kyō-ki,* Rinsen shoten, Kyoto.

Fujiwara Kanezane 1971 [1906–07], *Gyokuyō* (3 vols.), Meicho Kankōkai, Tokyo.

Fujiwara Sadaie 1970 [1911–12], *Meigetsu-ki,* Kokusho Kankō-kai, Tokyo.

Fukuda Akira 1984, *Shintō-shū setsuwa no seiritsu,* Miyai shoten, Tokyo.

Fukuda Hideichi 1972, *Chūsei waka-shi no kenkyū,* Kadokawa shoten, Tokyo.

Fukutō Sanae 1990, 'Heian jidai no sōzoku ni tsuite', *Kazoku-shi kenkyū* 11.

—— 1991, *Ie seiritsu-shi no kenkyū: sosensaishi, onna, kodomo,* Azekura Shobō, Tokyo.

Furukawa Hisashi (ed) 1954, *Nihon Koten Zensho,* volume 2, 'Kyōgen: Kawakami zatō', Asahi Shinbun-sha, Tokyo.

Gomi Fumihiko 1982, 'Josei shoryō to ie', in Joseishi Sōgō Kenkyūkai (ed), *Nihon josei-shi 2: chūsei,* Tokyo University Press, Tokyo.

—— 1984, *Insei-ki shakai no kenkyū*, Yamakawa shuppansha, Tokyo.

—— 1990, 'Sei, bai, en: onna no chikara' in Joseishi Sōgō Kenkyūkai (ed) *Nihon josei seikatsu-shi 2: chūsei*, Tokyo University Press, Tokyo.

—— 1991, *Fujiwara Teika no jidai: chūsei bunka no kūkan*, Iwanami shoten, Tokyo.

Goodwin, Janet R 1994, *Alms and vagabonds: Buddhist temples and popular patronage in medieval Japan*, University of Hawaii Press, Manoa.

Gorai Shigeru 1976, 'Jisha engi kara otogi-banashi e', *Bungaku* 44–49.

—— 1982, 'Chūsei josei no shūkyōsei to seikatsu' in Josei-shi Sōgō Kenkyū-kai (ed), *Nihon josei-shi 2: chūsei*, Tokyo University Press, Tokyo.

—— 1990, *Nihon no jigoku to gokuraku*, Jinbun shoin, Kyoto.

Gunma ken-shi, Shiryō-hen 1977–92, no 6, *Chūsei I*, 'Chōrakuji monjo'.

Gyokuyō (diary of Fujiwara Kanezane, covering the years 1164–1200) 1907, Kokusho kankōkai, Tokyo.

Haga Kōshirō 1960, *Sanjō Nishi Sanetaka*, Yoshikawa Kōbunkan, Tokyo.

—— 1981, *Haga Kōshirō rekishi ronshū*, 'Chūsei makki ni okeru Sanjō Nishi-ke no keizai kiban to sono hōkai', 'Chūsei makki ni okeru chihō bunka no taidō ', and 'Sanjō Nishi Sanetaka no Man'yō kenkyū', Shibunkaku shuppan, Tokyo.

Hanawa Hokinoichi (ed) 1928–34 [1746–1821], *Gunsho ruijū*, Zoku Gunsho ruijū kanseikai, Tokyo.

—— 1931–33, *Gunsho ruijū*, Zoku Gunsho ruijū kanseikai, Tokyo.

—— 1958, *Gunsho ruijū*, Zoku Gunsho ruijū Kanseikai, Tokyo.

—— 1959–60, *Gunsho ruijū*, Zoku Gunsho Ruijū Kanseikai, Tokyo.

—— 1969, *Gunsho ruijū* 11, 'Zappitsu yōshū', Zoku Gunsho Ruijū Kanseikai, Tokyo.

—— 1976, *Gunsho ruijū*, volum 3, 'Zappitsu yōshū', Zoku Gunsho Ruijū Kanseikai, Tokyo.

—— 1982, *Gunsho Ruijū*, 28, Zoku Gunsho ruijū kansei-kai, Tokyo.

Hara Katsurō 1929, *Nihon chūsei-shi no kenkyū*, 'Higashiyama jidai ni okeru ichi shinshin no seikatsu', Dōbunkan, Tokyo.

Harada Tomohiko 1980, *Kyō no hito, Ōsaka no hito*, Asahi Shinbunsha, Tokyo.

Haru Kazue 1984, 'Kurōdo no shokumu to shite no nikkyū to gessō', *Bungaku shigaku*, volume 6, Seishin Joshi Daigaku, Tokyo.

Hashimoto Hisakazu 1990, 'Chūsei seiritsu-ki no doki yōsō: kinai o chūshin to shite', *Nihon-shi kenkyū* 330.

Hashimoto Yoshihiko 1976, *Heian kizoku shakai no kenkyū*, 'Geki nikki to Denjō nikki', Yoshikawa Kōbunkan, Tokyo.

Hayashiya Tatsusaburō 1960, *Chūsei geinō-shi no kenkyū*, Iwanami shoten, Tokyo.

Hirade Kenjirō 1906, 'Jingū to Keikōin to no kankei', *Shigaku zasshi* 17(5, 9).

Hora Tomio 1956, *Nihon bokeisei shakai no seiritsu*, Waseda University Cooperative Press, Tokyo.

Hosokawa Ryōichi 1987, *Chūsei no Ritsu-shū jiin to minshū*, 'Hōkongō-in dōgo no shūkyō katsudō', Yoshikawa Kōbunkan, Tokyo.

—— 1989a, 'Kamakura jidai no ama to amadera', Chūsei no Ritsu-shū ji-in to minshū, Yoshikawa Kōbunkan, Tokyo.

—— 1989b, *Chūsei no Risshū jiin to minshū*, Yoshikawa kōbunkan, Tokyo,

—— 1989c, *Onna no chūsei*, 'Dōgo Saga Seiryōji yūzū dainenbutsu-e; Hyakuman', Nihon Editor School Shuppanbu, Tokyo.

Hosoya Naoki 1976, *Chūsei karon no kenkyū*, 'Yoru no tsuru saiginmi', Kasama shoin, Tokyo.

Ichiko Teiji (ed) 1958, *Otogizōshi, Nihon Koten bungaku taikei* volume 38, Iwanami shoten, Tokyo.

Ichino Chizuko 1982, 'Fushimi gosho shūhen no seikatsu bunka: Kanmon nikki ni miru', *Shoryōbu Kiyō* 33.

Iikura Harutake 1981, *Nihon komonjogaku kōza, Chūsei 2*, 'Tennō monjo', Yūzankaku, Tokyo.

Inagaki Yasuhiko 1981, *Nihon chūsei shakai-shi*, 'Shoki myōden no kōzō', University of Tokyo Press, Tokyo.

Inokuchi Yūichi and Horii Reichi 1974, *Gosho kotoba*, Yūzankaku, Tokyo.

Inoue Mitsusada et al (ed) 1976, *Ritsuryō, Nihon Shisō Taikei 3*, Iwanami shoten, Tokyo.

Inoue Nobutaka (ed) 2001, *Encyclopedia of Shinto*, volume 1 (Kami), Institute for Japanese Culture and Classics, Kokugakuin University, Tokyo.

Inui Sadahiro 1979, *Yōkyoku shūyō-shō*, Nihon tosho centre, Tokyo.

Ishii Susumu 1988, 'Genpei sōran-ki no Hachijō-in-ryō: Hachijo-in no chō monjo o chūshin ni' in Nagahara Keiji and Sasaki Junnosuke (eds), *Nihon chūsei-shi kenkyū no kiseki*, University of Tokyo Press, Tokyo.

Ishikawa Eikichi 1979, '"Genshi" no josei', *Josei-shi Sōgō Kenkyūkai Tsūshin* 7.

Ishikawa Yoshiyuki 1983, 'Insesuto tabū-kō', *Tokushima Daigaku gakugei kiyō* 32.

Ishimaki Yoshio 1918, 'Ise kanjin bikuni kō', *Geibun* 8 (10).

Ishimoda Takashi 1973, *Nihon kodai kokka-ron*, part 2, 'Man'yō jidai no kizoku seikatsu no ichi-sokumen', Iwanami shoten, Tokyo.

Itō Kunio 1980, 'Kanmon nikki no hitobito (2)', *Chūsei Bungaku Kenkyū* 6.

Itō Masayoshi 1989, *Yōkyoku zakki*, Izumi shoin, Kyoto.

Iwahashi Koyata 1975, *Geinō-shi sōsetsu*, 'Kusemai', Yoshikawa Kōbunkan, Tokyo.

Iwamoto Hiroshi 1968, *Mokuren densetsu to urabon*, Hōzōkan, Kyoto.

Iwasaki Kae et al (eds) 1993, *Shichijūichi-ban shokunin utaawase*, Iwanami shoten, Tokyo.

Iwasaki Yoshie et al. 1982, *Shokunin utaawase sōgō sakuin*, Akao Shōbundō, Tokyo.

Izumiya Yasuo 1984, 'Kibune engi ni tsuite' in *Shintō-shi ronsō*, Kokusho kankōkai, Tokyo.

Jinnō shōtō-ki, Masukagami 1965, *Nihon koten bungaku taikei* 87, Iwanami shoten, Tokyo.

Joseishi Sōgō Kenkyūkai (ed) 1982, *Nihon joseishi* (5 vols), Tokyo University Press, Tokyo.

—— 1990, *Nihon josei seikatsu-shi* (5 vols), Tokyo University Press, Tokyo.

Jugaku Shōko 1982, 'Josei-go no seikaku to sono kōzō', in Joseishi Sōgō Kenkyūkai (ed), *Nihon josei-shi 2: chūsei*, Tokyo University Press, Tokyo.

Kairaishi-ki 1979, in Yamagishi Tokuhei (ed), *Kodai seiji shakai shisō*, *Nihon shisō taikei 8*, Iwanami shoten, Tokyo.

Kamei Akinori 1986, *Nihon bōeki tōji-shi no kenkyū*, Dōhōsha, Kyoto.

Kamiyokote Masayoshi 1972, 'Tango no tsubone to Tanba no tsubone', *Nihon rekishi* 284.

Katō Etsuko 2004, *Sad marriage of (post-)colonialism, feminism and anthropology: or why Japanese sexual behavior is always intriguing*, unpublished conference presentation, Asian Studies Conference Japan, Sophia University, Tokyo.

Katō Mieko 1985, 'Onna no za kara nyōbō-za e' in Wakita Haruko (ed), *Bosei o tou: rekishiteki hensen*, volume 1, Jinbun shoin, Kyoto.

—— 1990, 'Chūsei no josei to shinkō: miko, bikuni, kurishitan', in Joseishi Sōgō Kenkyūkai (ed), *Nihon josei seikatsu-shi vol. 2: Chūsei*, Tokyo University Press, Tokyo.

Katsumata Shizuo 1979, 'Chūsei buke mikkaihō no tenkai' in *Sengoku-hō seiritsu-ron*, Tokyo University Press, Tokyo.

Katsuura Reiko 1984, 'Kodai no sentaku onnatachi', *Gekkan hyakka* 225.

Kawane Yoshiyasu 1971, 'Nihon-rei ni okeru koshu to kachō' in *Chūsei hōken seiritsu-shi-ron*, Tokyo University Press, Tokyo.

—— 1977, 'Kinai zaichi ryōshu no chōja shoku ni tuite', *Jinbun kenkyū* 29(4).

—— 1982, 'Chūsei zenki sonraku ni okeru josei no chii: toshi daichō no sekai to yuzuri-jō, baiken, zōzōmei no sekai', in *Nihon josei-shi 2: chūsei*, University of Tokyo Press, Tokyo.

Keikōin monjo, facsimile edition held at Tokyo Daigaku Shiryo Hensan-jo, Tokyo.

Kim, Yung-Hee 1994, *Songs to make the dust dance: the Ryōjin hishō of twelfth-century Japan*, University of California Press, Berkeley.

Kinoshita Masao 1967, 'Kyōto ni okeru machigumi no chiikiteki hatten', *Nihon-shi kenkyū* 92.

Kinpishō 1983, in Hanawa Hokinoichi (ed), *Gunsho ruijū*, no 260, 'Zatsu', Zoku Gunsho ruijū kanseikai, Tokyo.

Kishi Shōzō (ed) 1967, *Shintō-shū*, 'Kaisetsu', Tōyō bunko no. 94, Heibonsha, Tokyo.

Kitano Tenmangū shiryō kankōkai (ed) 1978, *Kitano Tenmangū shiryō*, 'Sakaya kyōmyō', Kitano Tenmangū, Kyoto.

Kiyooka E (ed & trans) 1988, *Fukuzawa Yukichi on Japanese women*, University of Tokyo Press, Tokyo.

Kobayashi Tomoaki 1974, *Zoku Chūsei Bungaku no Shisō*, Kasama shoin, Tokyo.

Koga-ke monjo 1982, Hanawa Hokinoichi (ed), *Zoku Gunsho ruijū*, Zoku Gunsho ruijū kansei-kai, Tokyo.

Kojima Shōsaku 1980, 'Keikōin seijun shūyō no jiseki to Keikōin monjo no rekishiteki igi' in Kokugakuin Daigaku Shintō-shi gakkai (ed), *Shintō-shi no kenkyū*, Sōbunsha, Tokyo.

Komatsu Shigemi (ed) 1987, *Nenchū gyōji emaki*, Chūō Kōron-sha, Tokyo.

Kondō Yoshihiro (ed), 1959, *Shintō-shū tōyō bunko-bon*, Kadokawa shoten, Tokyo.

Kondō Yoshihiro and Kishi Shōzō (eds) 1968, *Akagi Bunko Shintō-shū*, Kadokawa shoten, Tokyo.

Konno Tōru ed. 1993-99, *Konjaku monogatari-shū*, in *Shin Nihon Koten Bungaku Taikei* volumes 33-37, Iwanami, Tokyo.

Koresawa Kyōzō 1944, 'Oyudono no ue no nikki no kōsei', *Kokushi-gaku* 49, 50.

—— 1951, 'Kōkyo Oyudono no ue no ma no seikaku', *Nihon gakushi-in kiyō* 9(3).

—— 1952, 'Kōkyo Oyudono no ue no ma no seikaku', *Nihon gakushi-in kiyō* 10(1).

—— 1954, 'Mibu-in jihitsu Oyudono no ue no nikki', *Kokugakuin Zasshi* 55(2).

—— 1957–59, 'Oyudono no ue no nikki no kenkyū', *Nihon gakushi-in kiyō* 15(2) to 17(1).

Koyama Hiroshi (ed) 1960, *Kyōgen-shu*, Nihon Koten Bungaku Taikei 42-43, Iwanami shoten, Tokyo.

Kunida Yuriko 1964, *Nyōbō kotoba no kenkyū*, volume 1, Kazama shobō, Tokyo.

—— 1977, *Nyōbō kotoba no kenkyū*, volume 2, Kazama shobō, Tokyo.

Kuroda Toshio 1974, *Nihon chūsei hōken-sei-ron*, 'Sonraku kyōdōtai no chūseiteki tokushitsu', University of Tokyo Press, Tokyo.

Kuwata Tadachika 1931, 'Shūsei shōnin no ganmon to sono yurai', *Rekishi chiri* 57(5).

Kuwayama Kōnen (ed) 1980, *Muromachi Bakufu hikitsuke shiryō shūsei*, volume 1, Kondō shuppan-sha, Tokyo.

—— 1986, *Muromachi bakufu hikizuke shiryō shūsei*, volume 2, Kondō Shuppansha, Tokyo.

Kyōen and Nakajima Shunji (eds) 1973 [1179], *Daigo zōji-ki (zatsuji-ki)*, 15 vols, Daigoji Temple, Kyoto.

Kyoto-furitsu Yamashiro Kyōdo Shiryōkan (ed) 1984, *Inori to kurashi*, Kyoto-furitsu Yamashiro Kyōdo Shiryōkan, Kyoto.

Mackie, Vera 1997, *Creating socialist women in Japan: gender, labour and activism, 1900–1937*, Cambridge University Press, Cambridge and Melbourne.

Maeda Toshi 1977, 'Tabi nikki no josei', in *Jinbutsu Nihon no josei-shi*, volume 6, *Nikki ni tsuzuru aikan*, Shūeisha, Tokyo.

Makabe Yoshiko 1973, 'Kurashiki-shi Sakatsu: Mizue iseki' in *Kurashiki kōko-kan kenkyū shūhō* 8.

Maraldo, John C 1998, 'Buddhist philosophy, Japanese' in Craig, E (ed), *Routledge encyclopedia of philosophy*, Routledge, London, www.rep.routledge.com/article/G101SECT5, viewed 16.10.2005.

Masaki Tokuzō 1948, *Honnami Gyōjōki to Kōetsu*, 'Honnami gyōjōki', Geisōdō Shuppanbu, Tokyo.

Matsuda Kiichi and E Jorissen 1983, *Furoisu no Nihon oboegaki*, Chūkō shinsho, Tokyo.

Matsue Shigeyori 1943, *Kefukigusa*, Iwanami shoten, Tokyo.

Matsui Toshihiko 1968, 'Muromachi jidai ni okeru tōshō no josei no hyōgen', *Kokugo kokubun* 37–4.

—— 1979, 'Josei-gaku to josei-go', *Hiroshima Joshi Daigaku Kokubungakkai Kaihō* 6.

Matsumoto Neiji 1983, *Chūsei joryū bungaku no kenkyū*, Meiji shoin, Tokyo.

Matsumoto Yasushi 1983, *Chūsei joryū nikki bungaku no kenkyū*, Meiji shoin, Tokyo.

McCullough, Helen Craig 1966, *Yoshitsune: a fifteenth-century Japanese chronicle*, University of Tokyo Press, Tokyo, and Stanford University Press, Stanford.

—— (trans) 1984, *Kokin Wakashū: the first imperial anthology of Japanese poetry*, Stanford University Press, Palo Alto.

—— (ed) 1990, *Classical Japanese prose: an anthology*, Stanford University Press, Stanford.

Mills, DE (trans) 1970, *A collection of tales from Uji; a study and translation of Uji shui monogatari*, Cambridge University Press, Cambridge.

Minegishi Sumio 1989, 'Tōgoku bushi no kiban: Kōzuke no kuni no Nitta-shō', in *Chūsei no tōgoku: chiiki to kenryoku*, University of Tokyo Press, Tokyo.

Miner, Earl (trans) 1979, *Japanese linked poetry: an account with translations of renga and haikai sequences*, Princeton University Press, Princeton.

Miyake, Lynne K 1996, 'The Tosa diary' in Schalow, Paul Gordon and Janet A Walker (eds), *The woman's hand: gender and theory in Japanese women's writing*, Stanford University Press, Stanford.

Momose Kesao 1976, 'Ōnin-Bunmei no ran', in Asao Naohiro et al (eds), *Iwanami Kōza Nihon-rekishi 7, chūsei 3*, Iwanami shoten, Tokyo.

Morell, Robert E 1985, *Sand and pebbles (Shasekishū): the tales of Mujū Ichien, a voice for pluralism in Kamakura Buddhism*, State University of New York Press, Albany

Morita Minoru 1987, 'Tō Han-kei chūsei no seisan to ryūtsū' in Nihon Chūsei Doki Kenkyū-kai (ed), *Chū-kinsei doki no kiso kenkyū*, volume 3, Nihon Chūsei Doki Kenkyū-kai, Takatsuki.

Morris, Ivan (trans) 1967, *The pillow book of Sei Shonagon*, Columbia University Press, New York.

—— 1971, *Sarashina Nikki: As I crossed a bridge of dreams: recollections of a woman in eleventh-century Japan*, Dial Press, New York.

Mukō-shi-shi Hensan Iinkai (ed) 1985, *Mukō-shi-shi*, volume 2, City of Mukō, Kyoto.

Murakami Tennō gyoki 1982, in Tokoro Isao (ed), *Sandai gyoki itsubun shūsei*, Kokusho kankō-kai, Tokyo.

Nagakura Chieo 1978, 'Imagawa Yoshitada fujin Kitagawa-dono ni tsuite' in Imagawa-shi Kenkyūkai (ed), *Suruga no Imagawa-shi*, volume 3, Yajima-ya, Shizuoka.

Nagaoka Katsue 1958, 'Nonō miko no kenkyū', *Shinano* 10–12.

Nakahara Yasutomi 1965 [1453–55], *Yasutomi-ki*, Rinsen shoten, Kyoto.

Nakamura Ken 1975, 'Tōji keidai Kantō-machi no shihai' in Akiyama Kunizō and Nakamura Ken (eds), *Kyōto 'machi' no kenkyū*, Hosei University Press, Tokyo.

Nakamura Kyoko Motomochi (trans and ed) 1997, *Miraculous stories from the Japanese Buddhist tradition: the Nihon Ryoiki of the monk Kyōkai*, Curzon Press, Richmond, Surrey.

Natori Jōnosuke (ed) 1938, *Katsura-me shiryō*, Ōokayama shoten, Tokyo.

Nihon Chūsei Doki Kenkyūkai (ed) 1985–90, *Chū-kinsei doki no kiso kenkyū*, 6 volumes, Nihon chūsei doki kenkyūkai, Takatsuki.

Nishioka Toranosuke 1956, *Nihon josei-shi-kō*, Shinhyōronsha, Tokyo.

—— 1977, *Nihon josei-shi-kō*, 'Heian-ki ni okeru menoto no kenkyū', Shinhyōron, Tokyo.

Noritoki kyō-ki 1970, in Hanawa Hokinoichi (ed), *Gunsho ruijū*, Zoku Gunsho ruijū kansei-kai, Tokyo.

Odaka Yasushi 1985, *Oyudono no ue no nikki no kisoteki kenkyū*, Izumi shoin, Osaka.

Ōgimachi Machiko 2004, *Matsukage no nikki*, Iwanami shoten, Tokyo.

Okada Seiji 1982, 'Kyūtei miko no jittai', in Joseishi Sōgō Kenkyūkai (ed), *Nihon josei-shi, volume 1: genshi-kodai*, University of Tokyo Press, Tokyo.

Okuno Takahiro 1942, *Kōshitsu on-keizai-shi no kenkyū*, Unebō shobō, Tokyo.

Omote Akira and Katō Shūichi (eds) 1974, *Zeami, Zenchiku*, 'Seshi rokujū igo sarugaku dangi' and 'Go-on'. Nihon Shisō Taikei 24, Iwanami shoten, Tokyo.

Ōnishi Gen'ichi 1952, 'Ise no kanjin hijiri to Keikōin', *Shintō shigaku* 3.

Ono Masatoshi 1985, 'Shutsudo tōji yori mita jūgoroku seiki ni okeru kakki no sobyō' in Tokyo Kokuritsu Hakubutsukan (ed), *Museum* 416.

Ortner, Sherry 1987, 'Are women and men the same relation as nature to culture?' Mikami Hiroko (trans), *Gendai Shisō* 11(8).

Ōsumi Kazuo 1977, *Chūsei shintō-ron*, explanatory notes, *Nihon Shisō Taikei* volume 19, Iwanami shoten, Tokyo.

Otsuki Harutomi 1971, *Harutomi sukune-ki*, Meiji shoin, Tokyo.

Ōyamazaki-chō-shi Hensan Iinkai (ed) 1981–83, *Ōyamazaki-chō-shi*, 'Ōyamazaki rikyū Hachimangū monjo', Ōyamazaki-chō, Kyoto.

Oyudono no ue no nikki kenkyū-kai (ed) 1973, *Oyudono no ue no nikki no kenkyū: shūkyō, yūgei, bungei shiryō sakuin*, Zoku Gunsho ruijū, Kansei-kai, Tokyo.

Perkins, George W 1998, *The clear mirror*, Stanford University Press, Stanford.

Pigeot, Jacqueline and Keiko Kosugi (trans) 2001, *Histoire d'un pet: la déconfiture de Fukutomi*, P Picqier, Arles.

Reisen-chō kiroku, facsimile edition, Kyoto University.

Ritsuryō 1976, *Nihon Shisō Taikei*, Iwanami shoten, Tokyo.

Rodd, LR with MC Henkenius (trans) 1984, *Kokinshū: a collection of poems ancient and modern*, Princeton University Press, Princeton.

Said, Edward 1978, *Orientalism*, Pantheon Books, New York.

Sakurai Yoshirō 1976, *Kamigami no henbō: jisha engi no sekai kara*, Tokyo University Press, Tokyo.

Sanetaka kōki, diary of Sanjō Nishi Sanetaka (1455-1537) in Hanawa Hokinoichi (ed) 1958, *Gunsho ruijū*, Zoku Gunsho ruijū Kansei-kai, Tokyo.

Satō Shin'ichi 1971, *Komonjo-gaku nyūmon*, Hōsei University Press.

—— 1983, *Nihon no chūsei kokka*, Iwanami Shoten, Tokyo.

Satō Shin'ichi et al (ed) 1978, *Chūsei hōsei shiryō-shū Volume 1: Kamakura Bakufu hō*, Iwanami shoten, Tokyo.

Segawa Kiyoko 1971 [1933], *Hisagime: josei to shōgyō*, Miraisha, Tokyo.

Seidensticker, Edward (trans) 1994 [1964], *The gossamer years: the diary of a noblewoman of Heian Japan*, Charles E Tuttle Company, Tokyo.

Seikan-in no miya no-nikki (diary of Imperial Princess Kazunomiya, in the Kunaichō Shoryōbu (Imperial Palace Document collection).

Sekiguchi Hiroko 1977, 'Rekishi-gaku ni okeru josei-shi kenkyū no igi: Nihon kodai o chūshin ni', *Jinmin no rekishigaku* 52.

Shimamoto-chō-shi Hensan iinkai (ed) 1975–76, *Shimamoto-chō-shi – shiryō-hen*, 'Dōshi shussen no nikki', Municipality of Shimamoto, Shimamoto.

Shimizu Yoshiko 1966, *Genji monogatari ron*, Hanawa shoten, Tokyo.

—— 1979, 'Sei Shōnagon', *Kokubungaku* 24(4).

—— 1980, 'Nihon no joshi kyōiku', *Osaka-fu fujin mondai adobaizaa yōsei kōza kōgi-roku*, Osaka-fu kikaku-bu fumin bunka-shitsu, Osaka.

—— 1982, 'Chūsei joryū bungaku no keisei to sono haikei', in *Nihon josei-shi 1: Genshi, Kodai*, Tokyo University Press, Tokyo.

Shimofusa Shun'ichi 1968, 'Fushimi no miya Sadafusa', *Kokugo Kokubun* 411.

Shimohashi Takanaga 1979, *Bakumatsu no kyūtei*, Tōyō Bunko 353, Heibonsha, Tokyo.

Shinjōin monjo, facsimile edition by Tokyo University Shiryō hensanjo.

Shinma Shin'ichi et al (eds) 1959, 'Kyōgen kayō' and 'Hōshi ga haha', *Chūsei kinsei kayō-shū*, Nihon Koten Bungaku Taikei volume 44, Iwanami shoten, Tokyo.

Song Hui-gyong (Sō Kikei) 1968 [c 1420], *Nosongdang-ilbon-haengnok (Rōshōdō nihon kōroku)*, Zoku Gunsho Ruijū Kanseikai, Tokyo.

Sonoda Kōyō 1966, 'Emi-ke shijo denkō Part 1', *Shisen* 32.

Sonpi bunmyaku 2001, revised edition, Yoshikawa kōbunkan, Tokyo.

Sugawara Masaaki 1984, 'Kinai ni okeru tsuchigama no seisaku to ryūtsū', *Bunkazai ronsō* 1, Dōhōsha, Kyoto.

Suzuki Hiromichi 1981, Mumyō sōshi ron: josei-ron o chūshin to shite, Daigakudō shoten, Kyoto.

Tabata Yasuko 1982, 'Daimyō ryōgoku kihan to sonraku nyōbō-za', in Joseishi Sōgō Kenkyūkai (ed), *Nihon joseishi 2: chūsei*, Tokyo University Press, Tokyo.

—— 1990, 'Sengoku-ki josei no yakuwari buntan' in Josei-shi Sōgō Kenkyū-kai (ed), *Nihon josei seikatsu-shi*, University of Tokyo Press, Tokyo.

Taira Masayuki 1990, 'Medieval Buddhism and women' in Joseishi Sōgō Kenkyūkai (ed), *Nihon josei seikatsu-shi*, volume 2, *Chūsei*, Tokyo University Press, Tokyo.

Takagi Ichinosuke et al (eds) 1965, *Wakan rōei-shū; Ryōjin hishō*, *Nihon Koten Bungaku Taikei 73*, Iwanami shoten, Tokyo.

Takamure Itsue 1963, *Nihon kon'in-shi*, Shibundō, Tokyo.

—— 1966, *Nihon josei no rekishi* in *Takamure Itsue Zenshū*, Riron-sha, Tokyo.

Takeuchi Rizō (ed) 1967a, *Gohōkōin-ki*, Rinsen shoten, Kyoto.

—— (ed) 1967b, *Nochi no Hōkō-in no ki*, Rinsen shoten, Kyoto.

—— 1971–89, *Kamakura ibun*, Tokyo-dō shuppan, Tokyo.

—— (ed) 1974–80, *Heian ibun*, Tokyo-dō shuppan, Tokyo.

Takeuchi Rizō and Takayanagi Mitsutoshi (eds) 1974, *Kadokawa Nihonshi Jiten*, Kadokawa shoten, Tokyo.

Takie Sugiyama Lebra 1979, 'Tōgōteki josei kenkyū o mezashite', *Minzokugaku Kenkyū* 44(2).

Takigawa Masajirō 1976 [1965], *Eguchi, Kanzaki*, Shibundō, Tokyo. (First published in 1965 under the title *Yūgyō jofu, yūjo, kugutsume: Eguchi, Kanzaki*)

Tanaka Hiroshi (ed) 1976a, *Zeami geijutsuron-shū*, 'Fūshi kaden', Shinchōsha, Tokyo.

—— 1976b, *Zeami geijutsuron-shu*, 'Seishi rokujū igo Sarugaku dangi', Shinchōsha, Tokyo.

Tanaka Kōji-shi shozō monjo, facsimile edition by Kyoto University.

Tanaka Mitsuji-shi shozō monjo, facsimile edition by Kyoto University.

Tanasawa Naoko 1981, 'Furansu ni okeru 'onna no kotoba': josei-sei wa aru ka' in Josei-gaku kenkūkai (ed), *Josei-gaku o tsukuru*, Keisō shobō.

Tanji Yasuaki 1985, 'Tō Han-kei sue-ki ni tsuite' in Nihon Chūsei Doki Kenkyūkai (eds), *Chū-kinsei doki no kiso kenkyū*, volume 1, Nihon chūsei doki kenkyūkai, Takatsuki.

Tokitsugu kyōki 1965, in Hanawa Hokinoichi (ed), *Gunsho ruijū*, volumes 1–7, Zoku Gunsho ruijū Kansei-kai, Tokyo.

Tokoro Isao 1978, 'Ōkisaki no goki oboegaki', *Kokusho Itsubun Kenkyū* 1.

Tokushima-ken Kyōiku Iin-kai (ed) 1989, *Naka Shimada Iseki, Minami Shimada Iseki* (written by Fuke Seiji), Tokushima Prefecture Kyōiku Iinkai, Tokushima.

Tosa nikki 1990 [c 935], 'A Tosa journal' in McCullough, Helen Craig (ed), *Classical Japanese prose: an anthology*, Stanford University Press, Stanford.

Toyoda Takeshi 1983, *Collected works 3: chūsei no shokunin to kōtsū*, 'Nihon shokunin-shi', Yoshikawa Kōbunkan, Tokyo.

Tsubonouchi Tōru 1988, 'Chūsei Nanto no gaki, gashitsu doki' in Nihon chūsei doki Kenkyūkai (eds), *Chū-kinsei doki no kiso kenkyū*, volume 6, Nihon chūsei doki kenkyūkai, Takatsuki.

Tsuchida Naoshige 1959, 'Naishi-sen ni tsuite', *Nihon Gakushi-in Kiyō*, 17 (3).

Tsude Hiroshi 1982, 'Genshi doki to josei: Yayoi jidai no seibetsu bungyō to kon'in kyojū kitei', in Joseishi Sōgō Kenkyūkai (ed), *Nihon josei-shi 1: genshi-kodai*, University of Tokyo Press, Tokyo.

Tyler, Royall 1990, *Miracles of the Kasuga deity*, Columbia University, New York.

—— (trans) 2003, The tale of Genji, by Murasaki Shikibu, Penguin, Harmondsworth.

Ueno Chizuko 1990, *Kafuchōsei to shihonsei: marukusushugi feminizumu no chihei*, Iwanami shoten, Tokyo.

Ushiyama Yoshiyuki 1989, 'Chūsei no amadera to ama' in Ōsumi Kazuo & Nishiguchi Junko (eds), *Josei to bukkyō: ama to amadera*, Heibonsha, Tokyo.

Wada Hidematsu 1912, 'Rekishi-jō ni okeru menoto no seiryoku', *Kokugakuin Zasshi* 18(1).

—— 1983, *Kanshoku Yōkan*, revised edition, Kodansha, Tokyo.

Wakita Haruko 1969a, 'Chūsei shōkōgyō-za no kōzō to tenkai' in *Nihon chūsei shōgyō hattatsu-shi no kenkyū*, Ochanomizu shobō, Tokyo.

—— 1969b, *Nihon chūsei sangyō hattatsu-shi no kenkyū*, Ochanomizu shobō, Tokyo.

—— 1969c, 'Shōen ryōshu keizai to shōkōgyō' in *Nihon chūsei shōgyō hattatsu-shi no kenkyū*, Ochanomizu shobō, Tokyo.

—— 1969d, 'Shuto shijōken no keisei' in *Nihon chūsei shōgyō hattatsu-shi no kenkyū*, Ochanomizu shobō, Tokyo.

—— 1969e, 'Za no seikaku henka to honjo kenryoku' in *Nihon chūsei shōgyō hattatsu-shi no kenkyū*, Ochanomizu shobō, Tokyo.

—— 1977, 'Ano no Renshi' in *Jinbutsu Nihon no Josei-shi*, volume 5, *Seiken o ugokashita onnatachi*, Shūeisha, Tokyo.

—— 1978, 'Nihon kodai chūsei josei-shi oboegaki', *Rekishi Hyōron* 335.

—— 1981a, 'Chūsei Kyōto no tochi shoyū' in *Nihon chūsei toshi-ron*, Tokyo University Press, Tokyo.

—— 1981b, *Nihon chūsei toshi-ron*, University of Tokyo Press, Tokyo.

—— 1981c, 'Toshi kyōdōtai no keisei' in *Nihon chūsei toshi-ron*, Tokyo University Press, Tokyo.

—— 1982, 'Chūsei ni okeru seibetsu yakuwari buntan to josei-kan' in Joseishi Sōgō Kenkyūkai (ed), *Nihon josei-shi 2: chūsei*, Tokyo University Press, Tokyo.

—— 1983, 'Rekishigaku to josei', *Rekishigaku kenkyū* 917.

—— 1984a, 'Hino no Tomiko no jinbutsuzō', in NHK (ed), *Rekishi e no shōtai* 31, Nihon Hōsō Shuppan Kyōkai.

—— 1984b, 'Marriage and property in pre-modern Japan', *Journal of Japanese Studies* 10 (1).

—— 1981c, 'Tokusei ikki no haikei', in *Nihon chūsei toshi-ron*, Tokyo University Press.

—— 1985, 'Chūsei hisabetsumin no seikatsu to shakai' in Buraku Mondai Kenkyū-jo (ed.), *Buraku no rekishi to kaihō undō: zen-kindai*, Buraku Mondai Kenkyū-jo Shuppan-bu, Kyoto.

—— (ed) 1986, *Bosei o tou: rekishiteki hensen* (2 volumes), Jinbun shoin, Kyoto.

—— 1987 [1978–84], 'Sanjo-ron' in Buraku Mondai Kenkyū-jo (ed), *Buraku-shi no kenkyū: zenkindai-hen*, Buraku Mondai Kenkyūjo shuppan-bu, Kyoto.

—— 1988a, 'Chūsei no bungyō to mibun-sei' in Nagahara Keiji and Sasaki Junnosuke (eds), *Nihon chūsei-shi kenkyū no kiseki*, Tokyo University Press, Tokyo.

—— 1988b, 'Sengoku daimyō', *Taikei: Nihon no rekishi*, volume 7, Shōgakkan, Tokyo.

—— 1989, 'Nihon koku-ō Ashikaga Yoshimitsu no bunka seisaku', *Rekishi tanjō*, volume 5, Kadokawa shoten, Tokyo.

—— 1990a, in Nihon chūsei doki Kenkyūkai (eds), *Chū-kinsei doki no kiso kenkyū*, volume 6, 'Chūsei no shōhin ryūtsū to dokusen-ken', Nihon chūsei doki kenkyūkai, Takatsuki.

—— 1990b, 'Nōgaku to tennō and shintō' in *Bungei, Special Issue on Tennōsei: rekishi, ōken, daijōsai*, Kawade shobō shinsha, Tokyo.

—— 1990c, 'Chūsei kōki: machi ni okeru onna no isshō' in Joseishi Sōgō Kenkyūkai (ed), *Nihon josei seikatsu-shi* (5 volumes), Tokyo University Press, Tokyo.

—— 1990–91, 'Sengoku-ki ni okeru tennō ken'i no fujō' (in 2 instalments), *Nihon-shi kenkyū* 340 and 341.

—— 2002a, 'Nōgaku to Tennō, Shintō' in *Tennō to chūsei bunka*, Yoshikawa kōbunkan, Tokyo.

—— 2002b, *Nihon chūsei hisabetsu-min no kenkyū*, Iwanami shoten, Tokyo.

—— 2005, *Nōgaku no naka no onnatachi—onna mai no fūshi*, Iwanami shoten, Tokyo.

Wakita Haruko, Anne Bouchy, and Ueno Chizuko (eds) 1999, Gender and Japanese history, Osaka University Press, Osaka.

Wakita Osamu 1985, 'Harima Nozato Akuta-shi no katsudō' in Matsuoka Hideo Sanju Kinen Ronbun-shū Kankō-kai (ed), *Hyōgo-shi no kenkyū*, Kobe Shinbun Shuppan Centre, Kobe.

Wilson, William R (trans) 1971, *Hōgen monogatari*, Sophia University, Tokyo.

Wilson, William Scott (trans) 2002 [1979], *Hagakure: the book of the samurai by Yamamoto Tsunetomo*, Kodansha International, Tokyo.

Yamada Keiji 1990, *Yoru naku tori*, Iwanami shoten, Tokyo.

Yamada Takao (ed) 1959, *Konjaku Monogatari-shū*, Nihon Koten Bungaku Taikei 22–26, Iwanami shoten, Tokyo.

Yamagishi Tokuhei et al (eds) 1979, *Shin Sarugō-ki* (also *Shin Sarugaku-ki*) (by Fujiwara Akihira) in *Nihon Shisō Taikei 8, Kodai seiji shakai shisō*, Iwanami shoten, Tokyo.

Yamagishi Tokuhei et al (eds) 1979, *Yūjo no ki* in *Kodai Seiji Shakai Shisō*, *Iwanami Nihon Shisō Taikei 8*, Iwanami shoten, Tokyo.

Yamamura Kozo 1990, *The Cambridge history of Japan*, volume 3: *Medieval Japan*, Cambridge University Press, Cambridge.

Yamashina-ke Raiki 1967–2002, in Hanawa Hokinoichi (ed), *Gunsho ruijū*, Zoku-Gunsho ruijū Kansei-kai, Tokyo.

Yanagita Kunio 1989a [1997], *Josei to minkan densetsu* in *Yanagita Kunio-shū*, Chikuma shobō, Tokyo.

—— 1989b [1997], *Miko-kō* in *Yanagita Kunio-shū*, Chikuma Shobō, Tokyo.

Yasaka Jinja Shamusho (ed) 1978, *Yasaka Jinja kiroku*, Rinsen shoten, Kyoto.

—— 1994, *Yasaka Jinja monjo*, part II, Rinsen shoten, Kyoto.

Yokoi Kiyoshi 1979, *Kanmon gyoki: ōja to shūsho no hazama ni te*, Soshiete, Tokyo.

Yoshie Akio 1972, 'Ritsuryō seika no sonraku saishi to kōsuiko-sei', *Rekishi-gaku kenkyū* 380.

Yoshino Yoshie 1982, 'Muromachi jidai no kinri no nyōbō: kōtō no naishi o chūshin ni', *Kokugakuin Daigaku-in Kiyō* 13.

Yōshū fu-shi 1984–89, in *Kyōto sōsho*, Rinsen shoten, Kyoto.

Zeami, Zenchiku 1974, *Nihon shisō taikei*, volume 24, Iwanami shoten, Tokyo.

Works by Wakita Haruko available in English

Tonomura Hitomi, Anne Walthall and Wakita Haruko (eds) 1999, *Women and class in Japanese history*, Center for Japanese Studies, University of Michigan, Ann Arbor.

Wakita Haruko forthcoming, 'An age of 'superwomen': mistresses of merchant houses in the capital region from the fifteenth to the seventeenth centuries', translated by GG Rowley, in Summers, Anne and John Shaw (eds), *Woman in her place: essays in honour of the 80th birthday of Mary Prior*, Ashgate, Aldershot.

—— 1999, 'The formation of the *ie* and medieval myth: the *shintôshû*, nô theatre, and picture scrolls of temple origins', translated by Micah Auerback, in Wakita Haruko, Anne Bouchy and Ueno Chizuko (eds), *Gender and Japanese history*, volume 1: *Religion and customs/the body and sexuality*, Osaka University Press, Osaka.

—— 1999, 'The medieval household and gender roles within the imperial family, nobility, merchants, and commoners', translated by Gary P Leupp, in onomura Hitomi, Anne Walthall and Wakita Haruko (eds), *Women and class in Japanese history*, Center for Japanese Studies, University of Michigan, Ann Arbor.

—— 1993, 'Women and the creation of the ie in Japan: an overview from the medieval period to the present', translated by David P Phillips, in *US–Japan Women's Journal* 4.

—— 1991, 'Town festivals: medieval towns and seigniorical authority in medieval Japan', translated by James McMullen, in *Nihongo Nihon bunka kenkyû (Studies in Japanese Language and Culture)*, Osaka University of Foreign Studies 1.

—— 1984, 'Marriage and property in pre-modern Japan from the perspective of women's history', translated by Suzanne Gay, in *Journal of Japanese Studies* 10(1).

—— 1981, 'Dimensions of development: cities in fifteenth and sixteenth-century Japan', with Susan B Hanley, in Hall, John Whitney, Nagahara Keiji and Kozo Yamamura (eds), *Japan before Tokugawa: political consolidation and economic growth, 1500–1650*, Princeton University Press, Princeton.

—— 1975, 'Towards a wider perspective on medieval commerce', in *Journal of Japanese Studies* 1(2).

Wakita Haruko, Anne Bouchy and Ueno Chizuko (eds) 1999, *Gender and Japanese history*, volume 1: *Religion and customs/the body and sexuality*, volume 2, *The self and expression/work and life*, Osaka University Press, Osaka.

Index

onna-za (women's associations), 95, 121, 156
Ono no Komachi (*setsuwa*), 28
oracle (*takusen*), 28, 35–7, 58, 126
Original Silk Yarn *za*, 151
otogi-zōshi (late medieval period tales), 5, 47, 55, 57, 61, 63, 68, 158
Otozuru, 94, 154, 156
Ōyamazaki, 40, 143, 153, 209
Oyudono no ue no nikki, 4, 6, 7, 18, 102, 105, 123–4, 132, 162–97

patriarch, 52
patriarchal family, 72, 121, 128–30, 138
patriarchy, 12–17, 38–40, 69, 72, 107, 119–20, 127, 130, 157
patrilineal, 120
patrilocal marriage, 131
picture scrolls (*emaki*), 29, 43–4, 144, 152, 163, 199, 205, 217
pollution, 28, 31–2, 153
polygamy/polygamous (*ippu tasai-sei*), 3, 25, 30, 33, 128, 157, 159
Pond of blood hell, 31
possession/possessed (trance), 36, 37, 68, 77, 152–3
pottery, 4, 83–5, 130, 150
power, 2–3, 5, 12–3, 15–8, 21, 24–8, 40–1, 43–4, 48, 50, 52, 56, 58, 66–7, 69, 72–5, 78–9, 83, 89–90, 102, 106–10, 115, 117–9, 130, 132, 143, 152–3, 157, 165, 169, 171, 187, 190–3
priest's robes dyed in cloves, 89, 104, 106, 107
princely families (*miya-ke*), 18, 20–1, 41, 132–3, 135, 138–9, 167
property, 14, 16–8, 26, 40, 43, 72, 78–9, 81–3, 88–9, 91–2, 109, 117, 122, 127, 129–31, 133, 142, 145, 158, 213, 217
proselytising (*shōdō*), 27, 44
prostitution, prostitutes, 16, 48, 77, 91–2, 113, 115, 129, 154, 156, 158–9

Rakuchū rakugai-zu (*Sights in and around Kyoto*), 144, 150
regent, 17, 43, 50, 108, 165, 168
remarriage, 91
renga (linked verse), 23–4, 42–3, 103–4, 174, 207
respect for mothers/motherhood, 48–9, 52, 69, 120
retainer, 17, 103, 135
rinji (imperial decrees written by male courtiers), 22, 96, 98, 100–2, 106–7, 109, 116–7, 132, 159, 172–4, 178, 196
rites, 76, 140
ritsuryō system, 13, 15, 17, 19, 39–40, 74–5, 78, 80, 90, 92, 96, 102, 121, 123, 128, 130, 159, 172, 183, 193, 203, 209, 215
ritual role of women, 74, 118
rituals, 66, 75–8, 80, 156
Rokujō (Lady; character), 152
royal decrees (*densen*), 96, 102
Ryōjin hishō (collection of *imayō* songs), 61, 76–7, 83, 90–2, 204, 211

Sadafusa (Prince), 4, 7, 18, 27, 133–6, 138–43, 153, 160, 167, 210
sake brewing, 71, 75, 78, 85, 90, 113, 130
salvation, 27–8, 31, 37, 44, 53, 63, 190
Sanetaka kōki, 124, 138, 159–61, 196–7, 210
sanjo (areas set aside for outcast communities), 94–5, 115, 121, 153–4, 214
Sanjō Nishi Sanetaka, 23–5, 107, 124, 132, 136, 140, 160, 182, 201, 210
Sanjō Saneoto, 134, 140
Sano (Haiya) Jōeki, 86
Sanuki no suke nikki, 171